NORTH AMERICA
Fort Berthold
RRITORY
MINNESOTA
Lake
Superior
WISCONSIN
Mississippi River
Missouri River
Fort Randall
IOWA
(Horton's Crossing)
Anamosa
Des Moines
NEBRASKA
TERRITORY
Omaha
Council
Bluffs
Fort Kearny
ILLINOIS
St. Joseph
KANSAS
Missouri River
St. Louis
MISSOURI
0 100 200 300 400 500
Miles

D0408414

Strength of Stone

The Pioneer Journal of Electa Bryan Plumer
1862–1864

A Novel by Diane Elliott

TWODOT®

GUILFORD, CONNECTICUT
HELENA, MONTANA

AN IMPRINT OF THE GLOBE PEQUOT PRESS

Copyright © 2002 by Diane Elliott

All rights reserved. No part of this book may be reproduced or transmitted in any form by any means, electronic or mechanical, including photocopying and recording, or by any information storage and retrieval system, except as may be expressly permitted by the 1976 Copyright Act or by the publisher. Requests for permission should be made in writing to The Globe Pequot Press, P.O. Box 480, Guilford, Connecticut 06437.

TwoDot is a registered trademark of The Globe Pequot Press.

Text design: Linda Loiewski
Map credits: Louis Schmittroth
All illustrations by the Author

Library of Congress Cataloging-in-Publication Data
Elliott, Diane.
Strength of stone : the journal of Electa Bryan Plumer, 1862-1864 : a novel / by Diane Elliott.—1st ed.
p.cm.
ISBN 0-7627-2464-1
1. Plumer, Electa Bryan—Fiction. 2. Plumer, William Henry Handy, 1832–1864—Fiction. 3. Bannack (Mont.)—Fiction. 4. Women pioneers—Fiction. 5. Vigilantes—Fiction. 6. Sheriffs—Fiction. I. Title

PS3605.L446 S77 2002
813'.6—dc21

2002072058

Manufactured in the United States of America
First Edition/First Printing

Acknowledgments

The help and support of the following persons and organizations has enabled me to be as true to Electa's story as possible and to them I am deeply indebted: the staff of the State Historical Society of Iowa, Ellen L. Sulser, Archives Associate; Dr. Loren N. Horton, retired Senior Historian for the State Historical Society of Iowa and descendent of the Horton families who have been farming in Jones County, Iowa, since the 1850s. Dr. Horton graciously lent me use of his family name, thus Horton's Crossing was born; the staff at the State Historical Society of Montana, Helena, Montana; the staff at Renne Library at Montana State University in Bozeman, Montana, especially Mary Anne Hansen, Associate Professor of Library Science and Collections Librarian; the Staff of the United Methodist Church, Bozeman, Montana; the General Commission on Methodist Archives and History, Mark C. Shenise, Associate Archivist; the Iowa Methodist Conference Archives; the IWC Chadwick Library; Esther Wonderlich, Archivist; the Diocese of Great Falls–Billings Archives, Marjorie Sprang, Archive Assistant; Diocese of Great Falls–Billings, Rev. Jay Peterson, Vicar General; Janet Webster of the Guin Library at the Mark O. Hatfield Marine Science Center; the staff at Newport Library, Newport, Oregon; the Chouteau County Free Library, Fort Benton, Montana, Patti McKenzie, Reference/Research Librarian; the Schwinden Library, Montana Agricultural Center, Fort Benton, Montana; Henry L. Armstrong, Photo Archivist; Steve Cahalan, Editor of the Montana Standard; descendants of Martha Jane Bryan Vail, Mr. and Mrs. Norman Blosser of Findlay, Ohio; researchers Joyce Jensen, Billings, Montana; Beverly J. Kelly, Findlay, Ohio; W. W. Roath, West Union, Iowa; Barbara Senn, Helena, Montana.

The maps took form through collaboration with Ian Grivois, Computer Graphics Artist, and under the astute eyes and nimble fingers of Louis Schmittroth, cartographer, Web master (http://montana-vigilantes.org/hpinmt), instigator, and major catalyst for the creation of this novel.

In addition to the many researchers and staffers, I was blessed with the wisdom and support of my readers whose expertise includes antiquities, poetry, psychiatric nursing, engineering, photography, medicine, music, and art. Thank you Joan Chadwick, Joan Clark, Lee Faulkner, G. Leonard Kane, Linda Griffith, Majorie Smith, Jack Tkach and Karen Tkach; Mark Weber; and Jan Zimmerman. I owe the shape of this book to my editors Megan Hiller, Erin Turner, and Karin Utzinger.

Last, I wish to honor my great grandmother, Helen Annette Hjalvorson Souther, a loving staunch Methodist, 1876–1968, who has been a role model for my life as well as for my Electa. And my husband who, if he did not encourage the work at least did not stand in its way, and is my role model for Mr. Plumer.

Contents

ELECTA'S JOURNAL AND PERSONAL LETTERS CHRONICLE
A LOVE STORY. LIKE MOST LOVE STORIES,
STRENGTH OF STONE BEGINS AT A POINT IN TIME
BEFORE THE BELOVED IS KNOWN;
A TIME WHEN CIRCUMSTANCE COMBINES TO CREATE
A CLIMATE WHERE HOPE AND BREATHLESS EXPECTATION
CAN PIERCE A PATH THROUGH THE HEART.

13 May 1862

EVENING

I am over excited and cannot sleep. That's just as well, as today I purchased a small writing table. It's a cunning thing—this box that holds paper and writing equipage. It is constructed with a slanted hinged lid that one may write upon, and has a lock to keep the contents from spilling. I filled it with tablets and lead pencils. My desire is to record this moment with an eye toward the future. We (that is my brother-in-law James Albin Vail, sister Martha Jane, their two children Mary Eliza and Harvey, and myself) are about to embark on a wilderness adventure.

We have been hired by Lincoln's new Blackfeet Indian Agent, our very own Reverend Reed, to manage the Sun River Government Farm. We are to replace Agent Vaughn and his hirelings, who either have or are about to abandon the farm, which was established in '59 to civilize the Blackfeet, the Piegan and the Blood Indians. We shall be traveling deep into the Dakota Territory following the trail Clark and Lewis first recorded. As Mr. Vail and I are certified teachers we

hope to be able to teach the natives a bit more than agriculture and catechism. And I plan to record the whole of it with an eye, I hope, toward eventual publication. Personally, I can't help but think that the observations of a woman would not be less interesting than those of Clark and Lewis, and as I am one of the first women to take this trek, I do believe the task falls to me.

From Saint Louis to Fort Benton

14 May

Soot rode the waves below me and laced the ecru foam that lapped the shore we left behind. Late on Wednesday afternoon on the 14 of May in the year of our Lord 1862, at last, at last, my prayers were answered. At last, we began our journey! I have long prayed, let me see something of this world, allow me to taste it, measure it, weigh it. Dear God, with all my heart I thank Thee.

A great crowd of well wishers and idlers gathered on the levee, as the press had given much publicity to this undertaking. Martha Jane had taken her little Harvey and Mary Eliza to put them to nap in their cabin. I regretted they could not stand with me. After all, the *Emilie* is the first side-wheeler to attempt the 3,000-mile course from St. Louis to Fort Benton. It is a great pity those tots did not witness the shudder of this magnificent vessel as her engines came to life, nor watch the city of St. Louis slide into our past amid the cheers of people and the booming of cannon. Oh, what a waving of hats and handkerchiefs—and of course Old Glory flying above us! If I have children I shall never require they sleep while great events prevail.

Our ship is a luxuriously equipped steamer, and Providence has landed us fine cabins so far astern as to afford the children quick access to the back house. Mr. Vail tells me that 85 passengers with cabins have signed on and 53 more will be camping on deck. I think the greater portion of deck passengers are crew.

Yesterday morning the *St. Louis Democrat* reported most of the persons booked for passage on the *Emilie* are fortune hunters, except for us, of course. "Mr. Vail, a 24-year-old schoolteacher and farmer from Ohio, has accepted a position as manager of Sun River Government Farm, set up to 'civilize and Christianize' the Blackfeet, Piegan, and Blood Indians, by providing them agricultural equipment and instruction in farming." That same article closed with the wry comment, "We have little faith in the success of the enterprise." Personally, I suspect the outcome of our work rests in God's hands, not the editor's.

While I watched the goings on from the rail Mr. Vail waltzed about, visiting with first this person then another, ostensibly getting the lay of the land. He is as curious about the cargo, the people on board, and the dreams our good ship *Emilie* carries as am I. Fortunately for him he is not so shy as I.

"Miss Bryan, Miss Bryan!" Mr. Vail came to me. "Don't be standoffish now, Miss Bryan. There are people aboard who are wanting to meet you."

As we approached a small group of men, I could hear a sonorous voice pontificating, ". . . may have been the policy of the American Fur Company to oppose emigration to the fur producing region, but you can bet all this excitement regarding the discovery of gold in the Northern Rockies is good cause for them to change their tactics. You can bet they're not about to lose out on a lucrative passenger cargo."

Some vocal bass cut in, "I understand the *Spread Eagle* and *Key West* left, loaded to the gills, in spite of the company's finest captains having jumped ship."

A smug tenor interjected, "I'm pleased to be with a party whose leadership has the wisdom to join the opposition . . ."

"Miss Bryan, allow me the honor of introducing you to Messrs. Clow, Watkins, Mead, and last but not least, Mr. Thompson, who I'm afraid we have most rudely interrupted."

I felt like a pony on an auction block. Miss Bryan, this 20-year-old, old maid, up for grabs, see how tiny she is, see how bright her eye? Make no notice of that diminutive size; she can put her full five feet to the task as well as any. The profits of the trade, they well know. I suspect the balance may be tipped against the feminine side on the scale. It may be the mission of my sister and her husband to find me a mate. Nevertheless, 'tis hardly mine. Mr. Thompson took my hand. "As I was saying, Miss Bryan, our Captain Joseph LaBarge was for years in charge of the American Fur Company boats. He knows all the freaks and fancies of this changeable stream. This being his personal enterprise, I feel confident that his financial interest in the outcome of this venture will stand us in good stead. Wouldn't you agree?"

I pulled my hand from his, murmuring, "I'm sure you're right. I'm sure the new company will do well with its share of the Indian trade." Quite frankly I did not like his seeming familiarity. So I turned and solemnly shook the hand of each gentleman standing. "As pleased as I am to meet you, and as much as I'd like to stay and chat, I must get myself to the cabin to see if I might be of some little help to my sister. Mr. Vail, I'd be pleased for your escort."

Out of earshot, I addressed my brother-in-law, "Mr. Vail, I do have a problem with your new friend Thompson. I think he's much too bold, in fact I fear he borders on cheeky."

"Cheeky?"

"Yes, cheeky!" I can almost hear him condescend, 'were it not for their Government employee status, they would most certainly be on deck with the rest of the rabble that has to cook and otherwise fend for itself.'"

"He made no such allusion."

"Trust me. Trust my intuition."

"Miss Bryan, he seems to be a learned fellow. I trust he's only trying to be friendly. It's the frontier we're heading into. We need to be charitable."

"Charitable is as charitable does."

"Take care, dear sister-in-law. With your high standards and your intuitions, you might never land a husband."

I'll take my chances, dear brother-in-law. Thinks I, if I ever marry it will certainly not be to someone with no higher calling than a get-rich-quick scheme.

On the way to supper, Mary Eliza took little Harvey's hand. She fancies herself quite the little mother. All brushed and scrubbed and fresh from their naps they looked like a couple of cunning little cherubs.

Joseph Swift of Pennsylvania, one of two men hired to assist Mr. Vail at the farm, joined us at supper. Mr. Swift is but a teenager, actually yet too young to be called "Mr." However, in spite of his age he has the heft if not the girth of a full grown man. At first glance, he seems a bright enough fellow.

We waited a bit, wondering who is to give the blessing. Much to our chagrin we realized there would be no formal blessing.

Martha Jane, in that indomitable spirit that is so much the core of her person, quietly took charge. "Dear heavenly Father we thank thee for this beautiful day, our good fortune, and this bountiful repast of which we are about to partake, and we ask your blessing on this great journey upon which we have embarked. We ask that you watch over our good Captain and his crew and our fellow passengers. Lend your guidance to our president and all leaders of our country. We ask this in Jesus' name. Amen." Several fellow passengers seated at our table joined us in the Amen and, I believe, appreciated the blessing.

We commenced to eat a fine meal replete with cooked greens, root vegetables, beef, bread, pickles, and coffee. And what a fine way to dine! We eat in a salon that has tables lined at a slant on either side of the room and our staterooms have doors that open into it as well as the doors that open onto the deck. The service is quite lovely, a plain, white vitreous china and the simple pistol pattern silver. Above us we have lovely kerosene chandeliers and these are kept on of an evening so that the deck passengers can stay on and make use of the room. Dinner was accompanied by the hum of nearly 100 people, all of them talking at the same time. Even so, the shrill tenor of Thompson (three tables over, mind you) and some other loud boor bragging on the merits of their outfits could hardly be avoided.

"It is with great expectations we set out upon this journey, well equipped and willing to face all the dangers of navigation on the Big Muddy as well as all the savages who inhabit its shores. Indeed, with the exception of horses or mules, we are well equipped for a year's field work." Thompson's voice sounded as if it were strained through pursed lips.

I discerned the baritone's voice. "The party headed by Chapman, Clow, and Jones is admirably fitted out. They have four good mules with them and so has Colonel Hunkins."

"Nonsense!" exclaimed an agitated Thompson. "I have it on good authority, we will be able to purchase the needed beasts of burden at Benton cheaper than the cost of transport."

Little Harvey grabbed for his cup of milk, and no one was quick enough to save it from spilling. While Martha Jane took care of the scolding, I cleaned up after him, welcoming the diversion.

Our first day out and we've only managed to get as far as St. Charles. We've put up on the opposite bank and expect to be off by dawn. I'm ready to say my prayers and give myself to the hands of Morpheus.

15 May

T'was up before the dawn broke to watch the sun rise from the vantage point of the top most deck of the ship. On the one hand there was no protection from the infernal smoke and cinders pouring out the twin stacks, on the other hand that's exactly what made it a perfect steal-away—no others were wont to be there. From the lower deck I could hear the distant sounds of the voyagers as they went about their labors, and I rejoiced in the privacy of my thoughts. Not a week ago, I turned twenty. I could have taught another year in Iowa. My brother Daniel and his good wife Sadie begged me return, should the adventure prove not to my liking. And I could have married some Iowa farmer with the imagination of a turnip. Lord knows more than one came calling. But I think, stuff and nonsense! I'm the one who first thought of sister and her husband when we heard of Reverend Reed's appointment as Indian Agent to the Blackfeet and of his need for a government farmer. I'm the one who put the two parties in contact with one another. Granted, it was Daniel who talked Mr. Vail into leaving off teaching in Ohio and taking up farming in Iowa, but I'm the one who encouraged him to take the government farm position. I'm the one who inquired as to the particulars, discovering in the process that I would be able to finish out the school year in time to help Martha Jane with the packing. Had I not gone to live with Daniel's family in Iowa when, after Father died, we were forced to sell the farm in Ohio, we wouldn't be on this ship. Fiddlesticks to a life of child rearing, church, and no hope for an end to hard labor—not to mention a dull mate and the gossips! Fiddlesticks to life in a place where everyone knows more about who you are than you ever did!

The sun came up rosy over the rolling hills—as rosy as the possibilities of the life before me.

"Electa! What on earth are you doing up here at this ungodly hour?" Martha Jane found me out.

"Just woke early, Sister. It's hardly a sin."

"Better come down, before people begin talking."

Oh, sugar. I guess there's no getting away from it. I've lived too long with Martha Jane to argue.

"Just look at you, Sister, you're dusted with cinder and ash. I hardly understand you, stealing up to such a place."

To hear Martha Jane, one would think I'd never left home, never traveled on my own, hadn't spent the last two years teaching. Good grief! She's the one never left home alone, not I.

Breakfast and chores behind us, I spelled Martha Jane with the wee ones, reading them "Hansel and Gretel" out of Grimm's volume. Little Harvey was restless, but Mary Eliza ever loves to listen. She's not yet five and—unlike brother Daniel's son, Jamie D., who didn't even show an interest in reading till he was twelve—already she's beginning to pick out some of the words. She's a cunning little miss.

After talking Martha Jane into taking the children onto the deck for a bit of fresh air, wouldn't you know I no sooner sat down to write than Mr. Thompson, the foppish gold seeker from Massachusetts, came by, pulled up a chair, and began to jaw at me. He wanted to know how we were going to get on at the government farm, and, "Miss Bryan, aren't you afraid of the Indians?"

Although I hardly think it's any of his business, I told him, in tones rather stiff, I'm hoping, that the supplies and equipment we need to operate the farm as well as the supplies promised as annual annuities to the Blackfeet tribes were safely on board, and as for the Indians, they have signed a peace treaty.

Mr. Thompson laughed and said, "My! Aren't we a feisty little Irish Miss?" I'd have liked to scratch his eyes out, but I bit my tongue. It pains me that one is never given credit for the things they don't say.

"I see Miss Bryan is a scribbler such as I," the fop continued. "As secretary of our expedition I'm keeping an official journal of this trip."

I cannot but wonder what I was supposed to reply to this pompous donkey. Nevertheless, I prided myself on simply smiling, then dismissed him by turning back to my pad and pencil.

Alas, instead of working in my journal, I spent the afternoon writing to the folks back home and now I'm burning the oil long past dark with my scribbling.

At supper I had the good fortune of eating far from Thompson. When I complained to Martha Jane about him, all she said was, "Be nice, Electa, at worst he's harmless." I say, sugar!

16 May

Again, the *Emilie* set off long before dawn. After breakfast, Martha Jane, Mary Eliza, Harvey, Young Swift (already he's insinuated himself into our fold as our trusty farm lad), and I took to the deck for a bit of a stretch and fresh air. Mr. Vail staid behind to visit with the gentlemen at our table. We strolled one time around the cabin and Martha Jane called it quits. The children begged to stay on deck awhile longer. Martha Jane agreed so long as Mr. Swift remained with us. Together we watched the hills roll by as we steamed up the lower river past fire-ravaged buildings.

Mary Eliza asked, "Auntie, why are those places all burned?" I wondered how to answer such a one so young as she. How to explain war to one who's been told she must not torment her little brother?

"Mary Eliza, do you remember the map your father showed you when he was packing the books?" Her fine curls bounced with a sharp affirmative nod.

"I do. Daddy showed me our continent and he showed me our country and where we lived in it and where we're going. We are going to a territory."

"You do know that some of our states have slaves and some of our states do not, don't you?" She looked intently into the water, but nodded her head, so I went on. "When enough people move into a territory they want it to become a state. The states that do not have slaves don't want slavery in any new states. When President Lincoln was elected, the slave owning states became very angry and those states decided they would no longer be a part of our great nation. Our president said they could not do that and now they are fighting." Mary Eliza's brows were knit.

"Do you understand?"

"I think so. If Harvey took my slate and Mommy said I had to let him play with it, but I stamped my foot and ran away from home, then Mommy would come after me and she'd say, Mary Eliza, this is not an op-shon."

"Oh Mary Eliza, smart as you are, you should have been born a boy. You would have made a wonderful attorney." In truth she does remember more and understand more than the children twice her age I taught in Ohio.

Mary Eliza looked at me with something akin to awe in her expression. "Oh, Aunt Electa, the wind has made tangles of your hair and it is all dusted with smoke. I think it is turning you into an elf." She squeezed my hand and I told my little darling, "I am feeling most elfish as well." Returning her squeeze, I asked, "Shall we go to our room and see if we can be good brownies to your mother?"

Before we chanced to leave the rail we were joined by a fellow traveler I've been introduced to as Mr. Chick, but Chick who? I cannot remember. So many have been introduced. He stared at the ruins we were passing and drawled, "Damn Yankees, done this."

I quickly covered little Mary's ears. It's on account of just this sort of language that Martha Jane has hardly allowed the children on deck.

"Jest y'all wait and see. Jeff Davis gonn'a whup their. . . ."

Again, I covered Mary Eliza's ears.

"I beg your pardon, sir. If you care so much, why aren't you in the company of your illustrious Mr. Davis?"

"A woman with spunk. Ah allus say, Ah do like a woman with spunk."

I felt trapped. Desperately I looked about. Young Swift had wandered down the deck with Harvey and was of no help whatever. Whose eye did I connect with? Mr. Thompson's, that's who.

"Let me tell you little lady, Ah'd'a staid stateside if it waren't fo mah belov'd mama. Ma brothas all gone fo the good cause an Ah jest couldn't bear ta break her sweet ha't."

Desperately I looked again to Mr. Thompson, and I was not disappointed to see him working his way toward us.

"Sides ma'am, it's all togethah the wrong kinda medal them folks is dealing in. Ah'm aufta da stuff what glittas, not lead. Haw! Haw! Haw!"

Good Lord, I felt as if a member of Nasby's congregation rose from Lock's ink, walked off the page and into my life. Alas, witnessed outside the confines of Lock's satirical "Nasby letters," I don't find him one jot amusing. Faith, I'm hard put to accept a schooled person siding with the southern cause. I find the vapid utterances of an ignorant bumpkin positively aberrant.

Mr. Thompson came right up and offered his arm. Leaving Swift and Harvey on deck, with Mary Eliza firmly in tow, I gratefully took it. I'd never dream such a gesture from him would bring me so much relief. On reaching the door of the Vails' cabin I thanked him for the rescue. Then, seeing him respond with a smug set to his face, I almost regretted the event. Oh well, at least I know what to expect from this one. I have learned my lesson, and in the future I shall not go about unattended.

Our progress has been impeded by several sandbars this day. Mid afternoon a storm came up. I spent the rest of the day reading the little book of psalms that once belonged to my mother. Come evening we're tied up on the bank opposite Jefferson City. This night is cold and the storm yet rages.

17 May

Today we were visited by a fierce north wind and we women were more than a little glad to have a "Women's Parlor" away from the rabble where we can gather to share in the comfort of a fire. Beneath our feet is a fine carpet where the little ones can play. Harvey amuses himself with a cunning little farm our brother James built him especially for the trip. The Arnold's daughter and Mary Eliza are playing mother with their "babies." They say Harvey is supposed to be the husband and take care of the farm for them. There are six women aboard, if you count the wives of Captain LaBarge and Chancellor Hoyt. The latter keep mostly to their "pent house" quarters in the texas, where even their meals are served them.

At supper, Mr. Thompson regaled us with news about his dog. Evidently, during last night's storm, the old dog, Jack (actually, some kind of a company mascot, I do think) became so frightened that they had to take him into their stateroom in order to pacify him.

By 2 pm the rain quit. The river is wide and today our progress was good in spite of a strong north wind that plagued us all morning. Put up below Lexington, I am overwhelmed with the destruction I see before me. And I shudder to wonder how many incompetent General Freemans are in the Union employ. The landscape speaks to the hunger and the thirst of his men who, under his orders to hold until relieved, fought to their death on this elevated arid plateau. The rude sentiments of that Mr. Chick Something and his cohorts loudly cheering the ruins—where just a few months before 28,000 Confederates compelled the surrender of 3,000 Union men and a city—yet rings in my ears. Their ignorant good spirits draw the cold on my flesh deep into my heart.

God forgive me. We are taught that we are all Your children, that we are all loved. I haven't yet found a way to love all Your children.

SUNDAY 18 MAY . . . QUITE CHILLY

WE LIFT OUR HEARTS TO THEE,
O DAY STAR FROM ON HIGH!
THE SUN ITSELF IS BUT THY SHADE
YET CHEERS BOTH EARTH AND SKY.

—John Wesley, 1703–1791

Thompson, having tramped the woods in the rain whilst we were wooding and then being much too long on deck yesterday, has taken a fever and has stomach cramps. Martha Jane dosed him with her special remedy: camphor, laudanum, and cognac brandy. In a short time he was past the knowledge of pain or, for that matter, of anything else.

Mid afternoon we came to St. Joseph. The boom of our cannon brought to the levee a great crowd of people. A good portion of the city lies in ruins. I cannot but wonder—how many years of hard labor became the fuel for these ideals turned into militant passion—how many dreams vaporized in the smoke of St. Joe's destruction?

The *Emilie* spent fewer than two hours loading and taking on passengers, ten more, I believe. We gave another salute as we steamed up the river.

19 May . . .Weather Cool, Countryside Abundant With Pretty Farms

Most of the country today was open with extensive bottom prairies. My brothers would like to farm in this country, I think.

Today Martha Jane made the acquaintance of a Welsh Minister, the Reverend Mr. John F. Bartlett. He has made his home in this country some five or six years and preaches a Presbyterian gospel. There is another preacher on board, the Reverend Francis. Unfortunately, he is of the Baptist persuasion, preaching the heresy of redemption by faith alone. Sister and the other women on board have set an appointment with Captain LaBarge in order to ask him to authorize Reverend Bartlett to give the blessing at mealtime and to hold services on Sundays. Knowing Martha Jane, they shall prevail. Thompson, feeling better today, entertained us with recollections of his adventures through the rain. It seems he talked to an old lady who occupied the woodman's cabin. She told him she and her husband had come to this place from the east coast. She said that the Indians made them no trouble, but that wolves and wild cats played havoc with their small stock. Harvey, bless his little heart, spared me with a request that I take him to our quarters and read him a story.

Reached the Iowa line about sunset. The deck passengers and the voyagers, those hardy souls who labor to keep this craft afloat and provide the services for our comfort (they being in charge of providing for themselves) built a great fire on the shore tonight. After partaking of their meal they commenced to play music. Some of the stateroom passengers, including Thompson, joined them in singing and dancing. Martha Jane and Mr. Vail being unwilling, I chose not to join them. But I did watch and listen for a while. Quite a colorful and melodic bunch—Creoles I'm told they are—and the Captain swears they are the best workers he can find.

Captain LaBarge sort of granted the women their request for prayer and services. It turns out there is, beside the two preachers on board, an old Catholic Priest. So they all will be preaching and sermonizing, and they are to work out the blessings among themselves.

20 May . . .
Heavy Frost At Dawn

Overcoats are in demand. Passed Nebraska City about 11 am; from the river she looks pretty. It is comforting to be passing through country that hasn't witnessed the torch. Even the grey rain that has returned does not diminish its peaceful countenance.

We reached the Council Bluffs landing at 7 pm. About 80 teams are encamped here, the owners of a mind to travel overland to the Oregon and Washington Territories. We are told that 1,500 teams, bound for the new mines, have already crossed the river. From the landing we can see the city, like a jewel on the prairie, by far the loveliest city I've seen on the trip.

We learn that the Fur Company's steamer, the *Spread Eagle*, is but two days ahead of us, and we feel certain to overtake her soon. It is our understanding that our Reverend Reed is aboard.

The great excitement of the day came in the form of four letters delivered to us by the captain, one for me from Sadie in Iowa and three from Ohio for the Vails—one from his mother, another from our sister Sarah, and the last from our baby sister Cornelia.

Sarah's babe has been abed with the croup nigh on two weeks now. She and Evie, her eldest daughter, have been nursing him night and day. And this when they'd just been feeling fortunate that they'd all come through the winter with their health. On the plus side of her ledger, the rest of the family is getting on fine, and although the ground is yet too cold for planting corn, beans, and such, it did dry out enough by the end of April that they were able to get their wheat in. Mrs. Vail says her husband, the doctor, has had a hard winter and she fears for his health as he is yet calling house to house to care for his patients. Cornelia writes that everyone is well in brother James' family, she "loves" school, has a best friend Nancy, and she's embroidering a handkerchief for me, but not to tell as it's supposed to be a surprise.

Horton's Crossing
8 May 1862

Dear Electa,

At supper we said a prayer for you on your 20th birthday. Husband says he remembers the day you were born. A cold and blustery one at that, but one no less blustery than the complaint he heard from you. He claims your squalling could be heard all the way to the orchard where he was pruning trees. Happy times those were, he says, and hopes for happy times for you in the year ahead. We all heartily second the sentiment! We have a good portion of the garden in. A few sprouts of spinach, peas, and radishes are already showing. Hope to finish planting in a couple of weeks—God providing the ground again dries out enough to do so. Jamie D. is in the middle of the spring session at the Anamosa High School. Ever since my sister Nellie's husband joined the Iowa infantry, all the talk between the lad and the Horton boys is for joining the Union forces. As for me, I'm glad he's in school and not gone to war. Ah youth! The rumor goes, with no end to the hostilities in sight, conscription is soon to follow. Mr. Bryan and I worry on how we will manage should he be required to report for service. We pray to have the farm paid for before year's end, God willing the crops be bountiful and the market price on hogs holds steady. Your friend, Esther, stopped in last Friday on her way home for the weekend and I shared with her your letter of April 20th. She sends her regards and says teaching isn't the same without you to compare notes with. Well, friend, it smells like time to check my rhubarb pies so I'll sign off.

With Greatest Affection,
Sadie

P.S. I cannot tell you how empty this house is without any companion of the feminine persuasion. My dear, if the Wild West does not meet with your approval, you are more than a little welcome to return to your home on the banks of the creek at Horton's Crossing.

More love and missing you—Sadie

Between the letters and the familiar landscape, I am almost homesick.

21 May . . . Cold Rain

We left the landing about 7 am.

River very crooked today and that matches the way I feel—cross, crooked, and out of sorts. I am cross because there are so many crude men aboard this ship. And I'm not only speaking of the roustabouts, though heaven knows we've our share of them. That aside, a plethora of the male persuasion on board does not fail to join them. When we stop for wood they not only gather it, as is their duty, but they shoot at everything that moves. Martha Jane and I had promised Harvey and Mary Eliza we would take them for a walk on land first time opportunity arose. Wouldn't you know the men spoiled it with their nonsense? They were so rowdy it was too dangerous to stay ashore. When he is with them, Thompson is as bad as the rest. Never mind that the weather isn't particularly cooperative either.

Over supper Thompson entertained us with his adventures of the day. This afternoon, while we were stopped at a wooding place on the Iowa side of the river, there, in the woods, Thompson found a log house, the owner of which told him he was from Virginia. (Oh my, what a run-on sentence that was. Good thing my students shall never see it.) He said the old man reckoned that if the gold mines paid, he would have to up and move on, too many people for him, they scared away all the game. Then the old man said that he had never seen a railroad engine, but that before he'd sold out and moved away, a telegraph line did once overtake him. From the laughter, I take it this was some kind of great joke.

22 May . . . Nasty Wind Until Evening

I commenced to read Hawthorne's *House of Seven Gables*. About 7 pm we reached Blackbird Landing on the Omaha Indian Reservation, a beautiful place. Many mounted Indians dressed in all their finery came cantering down to the boat, but having no interpreter we could not talk with them. On seeing them, Harvey cried, and Mary Eliza hid in the stateroom. The voyagers quickly dispatched the freight destined for the reservation mission and we were soon on our way.

There are beautiful bluffs on the Nebraska side and upon the very highest point is the grave of the great Chief Black Bird. According to Thompson, he died in 1800 and was buried sitting upright upon his horse. He was held in the utmost awe by his nation, for it was observed that he could foretell the approaching death of any member of the tribe without fail. The secret of his power lay in a quantity of arsenic supplied to him by a merciless trader. I wonder where on earth this man finds such information.

Mr. Harkness of LaBarge & Co. told us he had seen a flock of turkeys and a few geese while we were wooding at the mouth of the Little Sioux this morning.

We ran to a point near the Iowa line and tied up in the woods for the night. Would anyone believe it? The voyagers, after laboring since 4 am, are again dancing and making music.

Even if I had the constitution for it, I couldn't. God did not bless me with a voice for singing that anyone but Himself could enjoy. As for dancing, I've never learned how, and now I would feel very uncomfortable learning. When I think about it, I doubt there was a time I'd ever have felt comfortable learning to dance.

23 May . . . Weather Fine At Last

The country continues to be open, and sides of the valley are bounded by gently rolling hills.

Early morning, not far below Sioux City on the Iowa side of the river, upon a steep bluff we saw the post placed there to mark the spot where Mr. Hunkin's says Sargent Floyd of Clark and Lewis's expedition was buried.

Not long after, we put in at Sioux City. Stp'd half hr., time enough to post letters. Half hoped there would be some for us—but alas, there were none. I suppose I'd best get used to this. I must remind myself that the letters will come far and few between. I've been told that some will even go through Panama and come to us via Walla Walla, others will be sent by ship up the Mississippi and Missouri Rivers and others will come cross-country to Salt Lake City and into the Dakota Territories in that fashion. However they arrive, by the time we reach our destination they may come in batches with some of them as much as six months after their composition—some of them never.

Some two miles from town we passed the mouth of the Big Sioux River; after traveling another twenty miles around a big bend, we discovered it was only three miles by land back to the mouth of the Sioux.

The river is pretty with a deep woods on the Northeast bank.

This evening we are stopped at a place called Elk Point.

24 May . . . A Day as Fine as a May Day Should Be

Early afternoon we pass the James River. The bluffs are high and barren. I tell Mary Eliza we are now in Dakota Territory. She does not appear impressed.

We were detained on a sandbar just below Yankton for about one and a half hours. I went out with Martha Jane and the children to pick wildflowers. Mr. Batesson asked Mr. Vail if he could accompany us. Mr. Vail assented. He did not ask for my opinion. Had he, I would have denied the man his pleasure, for though he does not seem to be of the ilk of either a Confederate or a roustabout, his nails are broken and snarly, he smells, and his English is that of one of low breeding. Unfortunately, poor breeding never stopped a man from pursuing any woman, no matter her station. What on earth do they think they have to offer? Fortunately, I was able always to remain close to my own.

Yankton is the capital of the Dakota Territory. It sits on a beautiful, high rolling prairie. The Indians that met the boat were dressed in bright and varied costumes, quite pleasing to the eye. Babies are carried in cradleboards strapped to their mothers' backs. I think it a clever way to keep the baby safe and not hinder one's labor. Stopped there to unload some freight. Only took about twenty min., then continued on to Bonhomme Island where we tied up for the night.

Mr. Harkness mentioned that this was the point of Clark and Lewis's ancient fortifications, thus inadvertently prompting Thompson to regale us with another of his soliloquies. It went something like this, "The honor of the first exploration of the upper Missouri must be credited to Pierre Gaultier de Varennes, that is Sieur de la Verendrye, who with his sons, reached the mauvaises terres in 1742, and passed over to the Yellowstone. Verendrye was the son of Lt. Rene Gaultier Varennes and Marie Boucher, who were married at Three Rivers, Canada, September 26, 1747. She was but 12 years old at that time. These French adventurers were several years making their approach to the Rocky Mountains and spent several more in their explorations. In 1749 the father died on the Saskatchewan. . . ."

Sweet Harvey, my dear, sweet daffydowndilly, begged me put him to bed. How could I refuse?

Tonight the voyagers are cutting wood by torchlight. From my window I can see the lights bobbing about.

25 May . . . Morning Cool and Cloudy

O let Thine orient beams
The night of sin disperse,
The mists of error and of vice
Which shade the universe

—*John Wesley, 1703–1791*

Midnight I woke to gale force winds. Our ship rocked and shuddered as if she'd split apart. I hardly dared return to sleep.

Reverend Francis gave the sermon today. Enough fire and brimstone to keep the children awake for many a night.

Early morning we passed the mouth of the Niobrara River where many beaver have been cutting wood. Here we passed an Indian burial ground and we saw many antelope and deer.

On reaching the Yankton Sioux mission, we stopped to discharge freight for Mr. Hedges, the Sioux Agent. It looked as if there were at least five hundred tepees at the site. The Indians were going about their business in a most peaceful manner. On leaving, the sound of our guns broke any semblance of Sunday serenity.

Late in the day we reached Fort Randall. At the landing we were welcomed by a few Indians and some 300 Iowa volunteers who make up the garrison. Stp'd an hour and a half to discharge freight and take on two wagonloads of ice and other merchandise. Mr. Galpin, his family, and Dr. Burleigh, agent at Fort Randall, joined us. From the deck, I could see a farm above the fort. The fort is about a half mile back of the river so we didn't go in. Mrs. Galpin tells us that the government has a good steam sawmill and a gristmill in operation here.

Across the river there was an encampment of 100 lodges of Sioux near a belt of cottonwoods. We crossed the river in order to take on 35 cords of wood.

Mr. Thompson went off to visit the lodges with Madison Carr, a half breed who has been a passenger with us and claims to be a sub-chief of these Indians.

On his return Thompson told us he greatly amused the little Indian boys by playing on a big jews-harp and finally got a number to dance to his music. The men were finely formed, strong and lusty, and were clothed with a breechcloth and a robe thrown over their shoulders, so that any scars they had received in battle were as plain as the noses on their faces for anyone to see. The squaws wore cloth or skin shirts and leggings, sometimes ornamented with porcupine quills or beads, or both.

I overheard Mr. Thompson telling Mr. Vail that he was surprised and somewhat disappointed not to find among them a single squaw who could lay any claim to even passable good looks.

I cannot but wonder why he was disappointed. I cannot imagine finding any buck that would strike my fancy, but I'm sure the Indian maidens would not agree.

26 May . . . Showers

River full of small islands. After running up one channel for an hour, we had to return and try another. High bluffs along the river abound, barren and streaked with burned out layers of coal. Thompson, Swift, and I along with six other hardy souls climbed to the top of a high bluff only to find other similar ones of greater height beyond.

At Fiensy's Island the men found the cut wood, but had to carry it a quarter of a mile. The men took on all the wood the boat could hold, as this is the last place at which we expect to find cord wood. Henceforth they must cut their own fuel. This evening we were detained three hours on a sandbar. Tied up at Cedar Island. It is late.

Mrs. Arnold's daughter, the darling of the ship, is sick. I should not feel jealous of her popularity over our own Mary Eliza's. Mary Eliza, like me, is shy, and we do not let her run amongst the passengers. In all charity, I shall pray for her tonight, and when I say my prayers, I shall not forget to thank my maker for our good health.

27 May . . . Heavy Rain Last Night, Beautiful Today

Bluffs not so high and barren now. At breakfast, the conversation turned to the scarcity of wood, its high price, and the reasons for this state of affairs–that being the shortage of labor, as the men are largely either in the Rebel or Union armies. And, of course, Windbags is reminded of a story that I will repeat if only to laugh at when I find myself in better spirits. "The situation reminds me of a story of early days on the Ohio River, when wildcat money was used as currency, the larger portion being almost worthless. The captain of an Ohio River boat, seeing a fine lot of wood on the riverbank, hailed the supposed proprietor; "Is that wood for sale?" "Yes!" "How much a cord?" The granger asked, "What ye going to pay in?" "Oh! Gallipolis money!" "Then it's cord for cord!" Hummm . . . At table everyone laughed. But I still don't find it much amuses. Perhaps they mean like Confederate dollars or some other worthless paper. Even so, it's not amusing.

Late afternoon some of the officers spotted buffalo just below the Big Bend. Forty-some passengers, including Mr. Vail, Thompson, and a stray Indian, decided to spend the rest of the day in hunting, then walk across the neck and meet the boat on the other side.

We've put up till the morrow at the center of the Big Bend. It's a dark and soft as velvet night.

28 May . . . Fine Morning

Picked up our adventurous hunters before breakfast. Thompson reported, "We came to the river without seeing so much as a jackrabbit for our pains. Since no boat appeared, we built a flood wood fire and we picked up many fine specimens of fossil fishes. By nightfall many were frightened because the Indian abandoned the camp. He evidently feared our big fire would attract hostile Indians. On the fertile bottom across the river, we saw a large herd of wild ponies."

Made old Fort George before supper. The country is flatter than it has been and timber is scarce. Pointed out eight elk to Harvey. Laid up at Fort Henry Island, nine miles below Fort Pierre. Men out cutting wood.

29 May . . . So Cold We're Huddled about the Stove

A miserable day on all counts. Captain having trouble finding a channel through the shoals. They've put off all the passengers that would go to walk the livestock across the neck to Fort Pierre. About 50 passengers, including Thompson and Mr. Vail, consented to take the 12-mile hike. Captain LaBarge said the *Emilie* would pick them up by sunset.

As the men prepared to leave, I watched the most amazing spectacle. Thompson, on taking one of the big mules to dry land, fixed the mule's halter into a kind of bridle and mounted. In an attempt to join its mate (who by this time was some distance ahead) his steed took off like a shot. He had absolutely no control over the animal whatever and he certainly is no horseman. The *Emilie* was on her way in search of another channel, as from her deck I watched the mule dump him in the grasses along the riverbottom.

Unfortunately, the *Emilie* has spent the greater part of the day lying on sandbars and, between bars, running for more wood. Late afternoon, two miles below her starting point, they broke the tiller and had to make a new one. The boat was about to try another course when six Indians and four men from the land tour arrived by boat. As one might expect, Thompson was with them.

We were served his version of his heroic feat along with supper. He is hobbling around on a sprained ankle. But somehow I can't get up enough steam for sympathy.

Against a very high wind, the Captain took our vessel into a channel close to the bank on the west side. At nine we finally laid to. Bucking a wind turned to full-blown storm, seven men started in a yawl to take food to those who'd walked cross country. After three miles against tide and wind they turned back.

I write. The storm rages. The little ones sleep. And Martha Jane and I are each to the other a comfort in our worry.

30 May . . . Cold and Wet

Woke early to the sounds of the rifles. The men were shooting buffalo. Wanting to see another, I broke my vow not to roam without escort and took myself to the stairway leading to the lower deck. I was not halfway down when the sight below left me in a swoon, but I left off gripping the rail whilst I watched. Indians, squaws, and bucks were eating raw liver and gut with their bare hands.

Picked up Mr. Vail and troupes about nine o'clock in the morning. They were one cold hungry bunch of men. While eating a late but bounteous breakfast of fried bacon and corn bread, Mr. Vail told us that the 12-mile march across the hills felt more like 40 by nightfall.

Martha Jane wishes Mr. Vail would tell the details as does Thompson.

After breakfast, while Martha Jane and I remained in the salon waiting for Mrs. Arnold to join us, Thompson stopped by the table. He declared, "You do know, I'm sure, that the unborn fawn of elk and deer are a great delicacy of the Indians and that, when short of meat, they leave absolutely nothing but skin and bones of such game as they may secure." Then he smiled at me and departed.

There's one who noticed me on the steps, I'm thinking. Poor Martha Jane turned white. "What on earth was that all about?" She asked.

"Didn't you hear the men shooting a number of animals this morning? I think it's just Mr. Thompson's way of making sure we know all the details."

The *Emilie* picked her way over the shoals nearing Fort Pierre by noon. The old dog, Jack, pitched into an Indian cur that ventured on board the boat. During the melee, Captain LaBarge got badly bitten, and in his rage he pitched the old dog overboard and shot at him as he swam, but he reached the shore. Mr. Thompson says the dog will probably have many more stout battles establishing himself as a Sioux leader. Fiddle dee dee, thinks I, I'll bet he ends up Injin soup.

Because the river is too shallow to permit a landing at Pierre, we have tied up on the opposite bank a couple of miles below where one of the Sioux tribes has a village. Many of the men went over by yawl to spend the day in conference at the fort. On the bank an Indian widow stood beneath an elevated platform bearing the body of a dead warrior. Over and over she slashed her arms, and with blood dripping she wailed in sorrow over the loss of her husband. The men, watching, made most rude comments about savage modes of mourning. I betook myself below to leave the woman to her grief without my prying eyes.

About 1,600 Indians of mixed Sioux tribes are said to be living at the fort. Those who have come aboard are dressed in a wide variety of garb, from almost nothing to quite respectable. I am most fascinated by their hair. Some of the men have parts of their head shaven, others dress it fancier and with more jewelry than I have ever seen on a woman of any race. The other thing is the use of paint; they wear color like we wear clothes. Martha says, don't stare. I say, fiddlesticks, they stare at me. It is interesting.

Martha Jane, Joseph Swift, and I took Harvey and Mary Eliza for a walk along the shore. We found a great many kinds of mosses and pretty rocks, and we had a hard time convincing the children not to haul home every fancy they found.

The grieving Indian woman returns to haunt me. If you loved someone and that person died and you were not old, wouldn't you feel like cutting yourself? Wouldn't cutting yourself be less painful than the sorrow eating you? Might not the pain of the flesh help tie you to this physical world?

It's after dark and time to blow the candle out.

31 May . . . Weather Fine and Clear

Passed the mouth of the Big Cheyenne. Took two Indians aboard.

Today the men again saw buffalo. One came slowly down to the river, plunged in, and was nearly half way across before the boat came up to him. The ruckus the men set up with their guns sent us scurrying to our room. Hundreds of rounds were carelessly fired, which, had they reached their intended goal, would have rendered the carcass inedible. This time Young Swift was near and I, yet wanting a good look at the beast, begged an escort. The Captain tied up, and by the help of a winch he hoisted the huge beast on board.

Heavens, it is the largest, shaggiest, strangest creature I have ever seen. The men butchered it right on the deck. The Indians got the liver and guts. We ate its flesh for supper. Judging from the reactions of all parties, I suspect we each believe we got the better deal. That buffalo's flesh is as good as any I've ever tasted.

We witness fine rolling prairie today. Later (just above old Fort Medicine, of which nothing remains but an old chimney and one or two cabins nearly undermined by the falling banks of the river), we ran on a sandbar at the head of an island. After getting free we were obliged to tie up for the night.

Word came down that Captain LaBarge has prohibited indiscriminate firing from the boat in the future. He has placed Captain Galpin in charge of keeping the men on the straight. And none too soon, I think.

SUNDAY 1 JUNE . . . MORNING COOL AND CLOUDY

HOW BEAUTEOUS NATURE NOW:
HOW DARK AND SAD BEFORE!
WITH JOY WE VIEW THE PLEASING CHANGE,
AND NATURE'S GOD ADORE.

—John Wesley, 1703–1791

Passed the mouth of Grand River at 4 pm. Shortly after, a Mackinaw boat loaded with robes from Fort Benton came to us. It was commanded by one Jeff Smith. They were out of provisions. Mr. Harkness seemed content to resupply them. They told us a war party of Rees, on a mission to again attack the Yankton Sioux, were heading toward us. Some of our rebel sympathizers found their amusement in advising the party in the boat to be careful how they shouted for

"Jeff" unless they wished to get into some military prison down the river.

This evening Reverend Bartlett delivered a fine sermon.

2 June . . . Beautiful Day

Boat laid up two hours getting wood at an old Indian camp. Much fallen cottonwood lay about. It was cut by the Indians so they could feed the bark to their horses.

Indians and more Indians. Midmorning, we discovered on the riverbank ahead a large party who desired the boat to stop and take them on board. The Captain, considering that we were far from any aid in case of trouble, kept on his way. The Indians showed their displeasure by aiming their guns at us and brandishing their tomahawks, but when they saw our men getting the cannons ready for action they sent up peace signals.

All morning we have been in view of a long line of hills and moving toward the peaks along the Cannon Ball River. This river takes its name from the numberless, perfectly round stones that make up the streambed. Late afternoon, on reaching the Cannon Ball, we met the war party traveling in eight queer crafts Thompson calls Bull-boats. They fired a salute as a sign of peace, dexterously brought their boats alongside the steamer and all came on board. Several passengers, thinking we were attacked, threw themselves upon the cabin floor for safety from stray shots. When they learned the true state of affairs, they loudly disclaimed being frightened. However, I was watching from the upper deck and I was much frightened. These men were painted and looked very fierce.

After they left, Thompson told me that Red Fox, the Ree chief, said that the Sioux had stolen many of their horses, and he was going down to get even with them.

While the men were in conference with the Captain, I stole down to the lower deck where I had ample opportunity to study the architecture of their Bull-boats. They appear to be round crates of green willow, constructed like the framework of a big basket. A rim around the top is formed by weaving in the pliable tops of the willows. Over this frame, a tightly drawn whole buffalo skin, flesh side out, is carefully turned in at the top and securely fastened with sinews, thus forming a watertight bowl. When thoroughly dry, these crafts are very light and serviceable, and large ones will carry three men.

Convincing Martha Jane there was no danger, I brought Mary Eliza out to see the curious boats. She wondered if, perhaps, they were like the one in which the three wise men of Gotham went to sea.

At supper, Thompson related the particulars of the meeting between Captain LaBarge and the war party. "They seated themselves in a circle and each in turn took a whiff of smoke from the pipe of peace. Then, in the sweet and mellifluous accents peculiar to them, announced that they were glad to see us. Captain LaBarge told them of the great benefits they could reap by supporting the opposition company. Then he gave them presents of tobacco and trinkets. They told him that they were glad that there was to be opposition to the Fur Company and that they had an abundance of robes which they wished to trade for provisions and ammunition. They expressed their satisfaction with our Captain by joining in a dance and concluded their visit by shaking the hand of Captain LaBarge and calling him 'Father.'"

Colonel Hunkins told me that when on a horse-stealing expedition the Indians take the greatest caution, lying concealed in the daytime and traveling by night. They take great risks, because if they are not successful in getting horses they are obliged to take the footpath home.

We put in some 16 miles above the Cannon Ball River. I go to bed wondering if marauding Red Men in boats take those boats back by horse or if they abandon them—assuming they are successful of course.

3 June . . . Clear and Fine With a Strong South Wind

In this stretch, the hills are close to the riverbank, and the peaks beyond look to be much higher than any we have before seen. Today the children and I saw three elk. Mr. Harkness shot one. Now it will be our good fortune to dine on elk.

Finished *House of Seven Gables* and found it a satisfying story. Martha Jane says she read that it was, in part, autobiographical. I'll have to think about that. I am now reading *Adam Bede*. Martha Jane is reading Thackeray. Quite frankly I don't see the import of Thackeray's work—nothing but dilettantes frittering away their lives, living for things of no value, and being miserable all the more for it. Perhaps misery is the point. I like George Eliot better. It's the emphasis on the importance of duty to which I am drawn. That's a concept I can ascribe to.

Another war party of Rees heading south with the intent of engaging their enemy (the Sioux) came on board and drank many cups of strong coffee. I've learned that their true name is Arikara and that they live in villages all year around and raise corn, as do the Mandan farther north and all of the Indians to the south. That being the case, I wonder why the Blackfeet don't raise corn.

Late afternoon we passed some very dramatic square buttes.

4 June . . . Weather Fine, Strong South Wind, River Up 3–4 Ft.

We are traveling through fine buffalo country, there being at times as many as 500 in sight at once. We were awaked at daylight by the cry, "Buffalo! Buffalo!" and immediately the boat ran into a herd containing hundreds swimming in the river. The water seemed alive with them, old bulls, cows, and calves swimming in the eddies formed by the bulk of their mothers. The wheels of the steamer had to be stopped, lest the paddles be broken on the horns of the animals. The shooting was kept under control and only seven were killed (four of which were secured and hoisted on board). A yearling was taken aboard alive by some dolts who thought they could domesticate it. Wouldn't you know, the poor beast became so unnerved, it ran amuck. Captain, at least, had the good sense to order it shot. Numerous wolves follow the herds, providing targets enough for the marksmen.

Arrived at Fort Clark at noon. Thompson reminds us that Clark and Lewis spent the winter of 1803–4 here. The voyagers pulled down two of the deserted houses for fuel. North of and adjoining the fort were several circular pole and dirt houses still standing, each large enough to hold twenty or thirty Indians and four or five horses. Nearly the whole nation of the Mandans was swept away by smallpox in the mid 30s. Last fall, after another outbreak, they abandoned the village and moved to Fort Berthold.

The elevated platforms where they placed their dead had rotted away, thus skulls and other bones lay scattered about the prairie. There are a large number of mounds where the Indians have buried the bones of their dead. They do so only after the flesh is long gone. One corpse was yet on a scaffold, and I saw the corpse of a child wrapped in a blanket on the ground below a broken scaffold. A dozen or more graves, about a third of them enclosed by picket fences, pay tribute to the whites who have died here. Even so, this is a lovely spot; the ground rising abruptly forty feet, then continuing flat for another two miles where it blends into gently sloping hills. And you can still see the impressions left of the plots where they grew their corn.

The river is higher and swifter than before, in consequence many carcasses of dead buffalo, having been drowned, float downstream with the flood wood.

Passed the Knife River. Stopped a second time for wood at another deserted Indian village. Thompson brought Martha Jane and me some flowers that look a lot like lilies. My, what grace they lent our supper table. When he isn't talking, he can be sweet.

Just below Fort Berthold we tied up for the night on the opposite bank. Hundreds of Indians—Arikarees, Gros Ventres, and Assiniboines—have a village here. When the boat landed, the Indians were having a scalp dance celebration. Evidently their late excursion to Fort Pierre met with some success. Midnight and they're at it yet. Even at this distance, the beat of their drums knock like a second heartbeat inside me.

THURSDAY 5 JUNE . . . WEATHER CLEAR AND FINE

By 7 o'clock this morning we could see Fort Berthold in the distance. Within an hour we descried the *Spread Eagle* and we fired a grand salute as we came up to the landing. The river forms an abrupt bend that wraps around the fort. It is a commanding and beautiful spot.

Upon our arrival we found a great gathering of Indians of many different tribes assembled to do us honor. Many of the leaders came on board, held a powwow, drank immense quantities of coffee, and smoked the pipe of peace.

We learned our Reverend Reed is indeed on board the *Spread Eagle*, and is accompanied by the second government farm laborer, a Mr. W.W. Bixby of New York. We discharged freight until noon, thus, allowing the Reverend Reed and Mr. Vail an opportunity to hold council.

Martha Jane keeps the children either in the cabin or the salon most of the time. I wonder if she isn't harming them by doing so. I think it keeps them frightened of the Indians. Not that I don't hold some reservations in my own heart.

Above the fort we passed several Arikara villages and mid-afternoon, the *Key West*. Ran some 30 miles, then laid up next to the *Spread Eagle* at an old deserted Indian village on the left bank. Later, the *Key West* came up beside us and tied up for the night. All voyagers are working into the night gathering wood.

The Reverend Reed took supper with us. I asked him if he knew why the Blackfeet Indians didn't grow corn. He speculated they might be more primitive than their neighbors to the east. Or they might not be as intelligent. Or, perhaps, they just hadn't been exposed to farming. After all, the government farm had not been built until '59. This is only the third year crops have been planted. In other words, he had no idea. I'm remembering my history. I was taught that it was the Indians who taught the first pilgrims how to farm their new country. I was taught that most of the Old World seed did not fare well here, that the early Europeans would have perished had not some of them paid attention to planting such as corn, squash, and melons.

"Evidently they are very militant." The good man added, "Every agent I've spoken to says they are the scourge of the prairie." How very reassuring, thought I. "At Fort Berthold," he continued, "Running Elk, one of the Sioux Chiefs, stoutly objected to the boats bringing the Blackfeet arms, ammunition, and supplies. He claims the Upper Indians only use the goods to come down and make war on the Lower Indians. He may be right. Perhaps we shouldn't be bringing them supplies."

I cannot but wonder if the man's gone daft. "We were under the impression that these things: the arms, the ammunition, the supplies, and also a mission school and the government farm were a part of the 1855 treaty."

Mr. Vail cleared his throat and looked sharply at me.

God forgive me, I could not stop. "We understood that these Upper Indians gave the government a good portion of their land in exchange for these services and goods."

Smiling, Martha Jane stood, "Oh Reverend Reed, it's been so lovely having supper with you. I do hope you'll excuse us, but it's getting late and we must be putting the little ones to bed."

I then thought to myself, "There, I've done it again." Long ago, I learned to keep my mouth shut, and most of the time that's all I'm doing, but every once and a while . . .

"Electa?" When my sister uses that tone, at the same time declarative and questioning, I know it's past time I stop.

I stood. I smiled. I extended my hand to the Reverend. "So good to see you again," I lied. Lest I forget, I'd best remind myself, 'twas I who introduced them.

Martha Jane was so angry she said nothing. She didn't need to say anything. I was wrong in questioning her husband's employer. I washed Harvey's face and hands and helped him into his nightdress. Then, as Mr. Vail was occupied, Martha Jane returned to the salon to find the lad a suitable escort to the back-house. Nearly a month on the trip and he's still terrified of the paddle wheel below the back-house holes, even when it's not in motion.

After bedtime ablutions and prayer, after Reverend Reed has left and Mr. Vail returned, I removed myself to my cabin.

Dear God, forgive me my lie. I don't know what comes over me. You know I know my place. You know I am usually so shy. Please God, help me to be good, to see Your glory—to understand. Please watch over us. We know so little, and our journey is so long. And thank You, Lord, for securing Reverend Reed's passage to Fort Benton on a ship other than ours. Amen.

6 June . . . Foggy Morning

A fog rises from the river like steam, misting and swirling like stage gauze around gnarly, craggy, ragged formations of every fantastic shape imaginable. Within this diorama, small stands of dwarfed ash and elm make occasional appearances on the bank.

Finished reading, *Adam Bede* and began *Mill on the Floss*. Martha is almost finished with *Vanity Fair*. She says truly I should read it if only to round my education, make it current as it were. Perhaps, in spite of myself, I shall.

Sometime in the afternoon we passed the White Earth River, which is next to the most northerly point of the Missouri. This evening we are moving through the Vermillion hills where deep fissures and ravines cut fairy tale sculptures out of red and yellow rock.

7 June . . . Overcast, Country Yet Rugged

Early in the morning we met a Mackinaw boat containing ten men and a large lot of furs. The crew was anxious for war news, having heard nothing for some time.

We caught them up on the news up to the 14th of May—told them the Union forces were doing somewhat better after the disaster at Lexington, General Frémont having been removed in favor of a series of generals, ending with the appointment of General Halleck. In Arkansas, on the second of March, Curtis routed VanDorn, losing 1,351 to VanDorn's 5,000. We reported that the Union victory at Pea Ridge in Missouri left only a bit of guerrilla fighting in that state, and that General Grant had secured Paducah for the Union, and General Smith was holding the mouth of the Cumberland, thus securing a defensive line along the Ohio River. Further, Kentucky,

Tennessee, and New Orleans were in the hands of the Union. Most importantly, the Union Navy had routed the Confederate; thus the waterways are in the hands of the Red, White, and Blue.

The boatmen screamed mightily against our assessment of the war, claimed a victory at Shiloh for the South, and let us know that the South had not yet begun to fight.

In that case, what was that initial blow to Fort Sumter all about?

SUNDAY 8 JUNE . . . WARM DAY, SLIGHT BREEZE, COUNTRY CONTINUES RUGGED

> MAY WE THIS LIFE IMPROVE,
> TO MOURN FOR ERRORS PAST:
> AND LIVE THIS SHORT, REVOLVING DAY
> AS IF IT WERE OUR LAST.
>
> —*John Wesley*, 1703–1791

We passed the mouth of the Yellowstone early on this bright and beautiful Sabbath morning. The barren bluffs and hills that hemmed us in for several days have receded, replaced by beautiful green sloping banks between which runs a narrow, deep, and swift stream of clear water.

We tied up at Fort Union. These Indians and their horses, having come through a winter so severe that many of their number have starved, are living in a weakened condition. We are told they lost 500 of their horses to starvation. They do not go out without being well armed for fear of the Sioux. There having been little trading at this fort in the past year, we were on our way about 8:30 am.

Mid morning, far from any sanctuary but God's own, the sanctity of the day is met with due respect by the passengers and four

Indians traveling with us between camps. Reverend Bartlett's sermon inspired the least of us to open our hearts to know the work God seeks of us, and to know by the gift of this lovely day that we are His beloved children. And Thompson led us in one of my favorite hymns, "Abide With Me." Throughout the day, and even now, its strains remain with me. "Fast falls the eventide." The river is now narrower than it was before we passed the Yellowstone. "The darkness deepens/Lord with me abide/When other helpers fail and comforts flee/Help of the helpless, O Abide with me."

9 June . . . Splendid Day

Martha Jane doesn't seem quite herself today. Her energy seems low, but she assures me she's fine, just a little tired.

This morning we passed the wreckage of the Fur Company steamer *Chippewa*, which burned last year together with the supplies for the upper fort. We are going through harsh country, threading our way through great bluffs with sparse grass on top. The sky is so blue and not a cloud in sight. The sun is most blinding.

Mid morning we passed the Poplar River. The landscape has returned to prairie filled with buffalo and antelope. At noon our tiller again broke, but it was repaired in fewer than two hours.

At an old camp near Fort Charles we found a large pile of wood already cut and stacked. Someone had nailed a large pair of elk horns to a tree and had put up a notice that the wood was for the *Emilie* and that the place was "Elkhorn Landing." We wonder how far ahead of us our companion ship the *Shreveport* is.

Game of many varieties is plentiful and we feast upon antelope, venison, buffalo hump and tongue, beaver tail, fish, and birds.

In spite of the wonderful variety in our fare, Martha Jane ate practically nothing at supper and went to bed early.

10 June . . . Cool Morning, But Turned Warm, Hills Lower, Valley Wider—In Places Three Miles Across

After breakfast Martha Jane and I staid in our cabin and put our needles to work on the blocks for a quilt we are making. Mary Eliza and Harvey played with yarn and scraps and pretended to do the same.

Then a most terrible thing happened. I suppose I shouldn't even write about it, but this afternoon haunts me and I cannot sleep. Perhaps if I write it out I can purge my mind of it.

Martha Jane was wondering aloud if brothers Daniel and James Jr.'s crops had come up thick, when her face went white. At last she whispered, "Electa, go find Mr. Swift. Ask him if he will take the children for a romp in the fresh air."

I don't think I even answered her. I must have looked like a chicken with its head chopped off, searching for Smith, first on our deck then the one below. I found him at last, he coming up from the hold with Lord knows what for Mr. Vail. He asked if anything was wrong. I thought, "Yes! Yes! Yes!" But I knew that whatever might be wrong, Martha Jane would have my head if I opened my mouth. So I said, "No, we just need someone to spell us with the little ones so we can get ahead on our quilt blocks." He said he'd be down as soon as he finished his chore.

On my return, sister was sitting in the same position as when I'd left her except that her sewing was on the floor and she was gripping the sides of her chair. "Did you find him?"

"He'll be here momentarily," I answered and I prayed this would be true.

"What did you tell him?"

"I think I said we need someone to take Harvey and Mary Eliza out for a bit of sunshine. It's such a beautiful day. I said we were engaged in our quilting and we wanted to have something to show for ourselves before the day is out."

"Good. Now, fetch a kettle of hot water from the laundry."

I had done as I was told when Swift arrived for the children. Closing the door behind him, I turned in time to see my sister swoon. I caught her and helped her to the floor.

Then I noticed her skirt and the chair seat all covered in blood. Lord, I've never seen so much blood. Dear God, what is happening? Frantically, I searched my mind trying to untangle the situation.

"Fetch some towels, little sister. Get a blanket to cover me, and undo my clothes."

I was all fumble-fingers, getting her out of her garments. Once off, I started to put them in the basin when a glob of bloody tissue, greater than the size of my fist, slipped from her underclothes and onto the floor.

"No, no. Don't put them in the hot water." Martha commanded in that take-charge voice of hers. "We need to rinse them in cold with salt, just as we do our monthly rags." Suddenly I understood the problem was female, and that was why I couldn't say anything to Young Swift. I saw Martha shivering. I let her clothes drop back to the floor and put the blanket over her. She saw the glob on the floor and with some effort rolled to her side. Pointing to it she said, "Could you pick that up? Go ahead and use my undergarments, they're soiled already. I want a closer look."

As repellent as I found the task she'd put me to, I complied. Setting it on the floor before her, I forced myself to watch as she opened the cloth, spread it flat, and smoothed the mess in front of her with her finger. "I wasn't even sure I was with child," she murmured. "Not one day of the sickness and me always sick as soon as I'm caught that way." And I remembered the ghastly morning ritual she'd gone through when she was with Mary Eliza. "See, Electa, tiny as it is, see the arms, see the legs? Isn't it a marvel how complete it is, even when it is yet so tiny it could fit inside a saucer?" I looked at the glob and saw the curled up body; all head, belly and bent strings for arms and legs. I shuddered. Faith, it was the ugliest thing I'd ever seen.

"What shall I do with it?" I asked.

Martha Jane rolled flat on her back and stared at the cabin ceiling.

I went out to have a bucket of cold water sent to the room and when I returned Martha Jane had not moved. When I heard the knock on the door, signaling that the voyager in charge of laundry had left the bucket on the deck, I waited a bit, then moved the curtain just enough to see that no one was there. Quickly I opened the door, pulled the bucket inside, and locked it behind me. I stirred a cup of salt into the water and into that I placed her petticoats and her dress. She began to moan.

"What is it?" I asked. Her knees came up and she rocked them side to side moaning and straining while I, I could only stand there wringing my hands and calling, "What shall I do? What can I do? What am I supposed to do? Shall I find Mr. Vail?"

"No! Not yet. I don't want him to see me so. Wait till it's over."

Over? What more could there be? The beginnings of a baby were on the floor and my sister has lost nearly all her blood. "Martha Jane, I'm going for the ship's doctor."

"No! No, Sister, no. Never been to one, not even my father-in-law. Not going to one now."

Dear God, I thought, let this end. I wish she'd let me get help. Dear God, what more is left? "Martha Jane, what more are we waiting on?"

"Tissue," She gasped, "more tissue needs come out. Then it will be over. But it's like having a baby all over again, excepting this one didn't—I didn't know this one was with me—not till I felt the rush of fluids, felt it slipping, slipping. . . ." Then, again, she fell into moaning and rocking, and I thought I'd die of worry, of helplessness. When she was again still, she said, "My fine china bowl. It's in my trunk. You'll find it near the bottom. It's wrapped in my winter cloak. I want you to get it out. Put the baby in it, hide it where it can't tip over and where no one will see it. After dark, let it rest in the river."

I concentrated on what I could do, following her instructions, cleaning her garments. She moaned and rocked until her moans turned into screams and I wondered that no one heard her. At last she cried out, "Oh! Oh! Oh!" Each Oh! riding on a spurt of air, then she seemed to sink into the floor. "It's over. Now it's over."

I didn't know what to say. I just stood there like a stone and stared.

"Sister, I need you to help me now. Get our rags." Pointing to a great mass between her legs she added, "You'll need to place this in the bowl with the baby. Then we need to wash me and pack me down there to help stanch the bleeding. We need to work fast, Sister. They'll surely be returning soon." I worked faster than I ever knew I could. After packing her as best I was able, I helped her into a clean dress and got her onto the bed. Before I'd finished cleaning the floor, we heard a knocking on the door. The water was rife with blood and long past any usefulness. Wiping my hands on a rag, I opened the door a crack. Indeed there was Mr. Swift and the babies. "We've had a bit of an accident here." I slanted the truth. "Would you be a love and fetch us a pail of water?"

To my relief Swift agreed and took the little ones with him. I grabbed the full basin and, seeing my way clear, I tossed the dirty water overboard. When they returned I gratefully took the bucket from them and said, "I'll come for you, soon as I get this mess cleaned up."

Martha Jane told me she was relieved I'd kept my wits about me. After the room was returned to proper order, we tied a bandage about her upper arm and we resolved to tell anyone asking that she was showing me her china bowl when the boat bucked—that she'd dropped the bowl and slipped and fell on its pieces cutting herself in the process. Only then was she ready to talk to Mr. Vail.

As I write this, I am still shaking. I have just thrown the good china, miserable contents and all, overboard. T'is a waste of a good china bowl I think. I don't intend on ever getting married. I could never live through it. I'm not Martha. I'm not sisters Sarah or Mary. I'm just a very tiny woman. I'd be dead before the child was born. I don't have that kind of courage. There, I've said it. I've faced it. And I know the answer. Never, never marry!

I don't know where we've put up for the night.

Please, God, grant us the strength of a stone that we might make it through this journey.

11 June . . . Evening Rain, River Crooked

The river is rising very fast and is full of driftwood. An epidemic of fishing has struck the passengers, and some fished all night, catching more than 300 pounds. Early morning, we reached the mouth of the Milk River. Its waters are truly much whiter than those of the body it empties into. We left off several men there. They plan to go overland from here, gather in a lot of Indian ponies along the way, and on reaching Fort Benton they'll trade them to the prospectors. The hills appear more mountainous, assuring us that we are gradually nearing the end of our journey.

Spent the day in play with the little ones, in work on another block, and in trying to cheer Martha Jane. She seems a bit stronger today. I pray she will be fully recovered before we reach Fort Benton. Sixty miles across land could not serve her well at this time. Joseph

Swift has been a dear, running errands for us and taking the children about to get some fresh air.

We're tied up early tonight. Stopped by a storm.

12 June . . . A Cold North Wind Blows, Making Fires and Overcoats Necessary Comforts

River very crooked, valley getting narrower—high, rugged, wind—chiseled, fantastic-looking hills. Pine appears on the hilltops. Today we passed the halfway butte between Forts Union and Benton. On the horizon to the north the mountain peaks are marvelous and white.

Spent another day in the cabin. Finished another block. Martha grows stronger. Her appetite returned this evening.

13 June . . . Cold Rainy Day, North Wind Like Yesterday

Sandstone bluffs rise 200–300 feet above the river. Wood scarce, bottoms narrow, channels good. Was able to point out black-tailed deer, antelopes, and a beaver to Harvey and Mary Eliza. Too cold and windy to stay out long.

Passed the Musselshell River about noon. Harvey has developed the sniffles. Martha Jane continues to improve. I finished another block. Tied up near rocky point for the night.

14 June . . . Cloudy Day, Rain, Wind Gradually Changed to East

Today we saw mountain sheep climbing the bluffs, a lone wolf in a stand of trees, and waterfowl. The side canyons support stunted pines. Today Thompson brought me some prickly pears with the most wax-like flowers in a bowl he fetched from the ships kitchen. The flowers are both crimson and white. One needs handle them carefully though, for the needles on the plant are indeed most prickly. I've wedged the bowl inside my writing desk and I hope the flowers will dry there.

A government boat containing men from Captain John Mullan's command at the Bitter Root Valley, where the greater contingent of them have been finishing Mullan's Road, which stretches from Fort Benton to Walla Walla, came up to the *Emilie*. They reported the *Shreveport* about 50 miles ahead of us, at Dauphin's Rapids. The men, further, declared that experienced miners were taking out from an ounce to an ounce and a half per day—elating news to the gold seekers on board, I'm sure.

On each side, towering bluffs have closed down upon the river. The river is high, and it is with difficulty the *Emilie* progresses. In these parts the water is clear and sparkling and runs very swiftly and small rapids are met at every turn. We reached the first important rapids near night. The *Emilie*, trembling under a heavy head of steam, bravely entered the fight. For a half hour at a time, she hardly gained a foot in her progress. To add to her problems, it rained heavily and was very cold. The men fueled her boilers with tar pitch and finally succeeded in getting her over the crest of the fall. All on board cheered the victory.

We tied up for the night ten miles above the rapid. Forty or fifty of the passengers climbed to the top of one of the high bluffs. We hoped for a peek at the mountains. The view from the summit was marvelous and the winding river below looked more like an Ohio canal, but no snowy mountains could be seen.

Martha Jane took dinner with us this day.

And now the rain falls in a torrent.

Sunday 15 June . . . Weather Fairer During Day

> To God the Father, Son,
> And Spirit, One in Three,
> Be glory: as it was, is now,
> And shall for ever be. Amen.
>
> —*John Wesley, 1703–1791*

This morning our good ship worked her way over the second rapids before we passengers were up. Soon after breakfast our pilot announced that he saw the smoke of the *Shreveport.* We all cheered like lunatics, and the cannon was fired to give notice of our approach. The *Shreveport* was lying at the foot of the third rapids, and when the *Emilie* came alongside, mingled greetings, hootings, howlings, and cannon firing ended in a general pow-pow. After an hour of visiting, preparations were made for getting the boats over the rapids. The steamers lay at the foot of a long, steep, sliding bank with a buffalo trail, several inches deep in mud, running above the river. A cold rain added grief to the miserable conditions. At the Captain's command, most of the men debarked to the path in order to lighten the load. They stood in the mud and the rain, watching the efforts made to run the rapids. Using rosin and tar, belching a most unholy smoke from her tall funnels, she made satisfactory progress until she reached the very swiftest part, where she wavered and fell back. By signs, the men induced the pilot to work the boat over toward them and to throw out a line. They proceeded, then, to cordelle the boat over the crest into stiller water. After dropping anchor, the *Emilie* attached a long line to a keg and let it float down to the *Shreveport.* Thus, she enabled the *Shreveport* to make it over the rapids.

Mr. Vail was one sorry looking fellow after his day in the mud, but as Martha Jane says, "The body washes."

This evening the passengers from the *Shreveport* joined us to hear Reverend Bartlett's sermon; his theme being, "Faith and Works." James 2:26. "For as the body without the spirit is dead, so faith without works is dead also."

A light late afternoon shower paved the way for a clear sunset capped by a glorious rainbow.

Now it's raining again.

16 June . . . Rainy Day

Hills high and close to river all day, boat gets on slowly. When we reached Drowning Man's Rapids, the *Shreveport* and the *Emilie* repeated the same tactics that proved successful in navigating the earlier falls.

At sunset we met another Mackinaw boat containing more of Mullan's men heading for the States. They are going to Fort Union and there await the return of the *Emilie*.

17 June . . . Cold West Winds, Later Clear, This Day the *Emilie* Reached Fort Benton

About two miles below Fort Benton we came to the last of the rapids. There, the Indians discovered us. By the time the *Emilie* and the *Shreveport* labored their way over the rapids, nearly one hundred Indians had gathered on the banks. They formed a friendly escort for passengers and crew all the way to the landing. For once, Martha Jane allowed the children to watch. We saw old, battle-scarred warriors riding as if they and their horses were one item. Alongside them, young bucks in colorful costumes and faces painted mustard and black, performed feats of horsemanship, riding up and down the riverbank. Now little Harvey says he wants to grow up to be an Indian.

Through a break in the grey bluffs, the river forms a wide, inviting sweep that rises to kiss the level prairie Fort Benton is built upon.

About two o'clock in the afternoon the *Emilie* and the *Shreveport* ran their noses aground and we were arrived.

After an hour's stop at Benton, the *Emilie* moved a couple of miles up river to a point above the crumbling adobe ruins of old *Fort Campbell.* Here LaBarge, Harkness & Co. propose to build a trading house, the adobe walls of old Fort Campbell being a safe place of retreat in case of hostile attack.

After supper a group of persons that sailed up the river on the *Shreveport* joined us. It was a glorious evening, and we hiked to a spot a little more than a mile above Fort Benton. There, with much hoopla and fanfare they dedicated, in honor of the Captain, a new fort, Fort LaBarge. The flag was raised and Rev. Bartlett said a prayer for the success of the adventure and expressed hope that the new fort would be superior, in point of neatness and comfort, to those we've too often seen before. And then a great bunch of self-important fools spoke to the occasion amid hearty cheers for the new fort, the captain, the Union, and Old Glory. Of course it's all a great humbug, the point being, LaBarge & Co. is planning to build an outlet in this place for their personal trading, and it would be called Fort LaBarge whether or not the people put up a carnival in his honor. That aside, the children greatly enjoyed the outing, and it was a pleasant way to spend the evening.

Under star-studded night skies we returned to sleep, one last time, aboard ship.

18 June

It is a glorious day. The sky is blue as far as eye can see, with not so much as a cloud in sight. Martha Jane and I took the wee ones on a hike up a tall bluff. There, far to the west, the Rocky Mountains are distinctly visible. They look as if someone had dipped a brush in white and drawn them on a sky blue canvas. Mary Eliza says they're like a vision from a fairy tale.

By the time we'd turned our faces toward camp, the landing was dotted with clusters of white tents, members of each party setting up near each other. The picture below was further decorated with the tepees of a few Indians evidently not living inside the fort.

Mr. Vail is on the levee sorting out the government goods. Oh my, what a mess that is! All the freight brought by the *Emilie* and the *Shreveport* is piled any old way upon the riverbank. It looks a fright to me. I cannot imagine they'll ever get it properly sorted.

We are to take up residence at the agency quarters in the fort and there await the arrival of Reverend Reed. But first Martha Jane, the children, and I must await our escort.

Fortunately, Mr. Harkness has set up a great tent for a store to sell his goods and his business has been brisk. In the shade of his tent, we are waiting for our men. Ah! Harvey has spotted his father coming. We are rescued.

19 June

The *Emilie* left today, taking with her the Chancellor Hoyt, his wife, and some few others who took one look at the frontier and turned their minds against adventure. Not an option many have.

Benton. From the distance of the ship, it looked so orderly and fresh. Oh, My! It is worse than Berthold. The fort provides safety for a varied group of peoples, horses, pigs, dogs, and bugs, all living together as in a stew—and a foul one, at that, it is. Sanitation not withstanding, there are too many for the size of it. Well you might imagine the stench it makes. The agency quarters leave much to be desired. Martha and I spent the rest of yesterday and this day just cleaning it out. I'd have preferred a tent.

Now, I can't but wonder what on earth I was thinking. It's been said the only decent fort on the upper Missouri is Fort Randall. I didn't go into it, so I wouldn't know. Now I wonder what sort of place we're getting ourselves to. Ah, well! It's soon enough we'll be knowing.

I shall miss my good berth on the *Emilie* tonight.

Sunday 22 June

Come, said Jesus' sacred voice,
Come, and make my path your choice;
I will guide you to your home;
Weary pilgrim hither come.

—*Anna L. Barbauld, 1743–1825*

This day the *Spread Eagle* has arrived. We are joined by the Reverend Reed and Mr. W.W. Bixby. Mr. Vail first met Bixby on the 5th of June at Fort Berthold, the rest of us made his acquaintance today. The Reverend will be traveling with us to the farm. We are to be escorted by one named Mr. Iron, who is to meet us with the government ambulance and will be our escort to the Sun River farm.

The Reverend tells us that the Piegans and the Gros Ventres are at variance. Word was sent that he was to meet the Gros Ventres at the mouth of the Milk River and there deliver their annuities. Unfortunately no one met him and he has no idea where they are. After Reverend Reed sent word to all the chiefs to come in and talk with him, he presided over evening services.

23 JUNE

It's set. We leave tomorrow morning, and not a moment too soon. Reverend Reed may not know where his Gros Ventres are, but we know where some were last night. Last night they made a raid and stole 80 horses. Another prospecting party, fellow passengers on the *Emilie*, lost six to a tune of $550.

Iron, who turns out to be an Indian, appeared in our camp this morning driving the Sun River government ambulance, which is to take us to our new home. Evidently he has, for some years, been the person in charge of procuring game for the government farm. Reverend Reed explained that we especially needed him because the Blackfeet would not countenance our killing their buffalo. At least we women and children shall neither have to walk nor ride astride the 60 miles or so it is to the Sun River. In addition to the Reverend Reed, Thompson, who has purchased himself a mount and another fellow from Gould's mining outfit, will join our party on this trek. Thompson and he will rejoin the rest of Gould's party when they reach the Sun River.

Martha Jane and I have spent the last two days cooking. I don't know how she keeps going. I'm so tired, I could sleep on a bed of stones.

Sun River Government Farm

25 June

. . . Day before yesterday we traveled 35 miles and camped at a spring on a high prairie that extends to the foothills of the Rocky Mountains. We travel on the Mullan Road. On its way to Walla Walla it runs past the government farm, thus every emigrant and miner will be on it. In truth, the road is naught but a rutted trail.

Yesterday we caught up with the Gray party, who are heading for the Salmon River mines, and kept with them until we reached the farm at noon. The Sun River is about 200 feet wide and its banks are lined with grand cottonwood trees.

It looks as if the former tenants vacated at least a month ago and the condition of the farm matches my worst fears. One wouldn't know to look at it that the place was built just four years ago. Martha Jane and I spent the afternoon and long into the evening cleaning and scrubbing our new home. Lucky for us the men hauled water from the ditch so we could begin while they unloaded the supplies.

First we swept the cobwebs, dust, and loose chinking out, then we washed the logs, shelves, and table. Next we enlisted all hands in removing dusty musty old ticks, hanging them over the bushes and beating the dust out of them. Then and only then did we commence to unpack. Thank God the extra cooking we did in camp held out. Besides the horses and some hogs, we have some milch cows. First thing Thompson did on arrival was separate them from their calves. Before supper he milked them and that made our meager rations go down well.

The beds are most interesting here. In both bedrooms they are built right into the walls, one above the other. I shall be glad when new hay is mown and we can refill the ticks with fresh. The floors seem to be of packed earth. I asked Iron about them and he said they were made by mixing bird droppings with the mud and that's what gave them their hardness.

Iron seems a good man. His English vocabulary is equal to that of most of my students, but his vowels are strange to me and I have a hard time following him. Also, I wonder if he isn't sometimes pulling my leg? There have been moments when, before he turned away, I thought I caught a twinkle in his eye. But he is such a stoic, it must be my imagination.

All day today, Martha Jane and I unpacked and cooked and cleaned. The men have been surveying the farm. Mr. Vail frets that the tools are in disarray and some are missing.

Martha Jane and I worry as to how we're going to go about rechinking the cabin. In places the chinking is so completely out as to let a bit of the light come through. I suppose, if it's true about the floors, we could mix up more of the same and use that for chinking.

One thing perplexes me though and it is this, sometimes my dreams are haunted by the specter of Indians eating raw entrails yet steaming with the heat of the freshly killed animal.

26 June

Having completed his inspection of the farm, Reverend Reed has already left to return to Fort Benton. The man rather wearies me. Martha Jane says be charitable. Mr. Vail says we must each look to our own faults first. Sometimes I wonder if being a "good" person doesn't require some kind of blindness? Martha Jane would say, God puts each of us here for a reason and we must respect that.

This morning, Thompson tied a dish towel about his waist and churned our first batch of butter. Then, in a spot shaded by trees, he dug a hole in the irrigation ditch and fixed it with a big crock so now we have a cold keep for the summer. At supper we were treated to cold buttermilk, and I must say, in spite of all the troubles, things don't appear quite so grim.

That scoundrel Iron! He was indeed pulling my leg. This morning when Harvey spilled his cup of water on the floor and I went to sop it up, I discovered wood beneath the dirty crust. Now I have scrubbed until my arms, my back, and my head aches. This house is about 20 by 30 feet and I've scrubbed each and every inch of it.

We have three windows, a door, a chimney, and a fireplace. The house and a 20 by 40-foot storehouse have a gate between them and altogether they form the north side of the palisade. On the east end of the enclosure, four rooms (designated as "Indian houses"), 18 by 15 feet apiece, share a common south facing wall, and the first room also shares the east wall of the storehouse. Each of these rooms has a chimney, fireplace, window, and door. These rooms were built to accommodate Indian families while they studied agriculture. Even the storehouse has two windows in addition to its three doors. And yet, would anyone believe it, there's no back-house—not a one on the place? Since there's plenty of room for one within the stockade, Martha Jane and I about had a fit over it. Mr. Vail said he'd rectify the situation right soon. And I should hope so. It is one thing for the men to be living in the wilderness like savages, but for the women it will never do.

Tomorrow we plan to do the laundry. Martha Jane came up with the idea of using one of the Indian "houses" for a summer cook and wash house. She swept it out and started a pot of beans for tomorrow's fare.

It's hardly yet dark and I'm ready to wash up and say my prayers.

27 June . . . Rained All Day

This day brought more of Gould's party to the farm. I suppose we'll soon be losing Thompson to them. They are camped by the river and have engaged themselves in the recovery and repair of the government ferry boat so they might take the wagons over the river. Today the wee ones, Martha Jane, and I did the laundry. In anticipation of the great chore, Joe Swift was kind enough to rise before dawn, bring up several barrels of water and start a fire under a boiler. On account of the rain we had to string up the laundry all about our cooking/washing room.

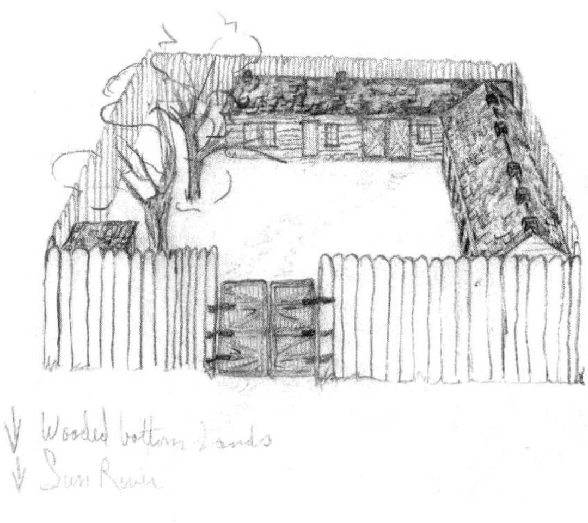

We entertained Mrs. Gould at lunch today. I do not envy her the trip ahead, but she is young and with the man she loves. I suppose that makes up for a lot of hardship.

Our men are out mending a section of the pasture fence that has fallen into disrepair. Time I stopped writing. Martha Jane got out a jar of pickled beets she'd brought from home, to honor a nice ham she found hanging in a cupboard in the storeroom. I'd best be mixing a batch of salaretus biscuits before the stove goes cold. The men will be soaked through on their return, and I'm sure they'll be most starved from their own labors.

28 June . . . A Splendid Morning

Late morning, Mr. Thompson came up to say goodbyes.

Come dawn, our visitors had discovered that one of the Gray parties' teams was missing. After a long search the strays were found far up the valley. As we women had hardly been out of the enclosure, Thompson suggested we accompany him to the ferry. Martha Jane demurred saying she still had too much to do, but insisted I do the honors for all the family.

This valley is large and today it was lovely. In an arc, extending from the river to the east and northward as far as my eye could see, miles and miles of grasses shimmered in the heat of the midday sun. This prairie arc bends 'round the palisade and ends in the northwest where the river woods begin. The wood creates a break mostly to the south and west of the farm. Great herds of little antelope and numberless deer dotted the landscape.

Thompson and I walked along the farm road, first north then east to the Mullan Road, then to the south and into the cool wood that lines both banks of the wide and lovely Sun River. And all the way Thompson entertained me singing the likes of "I know where I'm Going" and such. I shall miss that lilting tenor when he's gone.

In the shade of an old cottonwood tree, Thompson found us a nice set of rocks ensnared in its roots. There he bade we sit a spell, in this place just off the path and out of the way of the rest of the pilgrims, as it would be some time before we'd see each the other again. I chose to laugh and said lightly, "I suspect you'll make your fortune in a fortnight and we'll be hearing your jaw awagging before the body arrives."

Thompson laughed, then turned sober. "Electa, I do intend to come out of these wild lands with my fortune. I don't know yet how I'll do it. But I'm confident, after testing the lay of the land, I shall puzzle it out. I fully intend to make my fortune, and I intend to transport the fruits of my labors back to my home state, thereafter to live a quiet and grand life. What do you think, Electa. Do you dream of such a life?"

A thousand thoughts rushed through my head. Yes! Yes! Yes! I too expect to return home, marry well, and live a gracious life. And No! No! No! I could well imagine a life with Thompson. I could hear him, 20 years from now, endlessly retelling his "pioneer" stories, endlessly pontificating on the finer points of his intellectual correctness in the assessment of the situation. Sure as God's in heaven, he'd never shut up. Mr. Vail's admonition screamed through my brain, "Miss Bryan, with your high expectations and your intuitions, you may never land a husband." Oh sugar!

And then it happens. I have been staring into the wood where, not ten feet from us, I discern two lovely creatures where before I only saw the forest leaf bed. "Look, Mr. Thompson," I whispered nodding toward them. "Do you see the fawns lying there?"

Thus I broke the awkward spell, and being recovered of good senses, Mr. Thompson bade me farewell until we're to meet again.

I watched the company safely ferry the wagons across the Sun, the stock swimming after.

Turning, I beheld the palisaded farm buildings. Fifteen feet high stand the rough, upright poles that offer us protection and as I walk I sing, "A Mighty Fortress Is Our God."

Tonight, I know, I'll come into sleep at peace with myself.

SUNDAY 29 JUNE . . . AH! SUNSHINE

> THOU WHO, HOUSELESS, SOLE, FORLORN,
> LONG HAST BORNE THE PROUD WORLD'S SCORN,
> LONG HAST ROAMED THE BARREN WASTE,
> WEARY PILGRIM, HITHER HASTE.
>
> —*Anna L. Barbauld, 1743–1825*

What a lovely day this day came to be. Friday it rained all day and yesterday, after a beautiful beginning, the skies again turned grey and dumped more rain. Sister and I took to baking gingersnaps, ironing, and mending while the children chalked pictures on the wood floors. Their designs covered the whole dining area and we had a great time identifying the images in little Harvey's scratchings. But today! Today, we received letters from home.

A Mr. Morley arrived about eight this morning. He is with a large train on his way from Fort Benton to the mines on Gold Creek. They're camped about a mile off the river some eight miles below us. He says the recent rains have put the roads into a bad state, making a hard go of it for them. Tomorrow he wants to leave some of their tonnage in the care of Mr. Vail. He asked a lot of questions about the farm and I'm afraid there wasn't much to tell. So far the only Blackfeet we've seen is our Iron. I can tell he wasn't much impressed, and who could blame him? We haven't been here two weeks and I'm beginning to wonder what we're doing here myself.

About nine, two more visitors on their way to Fort Benton joined us for coffee and cookies. One was a merchant from Hell Gate who has with him five ox teams, of five yoke each, to haul his goods brought up on the *Spread Eagle*. Of greater interest, he brought letters. I received one from Daniel, Martha one from Cornelia, and Mr. Vail one from his father. The merchant spoke flatteringly of the mines they visited yesterday morning four and a half miles west of the mountains, and his companion showed us $500 in gold dust taken from the new mines on a branch of the Hell Gate River.

Mr. Vail Sr. wrote that his wife, bless her heart, much exaggerates his problems of frail health and overwork. The truth of the matter is quite in the reverse. It is the Mrs. who insists on working herself to exhaustion, knitting socks, making bandages for our soldiers, and advising all on the merits of sending tea and cloves to their boys. He asks, did you know a pinch of tea under the lip gains them energy on long marches (and, of course, diminishes the temptation toward the nasty use of tobacco) and one little clove can do so much toward keeping the mouth from drying out, and if chewed diminishes the pain of tooth ache? Unfortunately, he also sent a couple of newspaper clippings. The first, a short piece on a couple of robberies; one, the drugstore's—the other, the hat shop in Anamosa. The second clipping had on the one side "Useful Medical Hints" and on the other a treatise on rearing young children. As one can well imagine, sister bit her lip on that one. Had there been a fire in the stove I'm sure she would have tossed it in. As it were, I retrieved it from the wood box.

USEFUL MEDICAL HINTS

If a person swallows any poison whatever, or has fallen into convulsions from having overloaded the stomach, an instantaneous remedy, more efficient and applicable in a large number of cases than any half-a-dozen medicines we can now think of, is a teaspoonful of common salt and as much ground mustard, stirred rapidly in a teacup of water, warm or cold, and swallowed instantly. It is scarcely down before it begins to come up, bringing with it the remaining contents of the stomach: and lest there be any remnant of poison; however small, let the white of an egg, or a teacupful of strong coffee be swallowed as soon as the stomach is quiet; because these very common articles nullify a larger number of virulent poisons than any medicines in the shops. In cases of scalding or burning the body, immersing the part in cold water gives entire relief, as instantaneously as lightning. Meanwhile, get some common dry flour and apply it an inch or two thick on the injured part, the moment it emerges from the water, and keep sprinkling on the flour through anything like a pepper box cover, so as to put it on evenly. Do nothing else: drink nothing but water; eat nothing, until improvement commences, except some dry bread softened in very weak tea of some kind. Cures of frightful burnings have been performed in this way, as wonderful as they are painless. We once saved the life of an infant which had been inadvertently drugged with laudanum, and which was fast sinking into the sleep which has no waking, by giving it strong coffee, cleared with the white of an egg, a teaspoonful every five minutes, until it ceased to seem drowsy.

—American Medical Journal

REARING CHILDREN

Says Dr. Hall—**1.** Children should not go to school until six years old. **2.** Should not learn at home during that time more than the alphabet, religious teachings excepted. **3.** Should be fed with plain substantial food, at regular intervals of not less than four hours. **4.** Should not be allowed to eat anything within two hours of bed time. **5.** Should have nothing for supper but a single cup of water drink, such as very weak tea of some kind, or cambric tea of warm milk and water, with one slice of cold bread and butter—nothing else. **6.** Should sleep in separate beds, on hair mattresses, without caps, feet first well warmed by the fire or rubbed with the hands until perfectly dry; extra cover on the lower limbs, but little on the body. 7. Should be compelled to be out of doors for the greater part of daylight, from after breakfast until half an hour before sundown, unless in damp weather, when they should not be allowed to go outside the door. **8.** Never limit a healthy child as to sleeping or eating, except at supper; but compel regularity as to both; it is of great importance. **9.** Never compel a child to sit still, nor interfere with its enjoyments, as long as it is actually uninjurious to person or property or against good morals. **10.** Never threaten a child; it is cruel, unjust, and dangerous. What you have to do, do it, and be done with it. **11.** Never speak harshly or angrily, but mildly, kindly, and, when really needed, firmly—no more. **12.** By all means, arrange it so that the last words between you and your children at bedtime, especially the younger ones, shall be words of unmixed lovingness and affection.

Poor Martha Jane. She took it as an insult to her motherhood. But I doubt he meant it that way.

Cornelia sent me the handkerchief, a sweet piece trimmed with tiny pink and white roses, and Martha Jane a letter. In one sentence she informs us that little Albert is quite sick with the measles, she came in first in her class spelling bee, and for a reward James took both Nancy, her dearest friend, and herself to Fishers and treated them to an ice-cream sundae. Ah, sweet youth!

HORTON'S CROSSING
16 MAY 1862

Dear Sister,

I pray all is as well with you and Martha Jane and her family as seems to be with us. Sadie's father finally accepted our invitation to come live with us. He sold out the last of his stock at the store in Anamosa and has put his house up for sale. I know he does not like to do it, as the prices are not good with so many gone to war. But he will be better cared for here than rattling around alone in that house.

The weather has been more cool than desirable for growing crops. We've even had to keep the fire lit in the house. The other night the mercury sank down to 6 degrees above the freezing point. At this rate the plants just sit and do not grow. It rained early in the week and we are in no danger of drought for the month to come. I only hope it warms up soon lest the unsprouted seed rot in the ground.

The paper reports that the pope is dying, the Mexican Army is losing to the French (the French have been saying they invaded Mexico to save them from American aggression), two of Fredrick Douglas' sons are now non-commissioned officers in the Massachusetts 34th, and the war looks to be no closer to an end.

On a happier home note, Jamie D. is growing into a strapping boy and is a great hand. A man with but one child could not ask for a finer son.

Sadie sends her best to you and the rest of the crew in the territories, as do I.

With Affection,
Your Brother
Daniel

Oh, my! These letters took over six weeks to work their way here. Come winter it will be worse, I'm sure. And doesn't the distance from the States to the Territories seem a far stretch when we open these travel-worn letters from home?

Prior to his departure, the Reverend Reed delegated limited authority to Mr. Vail in order that he might hold services at Sun River as well as bury, baptize, and marry. In the absence of our pastor, this evening Mr. Vail gave the sermon for our Sunday service and led us in prayer. It was a good sermon, reminding us of our need to prevail over fires we need pass through, that we may be strengthened like iron to do service for the Lord.

Sometimes I wonder at the strangeness of joy and sorrow that comes at the same time when something so good as a letter from home is put in our hands.

30 June . . . Weather Like Yesterday, Quite Warm

While Martha Jane and I worked at laundry, Morley spent the morning reducing his load. He left over a thousand lbs., amounting to about a third of his cargo, in Mr. Vail's care. If this keeps up, Martha Jane and I shall have to give up our nice laundry/cookhouse.

By noon, two more trains had joined with Morley's and they all proceeded to cross on the ferry.

I'm feeling restless. I too want to cross the river on the ferry. Mr. Vail says, work and weather permitting, one day we shall.

3 July

Today Iron appeared out of nowhere with a nicely dressed-out deer for us. He showed us how to dry it for winter storage. The air in this country is very dry, and often during the day it is so hot you do not need to use salt to preserve meat. What you do is slice it in slabs, not too thick of course, put it on a scaffold, and in a few days it's shrunk to less than a quarter of its size and can be stored in any dry place that's safe from rodents. I think we should try to smoke some, in the manner of a ham. Back in Ohio we had a neighbor who did this with some of his ducks and they were delicious.

Iron does not actually stay within the palisade, and I don't know where he lives. Periodically, he shows up with meat for us, and then he's gone. Occasionally, he stays a day or two, most often not, then he disappears without so much as a word. Vail, Swift, and Bixby are cleaning what little acreage they can salvage of the plantings. Iron tells us the fields flooded three times this spring. From what I've seen, only a miracle will raise up any garden vegetables this season. To think, back home the peas are already coming on, not to mention spinach, lettuce, and radishes, which have been up over a month.

Sunday 6 July

Ye who, tossed on bed of pain,
Seek for ease, but seek in vain:
Ye, by fiercer anguish torn,
In remorse for guilt who mourn.

—*Anna L. Barbauld, 1743–1825*

According to the Reverend Reed, a Piegan chief, Little Dog, has a farm some four miles down river from us. After morning worship, this day, we took a picnic lunch and the ambulance to his place. It is much overgrown, and there was no sign of anyone being near it for some time. To date the only Piegan we've seen is Iron. And I doubt he counts as a true Indian.

Sunday 13 July . . . A Glorious Day

Hither come, for here is found
Balm that flows for every wound,
Peace that ever shall endure,
Rest eternal sacred, sure. Amen.

—*Anna L. Barbauld, 1743–1825*

All week the weather has been fine. All week Martha Jane and I worked our routine, washing, ironing, baking, churning, cleaning, sewing. Not one pilgrim knocked on our door. On this day of worship and rest we packed a picnic and took the children to the river to fish. Both caught nice speckled trout and we fixed them for supper.

14 July . . . Crisp in Morning, but Sweaters off by Midday

Good day for laundry and baking.

16 July . . . Weather Fine and Cool

Inside we're more than toasty with the fires going to heat the irons. I press the clothes and Martha Jane bakes.

17 July . . . Weather Fine, Picked Service Berries

18 July . . . Rained

The Reverend Reed and a small group of men on horseback arrived from Benton this afternoon. Last week, over 100 principal men of Piegan, Blood, and Blackfeet tribes came in and talked to him. He said they were most upset by the great numbers of white men coming through their country. The Reverend assured them that the white men already have more land than they know what to do with, so they needn't worry. He said they had a pleasant council, and after receiving their gifts of tobacco and some provisions, they departed. They plan to go north some 150 miles or so to make a medicine lodge and kill some buffalo. In about a month they will come back to the fort to collect their annuities.

Sunday 20 July

The spacious firmament on high,
With all the blue ethereal sky,
And spangled heavens, a shining frame,
Their great original proclaim.

—Joseph Addison, 1672–1719

Our Reverend gave a good, old-fashioned Methodist sermon, heavy on duty, honor, and good works. When we lifted our puny voices in disharmony, I longed for the choral guidance of Thompson.

21 July . . . Clear and Warm

Good day for laundry and baking.

The Reverend and his fellow travelers left early for Fort Owen to visit with the Major there.

We've been in this place over three weeks now. 'Tis three weeks hard labor and none of it gone to the cause we were sent for. Where are the Indians we were to teach? Where are my little children? The classroom of my vision? God's ways are certainly mysterious, and faith, in time God shall reveal his purpose.

22 July . . . Weather Fine

Picking service berries. Now this is pie! Also a nice bucket of currants, and have made a pot of jelly of them.

23 July . . . Cold, Some Rain

It's Wednesday and a party of men has arrived with a wagon and three yoke of oxen to retrieve the provisions left here by Mr. Morley. They are accompanied by another, even larger party making quite a gathering of men. And all of them expecting coffee of course. Having left their camp on Gold Creek on the 20th, they seem to be making good time.

They say they're working with a party in Gold Creek Canyon and report the weather fine, though perhaps in the valley of the Hell Gate River it is a bit cooler than it is here. They are camped near the mouth of Gold Creek, where there are four cabins, three of them occupied by whites and their Indian wives. A Mr. Stuart occupies one. He is an old Californian who has been there for some years.

Morley and two others are working on a shaft about four miles from the main camp. He says they believe that this shaft, through layers of burnt quartz graves, and interstices filled with clay, is the arterial. They have gone down fifteen feet and have great hopes for it.

They reported that a party that had come up the river on the *Shreveport* has divided and some have gone on to the mines over on the Salmon.

Mr. Vail asked if they'd met up with Thompson. Indeed they had. The enterprising Thompson engendered a rash of stories causing us all to laugh till the tears rolled. Not being a storyteller myself, I cannot do them justice, but true to form, he has organized a church choir. The past two Sundays about 50 miners have had wonderful services, the Reverend Francis preaching hard sermons, and the singing accompanied by an excellent violin.

Thompson and a portion of his party have situated themselves at the junction of the Little Blackfoot and Deer Lodge Rivers; having rented there a deserted log cabin from Johnny Grant. The place has a good corral of which Morley is particularly envious, especially since he had to delay this leg of his trip an extra day, their oxen having strayed.

We wondered if the man they hired to bring up their wagon had found them. Morley told us that last they heard, he had succeeded in getting their wagon into the Deer Lodge Valley and that some of Gould's party had gone over to Johnny Grant's new place several miles up the Deer Lodge near Cottonwood and brought the stuff over to their headquarters.

It seems that hundreds of this Johnny Grant's cattle graze the whole valley. And one day, Thompson, noticing some wild cows with calves nearby, enlisted the aid of others, and succeeded in capturing two calves and putting them into the corral. The mothers followed and thus were also taken. By dint of their mother's courage and by gentle persuasion, he was able to enlist their cooperation to such an extent that he could milk them. At least twice each day the cows come to their calves and thus he is obtaining a sufficient supply of milk for their camp. They say he's even churning the cream by shaking it in a pickle jar. Ah, Thompson. If only you could keep your mouth shut.

They say the Gray party, already discouraged by the amount of work it took to make a showing, decided to sell out their surplus supplies and move on over the mountains to Walla Walla or some other good point and purchase a hotel.

It seems that the two Stuart brothers had at one point opened up some good paying mines showing from seven to twenty dollars per day for each man. But the bedrock lay from 12 to 15 feet below the surface, and the time necessary and the cost of doing this stripping before reaching pay dirt was more than many a man had bargained for. They tell us we can expect to see a fair few of those disgruntled fellows (who seemingly expected to pick up nuggets upon the bars in the streams) passing our way on their return.

Churned a great batch of butter.

24 July

Today Iron showed us some brushy trees along the edge of the wood about a mile north of the farm. They are loaded with a red berry that is not too sweet but has a good flavor, similar to that of currants—but this shrub is not at all a currant, instead, it has great thorns along the branches. He showed us how to put a blanket below the tree and shake the branches. In this manner we acquired great buckets of the fruit in a very short time. He calls them buffalo berries.

26 July

The red berries we picked the other day are already mostly dry. Dried they are much sweeter. A nice tart taste. Buffalo berries.

Sunday 27 July . . . Picnic Weather Perfection

> The unwearied sun, from day to day,
> Does his Creator's power display,
> And publishes to every land
> The work of an almighty hand.
>
> —*Joseph Addison, 1672–1719*

Yesterday Mary Eliza cracked walnuts and staid with the project until she had enough meats that we could bake an oatmeal pie. Martha fried up a couple of nice sage hens, compliments of Iron, and made a pot of beans with ham. To that she added a dish of lambs quarters (I'm coming 'round to liking them better than spinach), a jar of pickles from home, together with a batch of cookies.

She'd packed the lunch in Harvey's little tin trunk and tossed it on the ambulance. When we sat down to eat, Martha Jane stunned each and every single one of us by pulling out a jug of cold lemonade. We could not have been more astounded had we gone up in a tornado. Last year a friend of hers taught her how to make a lemon juice base that will keep indefinitely. After squeezing the juice, add to it the grated zest from the peel and thicken it with as much sugar as it will hold. Then you just pack it into bottles and stop its top with a rubber. One never knows how next this enterprising sister of mine might surprise us.

True to his word, Mr. Vail, Young Swift, and Iron hitched up the gov't farm ambulance and ferried us across the river. We left the antisocial Mr. Bixby to watch over the farm. Mr. Vail drove the ambulance whilst the rest of our men rode their ponies.

After we crossed the river and climbed the first rise, Crown Butte hove into sight. It has fascinated me since I first saw it. Having set out early, we reached its base by mid morning. Leaving our horses and ambulance on the flat, we followed our good Indian, Iron, to a path leading to the top. Our ascent was no easy task. With our restings it took near till noon to accomplish the task. Mr. Vail ended up carrying Harvey, and Young Swift took charge of Mary Eliza. She would not suffer herself to be carried (I'm no longer a baby, she says), so he patiently helped her up the worst parts. Martha and I took turns with the picnic trunk, which long before we reached the summit, I'd decided was pure nonsense to have dragged it along. The Butte rises over some 600 feet above the surrounding prairie. I don't know about the rest, but as for me, had it not been for pride, I'd have turned tail homeward halfway to the top.

But oh, my! What a view! Mr. Vail estimates the top to be some four hundred acres. I expected it to be flat, but it is not. Instead, the ground unfolds in undulating swells, and at its edges a precipice of rock rises some 30 to 40 feet higher. Indeed, it was a magnificent place to worship our Lord.

After service, Iron took us up a path to the top of one series of rocks to a place we could sit and view the country. From here we have an eagle's eye view of the prairie all the way to the Rocky Mountains. Looking down, the butte's sides form a steep slope to the prairie, one can get a good view of the country. The land between this butte and the mountains is broken into all sorts of fantastic shapes: buttes, ravines, storybook valleys, the whole nearly absent of timber. And the mountains—I cannot do justice to them in words. They wear jagged caps of snow that in some places extend halfway down their sides. In spite of some 40 miles distance, we see clearly the snow broken by fingerlike ridges of rock.

Near to dusk we returned to the farm. The little ones were already asleep and did not wake even through the changing into their nightdresses.

I go to sleep thanking God for His wonderful creation and for giving me life in order I might see it.

29 July

I made my own experiment today and put those dried red berries into the oatmeal cookie dough in the same manner one would if they had raisins. Everyone, even Iron, said they were quite tasty. Iron usually passes on dessert. He practically lives on meat alone when he is with us.

SUNDAY 3 AUGUST . . . WARM, SUNNY DAY

> SOON AS THE EVENING SHADES PREVAIL,
> THE MOON TAKES UP THE WONDROUS TALE,
> AND NIGHTLY, TO THE LISTENING EARTH,
> REPEATS THE STORY OF HER BIRTH;
>
> —*Joseph Addison, 1672–1719*

Reverend Reed and entourage returned from their adventures over the mountains. He tells us, day before yesterday, while yet at Gold Creek word came in that a fellow found good color on a creek that flows into the Beaverhead River as recently as the 28th of July. The words were hardly out of the messenger's mouth before many of the Gold Creek men left those diggings for the greener pastures. The Reverend finds this "chasing after gold and rumors of gold an ungodly misdirection of man's energy."

Unfortunately for the Reverend, Major Owen was not at the fort as he had taken himself to Walla Walla. We begged the good pastor to deliver the Sunday sermon and he graciously consented. Even our good Iron staid to hear him speak. His theme was "Mysterious are the ways of God." He told of the strange deities the Blackfeet worshiped and how we have been brought into this wilderness to bring the heathens to the one true God that they might be received in heaven even as we have been offered that opportunity.

5 AUGUST . . . ANOTHER WARM, GLORIOUS DAY

Mr. Swift brought the children each a horned toad and showed them how to catch food for the little critters by sticking their hands into an anthill, of which we have several within the palisade. The ants run up their arms and they quickly brush them off into the box where they hold the toads captive. It is amazing how many hours they can wile away watching the toads eat the ants. Would that I could bottle that kind of concentration and feed it to a room of students.

Sunday 10 August

> While all the stars around her burn,
> And all the planets in their turn,
> Confirm the tidings as they roll,
> And spread the truth from pole to pole.
>
> —*Joseph Addison, 1672–1719*

All week Iron has been bringing us buffalo. All week we have been putting by corned buffalo—great crocks of it. We also pickled some tongues and dried of it a great quantity.

When I mentioned how much we all miss the good Reverend's Sunday services, Iron's usually stoic face turned dark. When we found ourselves working alone, I asked him what I'd said to disturb him so. He spat the words, "Your reverend knows nothing."

I defended Reverend Reed saying, "He is only human and thus he certainly does not know everything, but it does not follow that he knows nothing." Iron grunted. I was reminded of the silly conversation we'd held at Fort Berthold and decided to press Iron to clarify his statement. He then asked me if I knew the story of how the Blackfeet received the Sun Dance. In truth I did not, and I asked him to tell it to me.

"A long time ago, a long, long time ago, when the earth was first born and when the first Blackfoot persons walked on the earth. the Great Mystery held a talk with Tailfeathers Woman. Tailfeathers

Woman was the first person the Great Mystery talked to. The Great Mystery taught her that the sun is the source of all power. That it is right for his people to celebrate the renewal of life by the sun. The Great Mystery commanded her to oversee the construction of a sacred lodge each year when the prairie grass turns deep green and the cow parsnips grow high. The center pole of the sacred lodge links all of the Great Mystery's home in the skies to earth. Then the Great Mystery told her the acts, the dance, and the prayers that must be carried out to the beat of the tom-toms. And everyone is to put paint on his face and to make a special headdress and to carry bells. In this manner, each man prepares his spirit for the next year and in this manner we remember our ancestors and the wisdom of the Great Mystery."

I told Iron I thought it a beautiful myth, as wonderful as any the ancient Greeks told and would have asked for more, alas, before I'd finished the sentence, his face again closed. So I just thanked him.

Now that's a story worthy of my pencil.

SUNDAY 17 AUGUST . . . MIDDAY GOOD WEATHER

WHAT THO' IN SOLEMN SILENCE ALL
MOVE ROUND THE DARK TERRESTRIAL BALL?
WHAT THO' NO REAL VOICE NOR SOUND
AMID THE RADIANT ORBS BE FOUND?

—Joseph Addison, 1672–1719

All week we have been picking wild gooseberries and raspberries. The gooseberries are different from any I ever saw. They are large, oblong, and when ripe are a dark color almost like the color of whortleberries and are very sour like ripe currents. They make a tasty pie, not to mention jam. The raspberries are not as sweet as those at home and tend a bit toward the mealy side. Although Martha Jane made a nice cobbler with them, I like them best in jam.

18 AUGUST . . . WARM DAY

Gray's train came through today. They had gone all the way to the Salmon River looking for gold in the ground then spent time looking for some enterprise where they could make their pile. They said, "miners are leaving the Salmon in swarms." To a man they gave a hard account of doings out there. Thoroughly disgruntled, they're heading back to the States on horseback.

20 AUGUST . . . WARM DAY

22 AUGUST . . . ANOTHER WARM DAY

Found a stand of choke cherries and made a batch of syrup.

23 AUGUST . . . THUNDER STORM, LATE AFTERNOON

Martha Jane has spent the better part of the week sewing a new coat for Mary Eliza and I have been adjusting her old one to fit Harvey.

SUNDAY 24 AUGUST

IN REASON'S EAR THEY ALL REJOICE,
AND UTTER FORTH A GLORIOUS VOICE;
FOR EVER SINGING, AS THEY SHINE,
"THE HAND THAT MADE US IS DIVINE." AMEN.

—Joseph Addison, 1672–1719

25 AUGUST. . . VERY WARM AND CLEAR

28 AUGUST . . . NICE DAY, NOT SO HOT

30 AUGUST . . . MORNING PLEASANT WITH DEW—SLIGHT BREEZE

Yesterday, just after lunch, the most interesting company arrived in the persons of Major Owen, agent to the Flathead (the man has lived with them for 12 years!) residing in the Bitter Root Valley, and two other gentlemen. One of them a merchant who, having of late returned from Walla Walla, brought a letter to Mr. Vail from his father. The Sr. Vail said his wife was sending one up the Missouri and he was sending his by way of Panama and they had bets on which one would make it to Sun River the fastest. His letter was dated June 6th. He said he received his son's letter sent from St. Joseph, Missouri. The Doctor wrote of pleasant weather, his neighbor's barn being burned to the ground, the wonder of a bounteous crop of strawberries, a dreadful battle raging in Richmond, and of thousands upon thousands of stout-hearted men killed. And he sent a Nasby column, which Mr. Vail read aloud to the amusement of all.

The Walla Walla merchant asked of me so many questions I could hardly concentrate on what Major Owen had to say, and he seemed fascinated to meet another of Irish descent (as if my sister weren't of the same). Major Owen is a great fan of Mr. Vaughn.

On the choosing of the site, Major Owen concurred with Agent Vaughn that it should be good. At that time, he thought it might be even better than the Bitter Root location. Now, with the plantings Mr. Vaughn's man Paris put in last spring having flooded thrice, he's not so certain.

Mr. Vaughn, he tells us, was a great friend of the Indians, and they trusted him. Even at that, only Little Dog tried his hand at farming. After the spring floods, even he gave up. The problem, he said, was not only in the location, but in the nature of the Blackfeet themselves. They are warriors and hunters. The very idea of digging in the ground is as reprehensible to them as a life of prostitution would be to us. I found that a shocking revelation. I'm afraid I shall have to puzzle that one some time before I understand it.

I could not help but state my new-found sentiment. "All in all, I think it is a great shame that Major Vaughn was a Virginian. Had he been a loyal Yankee, things might have gone better for the Indians."

Major Owen dissented. "The problem being, those in the department at Washington know no more about the management of the Indian tribes than the Indians do about the cause of the present war. The department makes treaties neither side understands; then the department breaks the ones it does understand faster than the ink can dry. Take the 1855 treaty—settlers are inundating the Bitter Root Valley under the assumption that the Indians agreed to leave. Even Captain Mullan agrees our Indians understood they'd not molest the settlers, but they never agreed to leave the valley. Now the settlers feel any Indian is fair game." The way he tells it, he's just surprised the Indians have not already responded in kind and *en masse*.

Then I made a fool of myself asking the question that's haunted me for some time. "Do all Indians eat raw the entrails of the beasts they kill?"

Just as I feared, the men all laughed. But the good Major then found it in him to answer my ignorant question. "Indeed they do, especially in the springtime. After their long winter diet they are starved and in sore need of a tonic. The liver and that portion of the gut next to the stomach seem to do the trick in a way similar to the Eastern practice of eating dandelion greens in spring. Trust me, my dear, if you live in these parts long, one spring you too will come to the plate of raw liver with a new respect."

Martha Jane's lovely china bowl filled with chopped raw liver flew through my mind. Honestly, I think, I certainly hope not.

Martha Jane asked if they thought we'd be safe from attack. All three began speaking at once. The gist of which runs: the Blackfeet are hunters, and whereas they are known for their cleanliness and fine horsemanship, they are also feared for their warlike nature and their savagery. Even other tribes living within the area they roam are in constant danger of attack. With the present animosity exacerbated by the greatly increased number of emigrants passing through, it is very likely the friendly horse raiding could turn rapidly into something else. They find the introduction of intoxicants by notorious scalawags to be especially unsettling. In other words, peaceful as it is right now, I'm thinking perhaps we are not so safe.

Over pie and coffee, the topic turned to the war. Major Owen reported bad news. On the first of June, Robert E. Lee was given command of the army of northern Virginia, Joseph E. Johnston having been wounded in the Battle of Seven Pines. On the 26th of June, General Lee, reinforced by General Jackson's forces, engaged McClellan in a series of savage battles: June 26, Mechanicsville; 27, Gaine's Mill; 29, Savage's Station; 30, Glendale; and finally at

Malvern Hill on July 7th. McClellan then retreated. Major Owen seems to think Lee will be a hard man to defeat, especially since Lincoln keeps sending out the most incompetent men to lead this war. Major Owen says that if he wants to win this war he should be sending the likes of General Kearny and someone I've never heard of before, by the name of Stevens. Ah, well, I've never been in the military either.

Come time to start supper it looked as if there would be no end to their talking so Martha Jane invited them to stay. And stay they did. After supper Major Owen brought out his guitar and well repaid us with some tunes.

Even so, while I say my prayers, I am haunted by the vision of eating a plate of raw liver.

SUNDAY 31 AUGUST

GOD MOVES IN A MYSTERIOUS WAY
HIS WONDERS TO PERFORM
HE PLANTS HIS FOOTSTEPS IN THE SEA
AND RIDES UPON THE STORM

—*William Cowper, 1731–1800*

2 SEPTEMBER

Today Little Dog and his band are camped near the river. I have not seen him yet, but he talked to Mr. Vail. Mr. Vail says he seems to be of a decent sort. They talked about farming. Little Dog left his farm after the spring floods wiped him out.

3 SEPTEMBER

This morning a merchant from the Deer Lodge Valley reported there was quite a brouhaha in that place last week. Seems one man was shot, another hanged, and another sentenced to be hanged. The three had stolen some horses from Bitter Root Valley. The trio was playing cards in the shade of a tree when the sheriff, James Stuart, (who happens to be Granville Stuart's brother—the same person Thompson is renting his cabin near) came up and told them that they were his prisoners. One started on the run and the sheriff shot him dead. T'was said that when he started, he had a pack of cards in his hand and when shot, clasped the cards so hard that they remained in his hand after he was dead and he was buried with them in his hand. Can you imagine? The one that was hanged jumped off of the wagon as soon as the rope was put around his neck. The other has since been released. I asked our guest why they'd released the man if he was guilty, and he replied, "Oh you know how it goes. When tempers are high a hanging seems the way to go. But when every one cools down it doesn't look like the chap's truly in need of hanging."

Between tales of crazy men and avenging Indians, I cannot but wonder what shall become of this country.

Last night I heard the most beautiful music. It was soft as air and trilled deep like some reed wind instrument. This morning I told Iron about it and asked if we could have the master of the song come in and play for us. Iron's eyes lit up, he nodded his head, and exclaimed, "Oh, so soon the lady chooses to be courted!" Didn't we have a laugh over that one?

4 SEPTEMBER . . . WIND BRISK. COLD IN EVENING

5 September

We spent the greater part of the last two days picking both black and white currants. We plan to make jelly out of them.

Not a day passes when we do not see pilgrims on the road, by horse, cart, and on foot. All week the men have been cutting, splitting, and stacking wood in preparation for winter.

Little Dog, accompanied by several of his men, paid us a visit today and staid to dinner. Little Dog is well spoken. He dresses like any white man of position, wearing a woolen suit, a dark shirt, regular black shoes, and socks. In Saint Louis we saw many Indians, most in some mix of civilized clothing, but none like this. This man pays attention. More than that, he exudes an aura of self-possession the likes of which few men, Indian or white, can claim. It is a combination of strength and kindness he makes me feel.

His men wore moccasins, fringed buckskin breeches, and shirts. The shirts were more like tunics than shirts as we know them. Three of the men had roached hair on the top of their heads. It stood straight up some four or five inches. It was stiff. One wore his almost into a point. Then they had parts of their long hair braided with decorations woven into the braid. These three also wore a single straight up feather tucked into the hair at the back of their head. Some of the men wore sashes about their waists, and some wore a kind of sash over their shoulders. Some had pretty beads or porcupine quills embroidered on parts of their clothing. All of them, with the exception of Little Dog, had stiff hair. These men chattered in their own language, and two of them poked into everything, including my sewing basket.

Little Dog did not speak to either Martha Jane or myself. In fact he did not look at us. The men talked, we women served, and the little ones hid in the bedroom.

In order to teach the Indians anything, I think first you'd have to learn their language and their ways. Their language is filled with sounds I do not believe I could ever make. As for their ways, if God had intended me to know them, I'm sure He would have opened my ear to the strange sounds of their language.

Sunday 7 September

Ye fearful saints, fresh courage take;
The clouds ye so much dread
Are big with mercy, and shall break
In blessings on your head.

—*William Cowper, 1731–1800*

Little Dog and his band are still camped just outside the farm to the northwest. From the sounds of it, they seem to be a lively group, but they give us no trouble.

8 September . . . Evenings Getting Colder

9 September

Midday, Bixby killed a large rattlesnake. It was on the lane just outside the stockade. I shudder to think what it could have done to the children had it been within.

10 September . . . Rainy Morning, Tonight Cool, in Fact Frosty

Iron brought us three nice sage birds. Martha Jane baked them in sour cream. We've also had tender corn with our suppers for the last week, and that made for us a meal we shall long enjoy in our memories.

11 September . . . Cold Morning, Killing Frost Last Night

This afternoon Captain Fisk and his emigrant party set up camp on the Sun River about a mile and a half below us. Early evening Mr. Vail saw a group of them fishing the river. In the camp he saw a tent like he'd never seen before. They called it a "Sibley" tent. It is made of canvas, but built for a fire inside. From the outside, it looks much like an Indian tepee. He says it shelters as many as 12 men with room left for a stove and the center pole. Mr. Vail talked to one, Mr. Langford, who told him that a Captain Fisk was in charge of escorting the emigrant train west and that they had crossed the northern plains to Fort Benton, thus opening up an easier route to the gold mines. Mr. Langford made certain Mr. Vail knew he was an important official of the train. According to Vail, he puffed himself up to state, "Captain Fisk has hired me to take the position of second assistant in charge of commissary." Mr. Vail could not keep from chuckling, "He seems to be a man with quite a high opinion of himself."

12 SEPTEMBER . . . CLOUDY

Fisk's party has moved up river to our farm. Captain Fisk and the train's doctor delivered unto us this day mail that the agent at St. Charles had held until he found someone traveling this way. These from Cornelia, Mr. Vail's mother, and a former student who is leaving to join the Union forces. His father's letter, traveling at least three times as far as his mother's, beat hers by 12 days.

Fisk asked if we'd heard about the Sioux uprising in Minnesota. Of course we hadn't. When he arrived in Fort Union he received information that the Sioux killed five whites at the Acton trading post, and they've been terrorizing the countryside back there. He said they've killed hundreds of people and last he heard there was no end in sight. He wondered how our Indians were behaving. We told him, although our Piegans were at odds with the Gros Ventres, they've not been menacing us.

The doctor told us that about the 20th of last month they were visited by Squaw That Sits, first chief, and Star Rove, second chief of the Gros Ventres along with Rotten-tail, a Crow chief. A couple hundred Indians had come to be vaccinated for small pox. And he casually added that they'd heard that at least three people had been killed by those Indians whilst traveling down river in Mackinaws. That raises the hairs on my arms.

At their request, Mr. Vail took them on a tour of the farm. From Vail's report at supper, I sensed that they were not much impressed. Well, who would be? The wheat, what little there is of it, has not properly headed out, thus is not cut, and you can't see the corn for the weeds.

Oh, Sugar! What do we care? They can't begin to know what a deplorable mess we inherited when we came into this project.

According to Cornelia, our sister Mary's husband has joined the Union forces and Sister is sore lonely without him. James' boy,

Albert, is now quite well and wondering when he can play with his dear companion, Harvey, again. She (Cornelia) misses school and wishes the school year lasted longer. Next week she goes to Mary's house to help with the children while they pack to move their household into her Mother-in-Law's. She has begun a set of pillowcases for her hope chest, and wants a hoop to put in her petticoats for her birthday. All is well in brother James' family and they send their love. Mother Vail writes of rumor that Memphis was taken on the 7th by our gunboats and is much heartened by the possibility. She also sent more Nasby columns to lighten our day.

Oh, how I do wish I'd gotten a letter from Sadie or Daniel!

Lord, keep me from the sin of petulance.

13 September . . . Froze Again Last Night

Martha Jane and I were pleasantly surprised by a visit of two sisters from the train, one of whom brought her new baby with her—a beautiful little boy who fascinated both Mary Eliza and Harvey. Later we heard Mary Eliza telling her brother that she remembered when he was that small. Harvey became highly indignant and said, "Did not! I was never a puny thing like that!"

The ladies asked us if we weren't afraid of the Indians camped near. We replied we were sent to teach them, albeit they hadn't been interested in receiving. But they had not been hostile either. We were chalking our experience up to the old adage, you can take a horse to water, but you can't make the poor beast drink.

Then they showed us the little guns their husbands had given them in case they were taken. In that event, they were told they must shoot themselves and the baby first lest much worse be his lot.

It's almost dark and Fisk's party is still trading with our Indians.

Sunday 14 September . . . Looked Like Rain, Cleared By 9 AM

Judge not the Lord by feeble sense,
But trust Him for His grace;
Behind a frowning providence
He hides a smiling face.

—*William Cowper, 1731–1800*

By the time the weather cleared, the emigrants had crossed the Sun River.

We all spent the day by the fire, resting, reading and rereading our letters, and taking turns reading Mother Goose to the children.

15 September . . . Another Wash Day

Little Dog's village was gone this morning. I don't know whether that makes us safer or more in danger. It's not Little Dog I fear, it's not knowing what moves the rest of them. Why do they come? Why do they go? Where do they come from—go to? Do they have loyalties as we do?

It has been so cold at night, freezing in fact, that only about three acres of wheat and oats are standing, and what hasn't headed out has turned black. The men are thrashing what little made it ripe. They are stacking the straw for winter feed.

It looks as if a little corn will make it. Out of some 60 acres planted only 5 escaped the flooding. Most of the garden was ruined in the floods. But we did get a few squashes, a decent amount of beets, carrots, cabbages, and turnips, and about 100 pounds of potatoes. Out of ten acres we have retrieved less food than what can be grown in an Ohio garden. What wouldn't I give for a tomato?

The best thing about the frost is that it has killed the hoard of mosquitoes that have been plaguing us. Our greatest discomfort has been delivered to us in the form of the mosquito. They infest the whole country in both high and low places, so there's been no getting away from them. Still, we have got used to them. I trust one can get used to most anything.

16 September . . . Dull With Showers

We have picked up our quilting again.

17 September

We had just placed the weights on a crock of kraut we'd worked on most of the day when a dozen men from the Deer Lodge Valley came on horseback looking for Indians. They say the Indians have been raiding horses—so many horses that hardly a one of them has not felt the sting. They're looking for their horses and revenge as well, I think.

Sunday 21 September

> His purposes will ripen fast,
> Unfolding every hour;
> The bud may have a bitter taste,
> But sweet will be the flower.
>
> —*William Cowper, 1731–1800*

Reading Elizabeth Barrett Browning's *Sonnets from the Portuguese*. Would the world not have lost that soul last year. ". . . But there/The silver answer rang—'Not Death, but Love.'" Oh, to love! To be loved like that! Ah, that might be worth the price.

22 SEPTEMBER

Five of the men who came through looking for their stolen horses stopped in to tell us they'd been all the way to Benton and back. While in Benton, numerous reports were being circulated at the fort of attacks on the Mackinaws at the hands of Indians along the banks. Worse, before the passengers died, they had been made to suffer atrocities by their murderers and the Mackinaws had been burned.

We are much concerned with this. We would ask Iron what he thinks of the situation, but he has not appeared for several weeks. One moment Mr. Vail thinks maybe he should go to the fort and see if he can't hire us some protection; the next moment, he wonders if he should leave us alone on the farm.

Harvey and Mary Eliza have grown much too quiet. Martha Jane and I keep doing those things that need to be done no matter the circumstance. The men mend harnesses and rub boots and anything leather with goose fat.

SUNDAY 28 SEPTEMBER

BLIND UNBELIEF IS SURE TO ERR,
AND SCAN HIS WORK IN VAIN;
GOD IS OUR INTERPRETER,
AND HE WILL MAKE IT PLAIN. AMEN.

—*William Cowper, 1731–1800*

A fair-sized group of Indians is setting up a camp on the prairie just north of the farm. They are not of Little Dog's Band. Mr. Vail is sick with worry. He says he no longer knows why he brought us to this country and he fears he's made a grave mistake.

What can we do but pray for guidance and put our trust in God?

31 September

Yesterday two Indians came to the fort. Mr. Vail tried to communicate with them. He thinks they wanted something, but without an interpreter, who can say? They did not seem to leave angry, but who knows? Late this afternoon the sound of their drums kept us on edge.

1 October

Most of the night I stared into the darkness above my bed listening to the sound of the drumming and the shrieks. The times I dozed off, it was a momentary silence that woke me. They must have stopped before dawn, but I do not think it was long before. We go about our chores grey faced and grim. And we hold our breath when the men leave the palisade to fill the barrels with water.

This afternoon the drumming began again.

I used to think the Whitmans were heroes standing noble until death by the savage hand they hoped to bring to God. Now I see them quaking before the butchery they are about to participate in as victims. 1847 is not that long ago. How could I have perceived it as ancient history? Why did I think the world was now different? How could I not foresee the possibility that our lives might end in that selfsame situation? I've been frightened so long, I'm past caring.

3 October

Yesterday the drums fell silent. When we looked out today, the Indians had vanished. All that's left of them is crushed grass and fire rings. Now the silence deafens. Now the silence is heavy with our fear.

Sunday 5 October

> Rock of ages, cleft for me,
> Let me hide myself in Thee:
> Let the water and the blood,
> From thy wounded side which flowed,
> In my hand no price I bring;
> Simply to thy cross I cling. Amen.
>
> —*Augustus M. Toplady, 1740–1778*

We have thought on it and prayed. Our thinking is this: We are too small a number and none here is handy with a firearm, if we are attacked we shall perish all; if Mr. Vail goes to Fort Benton, we may be attacked and we will perish; Mr. Vail may be slain in trying to acquire help. In that event, he said, at least he would die with the satisfaction he had done all he could. We can all stay here quivering like mice in a hole, guarded by a cat, and there may be no attack. In which case we shall all have gone mad and none of this speculation will be relevant. In light of our deliberations, we have decided to support Mr. Vail's desire to try to find help. He leaves tomorrow morning. God willing, he shall return.

8 OCTOBER

This morning Iron returned with an antelope. The meat is quite strong compared to the deer. Martha and I spent quite some time mincing it along with a bit of buffalo fat. How I wish I had some dried apples to mix with it and make a real pie. Tomorrow I think I'll try substituting a goodly portion of those buffalo berries we dried last summer and see what kind of pie that turns out.

We had hoped Mr. Vail would be home today. We do not speak of the fear in our heart.

9 OCTOBER

I spiced the pies with cinnamon, ginger, and nutmeg. Hard to believe, they are quite tasty. I still miss the dried apples though. Swift has been occupying his time whittling little animals for the children. Martha Jane and I take turns reading aloud Dickens' *Christmas Carol.* I finished another patch. This afternoon Iron has brought us a brace of ducks.

Mr. Vail has been gone five days now and all is quiet. Except for chores and meals, Bixby stays in his quarters. He's the one who should have gone for help, I think. But then could he be trusted to find help? I don't know how he managed to carry on a conversation long enough to find himself employment.

We tried to push away the gloom and stillness of the day, playing Simon Says with the children. Bedtime now brings weariness without sweet-dreams respite.

10 October

Today I feel angry! Angry we live filled with a greater abundance of fear than any creature ought endure, to say naught of lives so short and death forever lurking but a breath away. For as long as I can remember, even when we were children, there was always the fear—will I die before I wake? Will my brothers, sisters, parents be with me on the morrow? Why did our God make this world so?

I churned the butter. I just had to. I plunged that dasher up and down with a vigor like to shake the living out of me. And yet, by the time I'd about frozen my fingers with the rinsing of the butter, and had patted it into wonderful waxy yellow globes, I was able to toss my anger into the yard along with the spent water.

What will we do if he is dead? Now the boats are stopped, no one is coming this way but the Indian. I will not be surprised if we see no white man, beside our own, before spring. Oh, my dear sister Martha Jane, oh, my darling Mary Eliza, my darling Harvey, how will you endure the loss of your beloved?

Dear God, help me through this night. Give me strength that I might be of service to You and to my family.

What is my strength,
that I should hope?
And what is mine end,
that I should prolong my life?
Is my strength the strength of stones?

—*Job 6: 11–12*

Sun River Autumn

11 October

He's back! Thank God. He's back.

And he's brought with him two competent riflemen and put them up in one of the Indian "houses."

So much to record, I hardly know where to begin.

Swift was filling the water barrels when he saw them coming. He threw open the gates yelling, "They're here! They're here!" And we all ran out to meet them. Mr. Vail rode in first on the govt. farm's little dun Indian pony and close behind came a man on a big buckskin. Last, William Henry Handy Plumer, astride a dancing bay mare he calls Lady Mac, short for MacBeth because, he says, she's so high strung she'll be the death of him. I don't believe it. He rides so one with his mount, he puts the agile Indian to shame. Besides the bay, he led a fine sorrel packed with his belongings.

Would you believe, Mr. Vail brought for us a good-sized sack of dried apples and a couple of hanks of yarn? How on earth did he ever get a hold of yarn, we wondered?

Turns out, one of the Benton traders, thinking some woman new to the territory might be wanting such, brought it up from St. Louis. Indeed he thought rightly. He brought to each of the children a piece of colorful hard candy. Didn't they think that was a treat? They haven't seen likes of it since we left the *Emilie*.

At supper we had so much to thank our Lord for that our food was nearly in danger of cooling before we were ready to eat.

We served a fresh haunch of the venison and the ducks with potatoes, squash, fresh corn, salaretus biscuits, sweet buttermilk, and of course, one of my mince pies.

To hear the men talk, one would have thought years had passed since they'd eaten a good meal. Even Bixby made some audible affirmation. Would you believe?

About four miles from the fort Mr. Vail's pony twisted his leg in a deep rut in the road, injuring it so that Mr. Vail ended up walking the rest of the way to the fort. And wouldn't you know, not another could be found for trade? Mr. Plumer doctored the dun with liniment and rest. Mr. Vail says those extra days laid over at Benton were akin to hell for him—so filled with worry for us he was.

In addition to Mr. Plumer, Mr. Vail has hired a Mr. Cleveland to help protect the farm. Mr. Plumer arrived at Fort Benton in hopes of taking a boat back to the States. I'm uncertain as to why Cleveland was there.

Benton is rife with reports of Indian action against the Mackinaw boats. It seems no one is willing to risk life running the river at this time. It is said that the Indians are capturing and burning the boats and then torturing the Whites until death.

The men bring news of the war—old news, but news just the same. The army of northern Virginia has crossed the Potomac River and has invaded Maryland. There has been a fierce battle at Manassas. Late in August General McClellan tried to stop General Lee on his path toward the capital. McClellan defeated, Lee marches on. And in Mexico, General Ortega has fallen. The men speculate the reasoning of the French Emperor is that the South will prevail and in that instance will support a French government in Mexico.

After supper Young Swift and Mr. Cleveland fairly leapt for the chance to dry dishes. Martha Jane and I thought it quite amusing. She quickly settled the dispute by tossing Young Swift a second dishtowel.

A prayer of thanks wells up like a song from some place deep inside me. Praise God. All is well with us tonight.

Sunday 12 October . . . Fine Fall Day

Come, Holy Spirit, heavenly Dove,
With all Thy quick'ning Pow'rs;
Kindle a flame of sacred love
In these cold hearts of ours. Amen.

—*Isaac Watts, 1674–1748*

This day we did nothing but eat, rest, visit, and give our prayers to God. What a wonderful spirit moves through us when we realize we have been carried through the storm.

13 October . . . A Glorious Day

I woke to the crackle and spit of the fires started in both fireplace and stove by my dear brother-in-law. Leaping out of bed, I traded my nightdress for my house frock. In my haste, I carried my shoes, to be buttoned up before the warmth of the fire. These days the children wake long before the sun is up, and we fit them for sleep and waking before the fire. In the chill of the morning, how I wish I was a child again that I might dress in the warmth of the chimney corner.

We have a long table with benches on either side and a chair at either end. Martha Jane and I concur that we now seat enough bodies at meal time to make the feel of a real family. The men come to table all rested. Mr. Plumer is an especial delight to the eye. He comes to the table fresh shaven (excepting for a close-cropped moustache that gives him a most distinguished air) and with more pleases and thank yous than any man I've ever known.

The day turned warm, as speckled cottonwood leaves fell in a carpet over the palisade yard. We have but two trees. Nevertheless, they do shade us in summer and gladden our autumn. I don't remember a time I've ever enjoyed a laundry day so much.

We served our usual washday supper of biscuits and beans along with one of my pies. Mr. Plumer said the fare put him in a most homesick mode. He said his family's custom was to have biscuits and beans of a Saturday night. His family lives in the state of Maine. He'd be there now, were the boats yet running the river. He is the youngest of seven, having three brothers and three sisters.

Martha Jane shared that we were also of a family of seven, but sister Cornelia was our baby. Cornelia is but a teenager, this year living with our Brother James in Ohio.

Mr. Plumer's father was a sea captain. He has been dead these past fourteen years, having died when Mr. Plumer was yet in his teens. While the father lived, they wanted for nothing excepting his company; the self same situation we found ourselves in when our father died. Of course, unlike us, he still had his mother. I think, in spite of his childhood discontent, he must have lived a beautiful life on their farm so close to the sea—with his mother, sister, and a few servants. Being consumptive, he could not follow his father, as did his brothers, to sea. Instead, he helped with the farm and tended to his studies—sometimes at the local academy, more often under the doting tutelage of his Aunt Rena.

Mr. Plumer came to California by way of Panama. His ship passed into San Francisco's harbor on the 21st of March in 1852. Fort Benton is as far as he has ever been into the interior of this continent. Thus we traded stories of oceans and prairies till we put poor Bixby and Cleveland to sleep.

After the work of the day I should be dog tired. Instead I'm feeling restless.

14 October . . . One Insufferably Hot Autumn Day

Martha set about baking bread and cookies, I to pressing shirts, whilst the men mended and reinforced our palisade.

Mr. Plumer was Swift's age when he set sail for California. His brothers all put to sea with the father, prior to their fifteenth birthdays. He grew up witness to their lively tales and the exotic merchandise they brought home. Longing for adventure, he pleaded with his mother to go to the gold fields.

Young Swift laughed, "I, too, pleaded with my family to allow me to go west. As I was last born, Mother was loath to let me go. But with brothers yet working with my father, what was left for me to do? Gold was not my goal so much as adventure."

My turn to laugh, adventure was sure enough my goal. We are beginning to feel a kinship like unto the three musketeers.

Mr. Plumer went on to say, "With the death of my father, the degringolade of our family fortunes ensued. Of all her children, I was perhaps closest to my mother. I love her as dearly as she has loved me. Whereas it is true, I wanted to find a means to take care of her, it is also true that the situation gave me leverage to break away to seek my just estate—to experience adventure—a chance to repair the failing fortune. Mother had read that California's climate was a catharsis for consumption and my brother, Willmot, a seafaring captain in his own right, agreed to remain at home and take over the agricultural affairs. Thus, with a promise I would always send a goodly portion of my earnings home, I was able to convince her to allow me to leave. These past ten years, through the mountains and valleys of my quest, I have always honored that commitment."

Young Swift has been openly admiring Mr. Plumer's horse and his riding skills. "How," he asked, "does a sea captain's son become so expert in the saddle?" Plumer modestly replied, "The year I turned five, father bought me a dandy Welsh Pony and hired an old German gentleman (who had trained horses for Prince von Bismarck before immigrating to the States with his youngest daughter and her new husband) to teach me the equestrian arts."

Evening, we lit the lamp and Plumer read to us while the men greased their boots and we worked on our blocks. We have been making a log cabin quilt for Martha Jane. I'm afraid when the day comes that I leave this place for the States I shall not care to be reminded of log cabins.

It's amazing how invigorating the air becomes as quickly as the sun begins to set.

15 October . . . Another Fine Day

Again the men spent the greater part of the day on the mending and fencing. Even so, Mr. Plumer found time to tutor Young Swift. I watched them work with the horse in the yard. Plumer showed him how to hold the reins so that he could not lose the horse even though it resisted and how to tip the horse's head a bit toward him with the near rein a bit shorter and to put his toe in the stirrup facing toward the horse's rear and swing up, his knee against the horse's side. In this way, when the horse took off with but toes of the lad's foot in the stirrup, he was tossed by the steed's motion right into the saddle—so neat the trick, the horse turning in a half circle instead of heading out.

"Be that as it may, according to Mr. Plumer," says Swift, "if a man thinks the bridle keeps the horse under control, then that man is riding the wrong end."

After lunch Mr. Plumer took Swift outside the palisade for a lesson in handling the gun. Cleveland commenced to tease Harvey, pulling on his nose with a decided tweak, then showing the lad the flesh side of his thumb slipped between his fingers, saying, "gottcha nose, ya little bugger. Now what ya gonna do?"

Incredulous and smarting, Harvey's lower lip began to tremble. Mary Eliza came to her brother's rescue. "Pay him no mind Harvey, your nose is as secure on your face as is mine. That's just his thumb. Look at it. Would Mother allow you to walk about with a nose that dirty?"

A dark scowl clouded Cleveland's face. He started toward the children and the two of them fled behind their mother's skirts. Martha Jane suggested they go out to play, which they obediently did. Trying to smooth out the situation, she poured more coffee into his cup. "I suppose, as are we, you're from a large family."

Directing his attention toward her, Cleveland cocked his head to the side and smirked, "And how was you deducing that?"

Martha Jane poured herself a cup of coffee and, smiling, joined us at the table. "Our brothers used to tease us, just so."

She glanced toward me. And I quickly assented. "Oh my, yes." Truth is, our brothers were working like men by the time we were old enough to be teased—had such been allowed.

"Now tell us," she continued, "what was your childhood like?"

"Tell the truth, ma'am, I never had one. My brother and I were put out to labor as soon as we could carry a pail."

"Labor can be good for a child, so long as it is tempered with play and good family," I added, for I am curious and I hoped to help draw him out.

"My family couldn't keep themselves, to say nothing of us. Brother and I was traded to a neighbor, our labor in exchange for father's whiskey. And that's more'n I wanna say about it."

He drained his cup and stood, smiling at me. "You see, Miss Bryan, unlike some others we know, I am a self-made man." With that he left the room.

At supper, Cleveland attempts to wear his best manners. Plumer puts on a white shirt with a sailor-knotted black scarf tucked under the collar. He covers his pistol scabbards and white linen with a black broadcloth coat. His manners are not something he wears for the occasion. His manners, like his good language, are an inseparable part of him.

Mr. Vail and Joe Swift described for Mr. Plumer our trip up the Missouri. Plumer was most interested in the length of time it took and how the boat got on. The steamer bound for Panama took 14 days. In the first week of May they reached the Port of Aspinwall then trekked across the 40-mile isthmus, four days by mule, to Panama City where they waited at the Grand Hotel for the steamer to San Francisco. The third leg of the trip took another 12 days. He said he could hardly remember which was worse, the squalid existence in Panama or the trip endured on the *Golden Gate*, which carried twice the passengers it was built to hold.

This evening we got up a game of Botticelli. Bixby and Cleveland bowed out to hole up in their cabins. Joe Swift, Mr. Plumer, and I are last to finish the game, me stumping Swift with Queen Elizabeth's mother, Anne Boleyn.

16 October . . . Another Hot Day

After breakfast, I set Mary Eliza to working on her slate. She knows her numbers well enough that we have commenced with simple addition. Mr. Plumer took notice and said he thought I was a natural-born teacher. I did tell him that I was not alone responsible for her advanced education, as her father was also a teacher, and the child had shown an interest in figures and writing at an early age.

Plumer ventured that he, too, had enjoyed both numbers and letters as a child and that it had put him in good stead when, on his arrival in San Francisco, he took up employment as a clerk.

Over supper Mr. Vail asked him his impression of that city. He said that a person with capital could make his fortune there in any industry he had a talent toward. Begging a talent, a man could erect buildings and let out rooms. The demand for living space was so great, he was fortunate in finding a place in a rooming house close by the mercantile where he worked. "It did not take me long to discern that any man investing there was bound to make excellent returns on his money, but the price of property was such, I knew that man was not to be Henry Plumer."

Plumer claimed providence in meeting a fellow native from Maine before the first year was out. The man had located a promising piece of land three miles north of Nevada City and anticipated some good mining not far from the river running through. Plumer said, "In any case, we surmised we would have the ranch to fall back on for sustenance and security. We planned and plotted our way into a partnership, thus, we began our first adventure."

Mr. Cleveland cleared his throat, smirked at Mr. Vail, then rather pointedly asked, "Ever noticed, Mr. Plumer talks as much as a woman?"

Thinking he was feeling left out, I'm sure, Martha Jane brightly asked, "Mr. Cleveland, what brought you to Benton?"

"Out here, ain't nobody's business where a fellow comes from, or where he's goin', and it ain't polite to ask," he snarled.

Plumer looked sharply at him and said, "I think Mrs. Vail was attempting polite conversation. It's a form of kindness, Cleveland." That shut him up. I don't understand how such extreme opposites can bunk together.

It is interesting. Three fingers on Mr. Plumer's left hand are curled. It is curious I never noticed it before. But he wears his disuse of those fingers as naturally as his nose.

I suspect, were the man a hair-lip, it would not be the feature one would either notice first nor remember.

I feel so wide awake this evening I'll need God's guidance just to put me to sleep.

17 October . . . Hot Day, Cold Evening

After supper, dishes were washed and we sat talking over coffee. I sat kitty-corner from him, which is better than across from him. I don't know what it is, but when I am across from him I do not dare look his way for fear he will look into my eyes and find me bold. And yet I cannot keep myself from looking at him out of the corner of my eye from afar or just at some article of clothing on his person. Over coffee my eye rested again on that hand and I longed to touch it. I felt the longing, but truth I wasn't thinking on it, when Cleveland blundered, "Wanna knowed how he done it? Tell her Plumer. Tell her how you wrecked that hand."

Mr. Plumer tilted his chair back, put his hands behind his head, and said, "It's your story Cleveland, you tell her . . ."

"Some years ago, not long after I'd just come to the California diggins to claim my pot of gold, Plumer here was Sheriff of Nevada City."

With this information, Swift's eyes grew as wide as my amazement.

"Anyways, he was in this here show house. He'd gotten restless. You ever notice, he can't stay put for long, but what he has to get moving? Anyhows, he's standin' on one of those platforms they set up for the press and other high mucky-mucks. When he jumped down, he hooked that little finger on the back of a seat. He broked the bone, an' that little finger was just hanging there by one bit of skin. The doctor sewed it up an' like a reptile he healed. Not that it mattered much, everbody knowed it was already made bent and useless by some other accident. Weren't it?"

"It was." Mr. Plumer leaned forward, his crippled hand unselfconsciously on the table while his other hand carried his coffee to his lips. Breathlessly we waited for him to enlighten us as to the first crippling. "I well remember that evening, another November night such as this. I wasn't a sheriff. Wasn't yet a marshal. Interesting how stories come down through time slant, is it not? My choice of entertainment that night was *Othello*, a seriocomedy of Henry V and this vaudeville trifle at the Melodeon. I was in the mood for a trifle.

"*The Democrat* had recommended the program as well worth the half-dollar admission, saying 'the jig dancer and mockingbird imitator having no superiors in their line.' And though I quite agreed with their evaluation, indeed, the execution of the banjo solos was better than any I've seen in that line of entertainment, I ought to have known myself better than to go. That sort of thing doesn't hold my attention. Unfortunately, I'd seen *Othello* preformed so many times, I was not drawn to another. Cleveland is right in that I was bored."

Swift could not contain himself. "But the first accident, how did you first injure that finger?"

Mr. Plumer smiled. "Remember my telling you how to hold the reins when mounting?"

Swift eagerly nodded, "Yes, hold the reins between the fingers and grip a bit of mane in the palm of the hand."

"Good. I was yet a young lad when one day I didn't. My pony bolted, my fingers tangled in the reins, I broke one. Hold the reins as I've taught and you'll keep yours."

Swift and I were awed by the story. Cleveland seemed disappointed.

After supper Swift read while Messrs. Vail and Plumer cleaned their guns. Martha and I stitched.

I cannot help but watch Mr. Plumer's movements. His hand works so naturally and yet, I feel myself almost irresistibly drawn to touch it. Caress it. Dear Lord, what foolishness now comes over me? I do believe I need a good, brisk walk by the river. It's been over two weeks since we've seen a sign of any Indian, and the men seem to be working about the farm without looking over their shoulders so much. Perhaps it's time for me to follow their lead.

18 October . . . Crisp Autumn Day

The day's finest moment came when the men brought to the house several geese they'd shot near the river. I plucked the down into a pillowcase and would be happy if they shot many more.

The afternoon was unbearably lovely, and I asked to take the little ones for a walk to the river. I could see "no" rising in Martha Jane's eyes, and I added, "I don't know about you Martha, but I've been cooped up so long if I don't stretch my legs and get some fresh air, I'm going to become ill." She let us know in no uncertain terms that she believed it was yet dangerous and whatever else befell us she was not about to give her children up to the Indians through neglect. I felt like having words with her. Fortunately, I held my tongue. Swift came to my rescue, suggesting that we take a walk and that he ask Mr. Plumer to accompany us for protection.

We set out on our jaunt, he and Plumer both carrying shotguns. On two occasions, while walking through tall, bunched grasses beyond the farm, they flushed grouse. Watching Mr. Plumer hunt is like—what can I say? Once I was privileged to attend a concert of Schumann's music. The music wove a rich brocade of sound around me and it carried me into another world. Watching him hunt transports me to that same place. I close my eyes and replay the experience. The sun warm, a breeze so light I did not know it was there, but for listening to Mr. Plumer tell Swift he could expect any birds they might flush to fly into it. His body, every fiber of it alert, moved as if without aid of feet. And when I heard the whir of the wings, his body swung with the motion of the birds and the gun was like his finger pointing to them. And in the same instant it went off once, then again, and two birds tumbled to the ground. Picking them up he brought them to me saying, "For you, my lady."

God is my witness. I do not know how I kept from fainting. Even now, remembering, I feel light headed—almost ill.

Today's worst moment began after supper when Mr. Cleveland broke out a deck of cards, and raising an eyebrow toward Plumer, insolently asked, "You got the courage ta lose a game to me?" This happened in a heartbeat and Plumer stared at him as if not comprehending. Mr. Vail sputtered in rage. For a moment I thought he was going to expire of apoplexy. "We may be living in a lawless land," he thundered, "nevertheless, neither card nor hard liquor shall ever corrupt my house." Mr. Vail pointed to the door.

We have always held the view that the dual curses of gambling and drink ruin more men than either stupidity or sloth. But for him to have the courage to speak out like that—well, he has gained my respect.

Sweeping the cards into his grubby hand, Mr. Cleveland rose, then paused. "What about solitaire? It ain't gambling, but it's cards. So what ya got to say about that?"

"Leave this house, and come back when you can be civil." Mr. Vail held the door for him.

On his way out he sneered at Plumer, "House rules are lucky for you, ain't they, pardner?" Glancing at Swift he said, "Your hero can't play a game of cards worth. . . ."

Plumer interrupted, calmly, warning, "Watch your tongue."

Mr. Vail pulled the door tight behind Cleveland's departure.

Swift broke the uncomfortable silence that followed. "Is that true? I can't believe you're not as good at the cards as you are with your horse."

Plumer laughed as much at himself as Young Swift, I believe. "You'd be wrong. To be sure, I've played cards and I've tasted my share of whiskey, but I tell you true, no man has been harmed by abstinence, neither has he missed a thing by not indulging."

"How is it you and Cleveland came to be together?" I feel the fool for not being able to check my tongue about that which is none of my business.

"Mr. Cleveland is no friend of mine."

"But he claims you a friend—he speaks of friendship that goes back many years."

"He is correct in stating that we have known of each other for some time. I suspect friendship was perhaps more implied than stated."

I searched my mind and realized that what he had said was true. I am comforted to know they are not friends, although I can't, for all the world, imagine why.

This evening soon found both Swift and Mr. Vail whittling. Again, Mr. Plumer read from Dickens while we women stitched.

As I prepare for prayer and bed, the low quiet sounds of his voice play in my ear. I could listen to him talking, reading. . . . Oh what a fool I am.

Dear God, keep me in Your graces this night and always. Watch over this house and all residing in it. Amen.

Sunday 19 October . . . Light Snow

Prince of Peace, control my will;
Bid this struggling heart be still;
Bid my fears and doubtings cease,
Hush my spirit into peace. Amen.

—*Mary A. S. Barber, 1801–*

We served up a grand feast today, starting with the fried grouse and mashed potatoes. Mr. Plumer said my pies were as good as any he had ever tasted.

We passed the afternoon in a checkers tournament, which Young Swift handily won. I played my first round with Mary Eliza, the second with Cleveland, who had won a round off Bixby, then I lost to Plumer. I couldn't seem to concentrate on anything. I had the strange feeling that he might be of the same state. A foolish thought I'm sure, for he, unlike Cleveland, has not made the subtlest indication of interest in me. Now Cleveland, he stumbles and bumbles his way about, too often underfoot offering to fetch me this and fetch that. Glory, there's more wood in the house than the boxes will hold. And how many pails of water can one use in a day? I think he'd scrub the floors if I'd let him.

Martha Jane says the walk must have done me much good, as the color has returned to my cheeks.

This evening, farming, or rather the practices of farming, dominated the supper table talk. Mr. Plumer coaxed out of Bixby information that he worked for a gentleman in New York, raising vegetables, pigs, and milk cows. Then they got into a discussion about the best way to grub tree roots in preparing a field and the merits of different plowing implements in turning prairie. Plumer and his partner had good grazing ground in California, so they had a ranch instead of a farm.

Their ranch was in the Wilson Valley. The road leading from Nevada City to the Washington mining camp ran along one portion of the ranch. Mr. Plumer said it was an ideal location for pasturing cows and horses for both miners and town's folk. Also, he was able to indulge in horse trading with passing travelers. Even the mining adventures panned out, "From the start, we knew easy pickings had passed. There being a great deal of good quartz on the place, we proceeded to have a small stamp mill fabricated. In short order we were up and running. The enterprise showing good profit, we soon hired on a crew to keep the crusher running."

It would seem the man was born with the Midas touch.

The men have finished the fencing. They trust all is tight as can be made. I feel more secure in our greater numbers.

20 October . . . Crisp and Sunny

This morning I rose extra early to put together pies while we fired the stove to heat the wash water. Laundry goes well with so many hands helping. The men plunged clothes up and down with the washing paddles and hung them out to dry while Martha and I sorted, spot scrubbed, and wrung the water out of them. Swift, Plumer, and Cleveland all pitched in, saying that their clothes as well as ours were in the tub, therefore, not having another item on their agenda, they might in the least be helping. On hearing Martha Jane's under her breath reply, "Better take it while you can. This won't last," I had to curl my lips in and bite to keep my laughter silent.

That aside, I feel so ill of late and I have no idea what can be wrong with me. The strangest images pour through me. Today while rubbing a cloth against the board, I noticed it was a linen of Mr. Plumer's. Then I drifted into a place where I was alone and the shirt was not yet wet and I lifted it and held it to my nose and filled myself with his fragrance and my knees began to buckle.

"Electa?" Martha called out. "Are you all right?"

"Just a little faint." I replied. "Perhaps I need a bit of fresh air."

Cleveland came in on that note and suggested we take a walk. Martha Jane came fast to the rescue. "Not on your life. The next proposal will be for all to take a walk and I have no intention of finishing this laundry alone."

We all had a laugh at that and I sat a spell under the cottonwoods.

After lunch, Plumer and Swift went goose hunting. Cleveland again asked if I wouldn't care to take a walk. I evaded the question, pointing out that Plumer and Swift were out and thus it would be impossible, as we had no escort. To that Cleveland belligerently replied, "I'll bet you'd be interested in an unescorted walk if I were a man who'd made a pile, wouldn't you?"

Now, not only do I dislike this man, but I fear him.

After supper Mr. Plumer showed us a newspaper advertisement for the first bakery he opened with a partner, the United States Bakery. It was a fine advertisement, reading, "The proprietors of the United States Bakery, on Pine Street, under the Dramatic Hall, return thanks to a generous public for the very, very liberal patronage heretofore bestowed upon them. They have recently fitted up their building in a splendid order for the purpose of accommodating the public. Every article will be manufactured of the very best material with the utmost taste, care, and cleanliness. The best assortment of bread, cake, and pastry to be found at all times on hand, together with a well-selected stock of pie, fruits, etc., fresh peaches, apples, plums, figs, raisins, green peas, green corn, oysters, clams, sardines, tomatoes, and a good assortment of confectioneries, cigars, etc. Their aim is to make the best of everything and sell for a small profit. Live and let live. Plumer and Heyer."

He bought a little house on Spring Street, not far from the bakery. Soon after, he and Robinson were persuaded by one of the large companies to relinquish their rich holdings for a price pleasing to both of them. He said, "Didn't I feel cocky sending that money home with the note, ' . . . use what you need and hold the rest, that I might vest it in some business on my return.'"

Their bakery did well. They hired additional staff and expanded into catering. Then, the following year, his new partner, feeling pinched for space, thought he'd like to try his hand at another venture and suggested they sell. As the business was running smoothly, he figured he could handle it alone and so bought Mr. Heyer out. Not long after, he was offered twice what he'd paid for the bakery. This time he sold it and, using a quarter of the proceeds, again he sent a goodly portion home.

Next he entered into another partnership with Heyer. This time, a lively saloon they called the Polka. However, it seems neither of them cared a whit for keeping bar, and again they hired help. And good help it was that freed them up to take advantage of another opportunity. This time, a space was open on Broad Street that Heyer felt was an even better location than the first bakery and had just the right accommodations. He said, "Soon, we found ourselves with another flourishing business on our hands. And Heyer, as was becoming his custom, was bored and looking for capital, thus again, I bought him out. Within two months, I found myself in a favorable position to resell at a handsome profit and again I did."

With admiration Swift said, "Sounds to me like you were trading businesses the same way you traded horses."

Plumer laughed. His laughter is deep and full. It warms me through and through, even better than a glass of warm milk.

21 October

A chilly overcast October day made bright by Mr. Plumer who read aloud while I ironed and Martha Jane mended. Martha Jane fetched him the Nasby columns James sent to us from Findlay. We all laughed till our eyes filled with tears. Mr. Plumer read in the Sacramento press that even Mr. Lincoln got a charge out of the wit off the pen of this man when wearing the badge of an ignoramus confederate of a most serious demeanor.

When I handed Mr. Plumer his fresh-ironed clothes, our hands touched and I felt a jolt that fairly knocked me down. Looking into his eyes, I think I saw in them the same experience, but neither of us said a word.

Is this my imagination? Is this what Elizabeth Barrett Browning speaks of? His eyes, those fine grey eyes, all my life I shall remember becoming lost in those eyes. And when I looked away, it was as if while I was there the world had changed. If this be love . . . but of course this is foolishness, one cannot love what one does not know, and we hardly know each other.

Dear God, lend this foolish woman wisdom.

22 October . . . Sun Returned

Today my world has turned me upside down. Where do I begin? Where will this end? It was a lovely day and, with Martha's blessing, Plumer, Swift, and I slipped off to visit the river.

There we sat on the selfsame rock Thompson and I shared those many months before, and I pointed out the spot where the fawns had lain. I told them about the fawns and that I found them the loveliest creatures I've ever seen. Then Swift went down to the landing to check the crossing cable. Mr. Plumer said, "Electa, you are the loveliest creature I've ever seen." His words were too grave to leave any doubt to the seriousness of their intent. My heart pounded so violently I could hardly hear what he next said. But hear it I did.

"Miss Bryan, I am hardly worthy to care for you as I do. Even so, I can go on no longer without some resolution. I wish to tell you the worst about me. Then, if you desire, we will never speak of this moment again." I opened my mouth to protest, but he put his finger gently on my lips and continued, "Hear me out. I have gambled and lost. I have drunk of spirits until I had no spirit. Worse, I have lain with women I did not love. And perhaps more despicable to your eyes, but not mine, I have lain with women for whom I cared deeply—women called by some fancy ladies, by others ladies of the night. I have shot to their death at least two men, possibly I have been responsible for more. To add to my shame, I spent six months of my life in the hell of San Quentin. But I tell you, in no instance have I shot anyone in any manner except self-defense. I say this in truth and I believe I can prove it.

"Having said this, do you bid me stay my speech or leave?"

I could hardly digest the information coming at me like flakes of snow in a storm, but this I know: I did not want him to leave.

"Good Sir, I do not pretend to understand, perhaps even to comprehend, but if God can forgive all, who am I to condemn?"

And he wept. I have never before seen a man's tears. They are not like that of a child's, but like some great silent rock breaking. And I knew that in the sharing of that silence, I was forever changed.

I reached out, touching at last that hand I'd longed for, feeling at last the heat of his flesh.

I have entered through the portals of those grey eyes and I have felt a heart that beats to the same rhythms as my own. And I know this, if he is not worthy, neither am I.

Dear God, how is it I am filled with such great hopelessness and hope all of one moment?

23 October . . . Weak Sun Today, Afternoon Skiff of Snow

In the morning Messrs. Bixby and Cleveland went out to shoot geese. The men have taken my desire for goose down to heart. Mr. Vail says if he'd allowed, every man of them would have gone off to shoot a goose for Electa. He and Plumer spent the day mending the roof. Martha Jane and I started knitting socks.

At supper Messrs. Vail and Plumer debated whether several new authors would endure or were too contemporary to become classical. Usually I am ready to jump right into just that sort of conversation. Tonight I could hardly hear the words for a hot wind that seemed to circumnavigate my mind.

I dare not look at Mr. Plumer, and when I find him looking at me, my face becomes hot. There was not one opportunity today for us to be together without a great crowd. I am fair beside myself with longing to hear more of his story.

He has said he cares for me, but then he has said he cares for Swift as well. Is this caring the same? I am very fond of Young Swift, but I don't blush when he looks at me. He does not make me feel as though I might, at any moment, faint.

Heavenly Father, bless this house and keep it whole.

24 October . . . Snow

I plucked down all morning. We put the extra geese to boil in the laundry tubs. Tomorrow we will remove the cooled fat, strip the meat from the bones, and bring it to boil again, this time with minced onion and spices, then we will pack it in crocks, and after it is nearly cool we will seal them with hot beef lard.

After supper the sounds of plates and flatware seemed gathered into the melody the children sang while skipping around the table, "Hey Betty Martin, tip toe, tip toe; Hey Betty Martin tip toe fine." Before long, they had us all singing with them. We finished cleaning singing, "Mammy's little babies love short'nin, short'nin, Mammy's little babies love short'nin bread."

Mr. Plumer said, "Sounds like a political song to me."

At that we all had a laugh. Swift said, "I have a real political song for you," and commenced to sing "Lincoln and Liberty" to the tune of "Old Rosin the Bow." It wasn't long before he was teaching the words to the rest of us.

HURRAH FOR THE CHOICE OF THE NATION!
OUR CHIEFTAIN SO BRAVE AND SO TRUE:
WE'LL GO FOR THE GREAT REFORMATION,
FOR LINCOLN AND LIBERTY TOO.

WE'LL GO FOR THE SON OF KENTUCKY,
THE HERO OF HOOSIERDOM THROUGH:
THE PRIDE OF THE SUCKERS SO LUCKY,
FOR LINCOLN AND LIBERTY TOO.

THEY'LL FIND WHAT BY FELLING AND MAULING,
OUR RAIL-MAKER STATESMAN CAN DO:
FOR THE PEOPLE ARE EVERYWHERE CALLING
FOR LINCOLN AND LIBERTY TOO.

THEN UP WITH OUR BANNER SO GLORIOUS,
THE STAR-SPANGLED RED, WHITE, AND BLUE,
WE'LL FIGHT TILL OUR BANNER'S VICTORIOUS,
FOR LINCOLN AND LIBERTY TOO.

Then we sang, "Old Abe Lincoln Came Out of the Wilderness" till the monotony of it reminded us 'twas time to put the children to bed.

Picking up my knitting, I said, "It's so nice to be in a group where everyone is of the same political persuasion, unlike on the boat, where one hardly dared let it be known the side he stood on."

At that Cleveland began to laugh, braying like a donkey and slapping his thigh. "Plumer's no damn, excuse me ma'am, Republican! Was the Democratic party he joined, Democrats is what elected him."

I felt the color drain from my face. Carefully watching my stitches I asked, "Is that true, you are a Democrat?"

"I am."

"Then, how is it you can sing 'Lincoln and Liberty' with such convincing gusto?"

His wonderful warm laughter rolled over me. And I looked up to see his eyes sparkling and kindly.

"Miss Bryan, whatever my political persuasion, I am an American first. I offer no apology for believing that Douglas was less likely to divide us, or for my belief that the Republicans stand for what is best for the Big Whig, not the little man. By that, I do not mean that Republican interests have no place. We all need representation. We coalesce into parties in order to promote our individual interests. I toss my hat in the ring in support of the lesser among us because they have chosen me, and because I find their needs less well represented, and because I find them more interesting.

"Having said that, Lincoln is our president and I am loyal to him. Would that all could say the same."

"Well put," said Mr. Vail thoughtfully.

"But what of slavery?" asked I. "You say you are for the little man. Is not the slave the littlest of us all? Is not that an issue above whether or not the nation is one?"

"To the first I answer, yes. To the second, I must answer no. The issue of slavery falls under the category of justice. Justice is a mere concept. The concept evolves, and we keep striving toward its perfection through our courts and our laws. That is the legacy of our system. Might I remind you that is also President Lincoln's understanding of the situation?"

I wish I could convince him that he were wrong to be supporting the Democrats, yet he is so solid in his thinking. And he does not dismiss us, Republicans, thus there is nothing to argue about. I do not agree that the nation is more important than the slavery question. Perhaps it is not a matter of which is the more pressing; perhaps it's the question of how one goes about achieving the goal. Why does it distress me that he does not think as I do?

25 October . . . Snow

It being a perfect temperature, we bundled ourselves and the children and filled the yard with snow creations. Plumer helped me build a unicorn, but the horn kept falling off. When we came in, his face was white with cold and on his cheeks were two bright spots. I wanted to warm his face in my hands, take the cold away, stand near him. I had him remove his wet socks and hang them above the stove to dry and fetched him a basin of water to warm his feet. When the children took their nap, he left for his quarters to do the same.

In the evening Swift, Plumer, and I outlasted the others playing Botticelli. This time Plumer won. When Swift rose to leave, Plumer stopped him saying, "stay a bit, that we may talk."

While he stirred the fire, I made us hot spiced milk and Swift pulled three chairs near the fire. Plumer started speaking in that wonderful, even, resonant voice of his. "You are the dearest people I know. But you are both naive and innocent, as I am not. I trust you are in some small way finding me dear to yourselves as well. It is of this account I want you to know who I am, that I would not deceive you.

"This story begins when 1855 was coming rapidly to a close. My obligations to home were well covered for the time. I had profits enough to invest in San Francisco. Heyer was doing well in his new dealings. He commenced to buy me out of the "Polka," as well as the house and lot on Spring Street. Thus, I determined to repair myself to the City.

"San Francisco can be chilling, especially in the winter—that fog rolls up from the bay, chills the bones, and sets up a bad brew in the lung. As much as I longed to enter the fray in that city, within a month I knew I could not survive the climate. An internal debate began to rage alongside my fever; should I return to my family, or seek another place where the climate was better suited to my weakness? As much as I longed for family, I dreaded returning to those beastly frigid Maine winters. While in Nevada City, my health became so robust I'd forgotten what it was like to suffer each breath. Then again, I felt I'd panned that city out and fortune could not possibly remain a constant. I pondered whether to take myself to southern California and see if that might not suit my calling.

"By this time, I could not leave my rooms for the pain the air drew into my lungs. I staid holed up before the fire, hoping to get well enough to leave. That was my state when a group of acquaintances from Nevada City, members of the Democratic Party, came to San Francisco to look me up. They urged my return, that they might put me forward as a candidate for town Marshal. Another took me aside and mentioned that a young lady I'd made feeble attempts in courting was said to be pining my absence. I had assumed I was on the fringe of her ring of suitors. It was flattery that led me back to Nevada City, that is, flattery and climate."

Swift added wood to the fire, and I replenished our cookies and hot, spiced milk. "Heyer had opened yet another bakery. On my return, I reentered into partnership with him. Within six weeks my health had returned. In May the miners took the office of Marshal from its current holder and gave it to me by seven votes.

"The office didn't preclude other business interests. I enjoyed mingling with all levels of society and the great variety of labor. Basically, it was my duty to keep the peace, enforce the local ordinances, and collect the taxes.

"After the election, the hardest thing I had to do was to gain acceptance of my right, not to mention duty, to enforce the law. The former marshal acquitted himself admirably in his execution of the office, and he was especially comfortable with the businessmen. To complicate matters, Sheriff Wright immediately hired him on as a deputy. I think it fair to say there was no animosity between the new deputy and myself. Unfortunately, the election of a Marshal from the opposition party stuck in the craw of both merchants and Sheriff.

"The next month a great fire broke out, destroying 400 houses—even the fireproof brick buildings built after the last conflagration. Worse, we lost both our courthouse and jail—not to mention our latest bakery. The loss of the jail brought with it attendant problems holding prisoners. That came under the purview of the Sheriff's office, not mine. Be that as it may, the temporary quarters rarely held its prisoners.

"Sheriff Wright generally subscribed to passing petty complaints to me. However, there came a time when he asked me to go after a repeat offender of some desperate reputation. Having brought the man in twice before and not having received any remuneration for my services to the county, I was reluctant to retrieve him again, especially since he was in the company of two brothers who had been incarcerated with him.

"The sheriff and I came to a price for my services, with the caveat that he come along to help with the capture. I told him I'd already enlisted a deputy to work with me. I had some information as to where the men might be, and I felt that more people turned an unknown situation into a dangerous one. He wouldn't listen to reason and he was calling the shots.

"Don't ever let anyone tell you what you don't know won't hurt you. What you don't know may kill you. What I didn't know was that after agreeing with me that three people were the maximum manpower needed, he secretly enlisted three men to trail far enough behind that neither my deputy nor I would notice.

"I proceeded to collect our horses and my deputy. We went to fetch the sheriff, who dallied and delayed, attending to what sort of business I did not know.

"While we were waiting for the dawdling sheriff, a fellow came in and told me that two saddled horses were staked in a ravine near the cabin where we thought the men were hiding. What he neglected to tell was he had left a companion to watch the horses till the sheriff got to them. To make matters worse, a Squire Williams, self-appointed liege lord of the community, chanced upon that companion and after ascertaining the situation, informed him he would take over. However, the man neglected to tell him the authorities had already been sent for and left, saying if he should return he would whistle so as not to be fired upon. Next, Williams scurried about rustling up a party of three volunteers, armed them with revolvers and shotguns, and concealed them behind trees and in a ditch so as to form a semicircle around the horses. He told them he would give a command for those hidden to step out, order the prisoners to halt, and if they did not, all were to commence firing on them.

"Before the evening was out, Sheriff Wright was dead and the former marshal lay dying. I probably need not add, the escapees were not captured."

"What of Williams," asked Swift. "What happened to him?"

"What of Williams . . ." Plumer mused. "A Williams comes to reside in every community, always above the law, always supported by the obsequious gullible, they maintain their princely kingdoms. These self-styled nobles obey one rule: Never take responsibility for your actions. It's interesting how many obsequious pecksniffs bow to them in some desperate hope that a bit of their glow will rub off—lend them some shine. Nothing happens to the Williams' of this world. That is the how and the why they prosper among us.

"We rebuilt our business and continued to do well. I invested in several small claims that showed promise. I won the next election handily. The girl I'd been courting agreed to be my bride. We were looking about for a suitable house and wondering whether to build instead, when a Mr. John Vedder, a family man, approached me, wondering if I knew of a place he could rent. I proposed my house on Spring Street and moved into the National Hotel for the duration till the wedding.

"In August the Democrats, my supporters having successfully argued the convention, put forth my name as a candidate for the state assembly alongside that of a Mr. Walsh for senate.

"Since we were the majority party, we expected to sweep the ticket in September. And I do believe we would have, had it not been for the illustrious Squire Williams. He campaigned hard against us, wooing the losers of our primary and their friends into a coalition with his Know-Nothing Party. In this election we were all but erased from the ballot."

In the pause that followed Mr. Plumer's speech I mused aloud, "You've been rambling some time now. Your life could not be more entertaining to me than Robinson Crusoe's, but faith, I've not heard one word that would indict you in the crimes you allege."

"I'm warming to it," he replied dryly. Abruptly he stood, "But you're right; I've been rambling long." Then he took my hand and kissed it. "Good night, sweet lady. I look forward to the sunshine of your presence in the morning."

He, with Swift as close as a spur to his heel, was out the door before I stood. Now sleep does not choose me.

SUNDAY 26 OCTOBER . . . BELOW ZERO

THOU HAST BOUGHT ME WITH THY BLOOD,
OPENED WIDE THE GATE TO GOD;
PEACE I ASK, BUT PEACE MUST BE,
LORD IN BEING ONE WITH THEE.

—Mary A. S. Barber, 1801–

On leaving the back-house this morning I slipped and fell in the snow. Wouldn't you know, just at that moment, Mr. Plumer was coming out of his cabin. Before I could get myself straightened, he was at my side helping me upright, and when I was standing we were so near, for a moment, I was afraid he was going to kiss me. The moment passed, he helped dust me off. I suppose I should be ashamed, but now I wish he had kissed me.

Tonight at supper Mary Eliza asked each of us to tell their favorite color, hers being blue, Martha Jane's a dusty violet, Harvey claims red as does Mr. Plumer. Neither Bixby nor Mr. Vail would attest to a favorite, Cleveland said he liked the color of yellow, Swift surprised me, saying he liked a deep turquoise and, I of course, cannot make up mind in favor of forest green or VanDyke brown.

After supper the household retired early, all except Swift, Plumer, and I. I set a pot of tea to steep, and Plumer continued to relate the story of his adventures.

"On the 25th of September 1857, I shot and killed Mr. Vedder."

The words about relieved me of my breath. To steady myself, I poured the tea.

"John Vedder and his wife had a stormy marriage. The wife, by her own admission, had a vicious tongue and Vedder, by his admission, was in the habit of knocking her about and threatening her life. My first close contact with her came after she had sought advice of the wife of one of my champions, Mrs. Senner. Mrs. Senner put the notion to her that she seek me out for advice. I put her in contact with David Belden, a prominent lawyer and a member of the Democratic Club. And he, after listening to her muddled tale of love, abuse, and devotion, advised against divorce. About a week later, the owner of the Hotel de Paris called me in to settle a family dispute between no less than Mr. Vedder and his wife. Evidently Mr. Vedder continued to abuse his wife. She'd fled to the hotel and was residing there when he came with a gun and forcibly removed their two-year-old daughter. I enlisted one of my deputies, and we moved into a room across the hall from Mrs. Vedder in order to protect her from her husband until such time she could straighten out her affairs. At length she decided to leave the city. She asked if we would carry her baggage, then returned to the house to pack her belongings. Having my rounds to attend, I sent my deputy to the house to protect her from her husband in the event he should return.

"About 11:30 I came to relieve him and found them sitting on either side of the stove. As my deputy stood to go, I took his chair by the fire. I asked whether she'd made up her mind to leave the fire. She said she did not like to leave a fire. Then my deputy left through the street side kitchen door, leaving it open behind him. Again I asked if she were ready to leave. She replied that she was considering staying in the house. So I asked if she were not afraid her husband might come back and "disturb" her. To which she made no reply. I remember being weary. I leaned forward, pressing the palms of my hands against my eyes, my elbows pressing heavy against my knees. I pondered how I could maneuver this mess to a satisfactory conclusion.

"I heard rapid footsteps coming up the stairs to the back door. As I rose, pistol first, Vedder came through the door saying, "your time has come." In that time I had my pistol unloosed and we both fired. He stepped back. I took a step or two, firing two or three times more. He did not fire again. I left.

"I went to the jail and told my deputies what had happened. They asked who shot first and I honestly do not know, but I probably did. Then they asked if I'd killed him. Again, I didn't know.

"Of course I had. When this went to trial, the prosecution tried to paint the wife and me as lovers, thus justifying Mr. Vedder's attempted murder. They could not find one soul who had ever seen us alone, because before that moment we had never been alone. Even the hotel keeper testified he had never seen me in Mrs. Vedder's room other than when her husband was present.

"Had I not killed Vedder, he would have killed me. Yet, the jury found me guilty of murder in the second degree. Neither my lawyer nor I could believe it. Expecting acquittal, I had not resigned as Marshal.

"Now I was neither Marshal nor fiancé, but at least I still had my interest in the bakery and my house on 94 Spring Street in Nevada City.

"In April of '58 the California Supreme Court unanimously reversed the decision, citing prejudiced jurors. Another trial, with a change of venue, was held and unbelievable as we found it, we failed again to secure an acquittal.

"I was sentenced to 12 years at San Quentin."

The placing of a name on the man he killed is unnerving; it moves the telling from vague incident into reality. The slow unfolding of the whole story leaves me not unsure of him, yet somehow unsettled. He must have sensed that in me. Before he returned to his quarters, he asked if I would be willing to read the newspaper accounts of his time in California.

Of course I would, even if I did not love . . . how foolish—I do not.

"Heavenly Father. . . .

27 October . . . More Snow

This morning, in the midst of laundry, Mr. Plumer met me on my way from the back-house. Letting me understand that more would follow, he passed me a packet of news clippings, which I, feeling most honored to be the recipient of his most private self, slipped into my apron pocket.

"Tonight, after dark, watch for me to come this way again." My words astonish me. I have always been a private person, but now I have entered into new territory, a secret person as well.

Even with all the heavy work to be done, the morning passed at some snail's pace, and I dared not look at him for fear everyone would read my thoughts. All morning I longed to be alone with my packet of reading. At last, after lunch, I begged need of a nap. Sister smiled smugly and said, "Well, if you didn't spend the night burning the oil. . . ." I did not stay to listen to her speech.

Climbing onto the upper bed, I pulled a quilt to my chin and commenced to read. As I read the clippings, I was amazed at the number of escapades in which the man had engaged. As marshal, hardly a week passed when he wasn't bringing in some notorious bad man, and daily he was in the news enforcing this law or that, sometimes much to the merchant's dismay. Listening to him tell of his exploits, I wouldn't have known the half how modest he truly is. As he's told it, he's even glossed over his many mining interests. A remarkable man, to be sure.

When at last we were alone, I thanked him for giving me the opportunity to read the papers. He asked me if he was vindicated and I exclaimed, "My heavens, I am not surprised they found you guilty. The papers paint a picture of the Vedders so deep into the gutter it would be hard for anyone to understand how you could find yourself involved with such disgusting low life. I haven't a doubt you would do so on your firm principles, but there are few who understand the notion of principles, let alone adhere to them. But 12 years—how did you escape serving those 12 years? Here you are and you are neither old nor dead!"

Martha Jane came to the door and peered into the dusk. "Tomorrow," I whispered before she called "Electa?"

When I came into view she asked, "Are you all right?"

"A bit of indigestion." I replied. Which wasn't far from the truth.

How I wish I were holding him in my arms. How heavy must the very idea of dying a convict have pressed upon him. Dear God, I want nothing more than to take care of him and keep him well for as long as I love. Did I write that? Oh, that he would love me!

28 October . . . Grey Day

Baking gingerbread, I daydream of a kitchen of my own, of Mr. Plumer coming into the house, sniffing the air appreciatively, while I remove my apron. And then his arms are around me, and my head is on his chest, and I can feel his heart beating and he says. . . .

"Electa, you're going to wear out those eggs if you don't stop beating on them." Martha Jane shakes her head. "Where on earth were you?"

I laughed, "Jungle adventure. It's cold outside."

"Never satisfied."

When the men returned from chores, I did watch Plumer sniff the air. He said the gingerbread was good as his sister's. And he had always thought hers was the best. I dusted my floury hands on the back of my dress to pour the men some coffee. Plumer laughed and shook his head. "Just like my sister; always using the back of her dress instead of her apron!" In his voice I caught the sounds of awe and admiration. So I smiled.

When the men went out again, Martha Jane asked more than stated, "I take it you are growing fond of that man?"

I froze inside. If I say nothing, she will know. If I admit how I feel, she will ask me 21 questions I am not able to answer and might not want to answer if I were able. "He pleases me well enough."

"And that's all?"

"And that's enough."

"Well that's more than any other man has gotten from you."

She left it at that, but come evening she did not sit up with us and, of a purpose I suspect, enticed her husband early to bed, leaving me to Swift and Plumer and my knitting.

"On reentering the poisonous vapors of the bay the consumption returned, and I spent the following months confined in the infirmary. During that time more than 150 people, including some I'd thought were my enemies, petitioned for my release on the grounds there was no evidence I had not acted in self-defense. After my release, I discovered that one of the guards also sent a letter asking I be released. The prison doctors sent a letter stating they believed I would be dead within a year if I were held in that climate. I have no doubt that was true, yet I shall carry to my grave a sadness that the governor cited my health and not my innocence in granting my reprieve. I served six months in San Quentin, was pardoned, but I never will be free of the cloud of the verdict of my peers."

On his release from San Quentin, he returned to the house at 94 Spring Street and was cared for by the widow of his former partner at the Wilson Valley ranch.

"The bakery partnership was doing well and did not take much of my time and my former deputy, now marshal, appointed me deputy. I thought I was returning with, in the least, my former respect. This was not to be. It seems too simplistic to me, but some have said they thought a great many held it against me that I did not die after receiving a pardon on account of precarious health. Shut out from the company of my former companions, as my health improved, I became restless. I began to roam the city at night, taking in a bit of entertainment, a drink here and there, the sort of thing many a young man turns to when he's been set adrift. At this time I met one of Mr. Ashmore's Ladies. Mr. Ashmore's was residence to fancy ladies and actresses. The woman I became enamored of was both."

"What did she look like?" I blurted. I don't know what came over me, but I had to know, and my intuition told me if I didn't ask he would slide past it, and if I didn't ask now I never would. Still he sat, staring into the fire.

"Please," I said, "Tell me true, I want to know."

"She was tall, straight. Her features were as chiseled marble. Some might have called them harsh. Her eyes were clear blue. They sparkled when she talked. Her hair black. When she let it down, it hung to her waist in thick waves."

"What was she like?" I almost whispered.

I felt I could have read a book in the time between my question and his answer. "Well educated. She was a woman who could take care of herself, capable, competent, sufficient—she knew her mind."

I pressed on. "Did you love her?"

"We never spoke of love, nor marriage, nor family. She did take my name, calling herself Mrs. Plumer."

"But did you love her?"

"Miss Bryan, she was very kind to me. If I had been asked then, I would have said 'yes.'"

"But I'm asking now."

"If you insist. Yes. I did. I do. I always will."

My throat hurt so I thought I'd have to leave the fire. Well I asked. And he's been honest.

"I am not ashamed of this," he went on, "but the love I felt was a mixture of awe, lust, and respect. And she returned that to me. Today, I know love can be larger, deeper, and more profound than that. But it is what I felt then. That is what I shall remember."

He then turned his face to mine. "I would have rather I didn't have to tell you this." His eyes were bright as if much moisture filled them. "I think we need to sleep. Tomorrow? Tomorrow do I go on?"

I touched his shoulder and I wanted to say so many things, but all I could get out was, "Please, tomorrow." Then swiftly I left, lest I begin to cry. I heard the door close behind. And now I cannot sleep for the sight of his face before me, the strange longing inside me, and all my thoughts whipping through the night like fireflies.

How shall I ever compete with a courtesan such as the willowy black-haired woman? I wish he'd lied. No, then he wouldn't be a man I could care for. I wish I'd had the wisdom not to ask.

Dear God, guide my heart. I hardly have any wits left about me.

29 October

This morning I was feeling out of sorts—rather adrift. Cleveland came through the door first and seeing me said, "My! My! What a long sour puss we're wearing this morning. Have a tiff with your lover?"

The crude familiarity made me gasp, and for a moment I was afraid Plumer was going to speak out. Fortunately, Mr. Vail said, "I'll stand for none of that language in this house. If you overstep your bounds again, Mr. Cleveland, I must ask you to leave." Thank you, thank you, Mr. Vail.

Mid morning only Mr. Plumer came in for coffee. Even now I feel the moment as if it were happening. As I served him, Martha Jane and the wee ones sat by the fire, she serenading us singing, "Hush little baby don't say a word, Papa's gonna buy you a mocking bird." I sat kitty-corner from Plumer. "And if that mocking bird won't sing, Papa's gonna buy you a diamond ring." He ran the tip of his index finger across the back of my hand. "And if that diamond ring turns brass . . ." Soft as a feather he began to stroke the back of my hand with the tip of his fore finger. "Papa's gonna buy you a looking glass, and if that looking glass gets broke, Papa's gonna buy you a billy goat." As he stroked, my breath fair departed my body. "And if that billy goat won't pull, Papa's gonna buy you a cart and bull . . ." I hardly dared look up. "And if that cart and bull turn over . . ." But when I did, I saw desire in his eyes. "Papa's gonna buy you a dog named Rover . . ." A desire that wiped the slate clean. "And if that dog named Rover don't bark . . ." It no longer mattered whom he'd loved in the past. "Papa's gonna buy you a horse and cart . . ." Or whether she was most gloriously beautiful. "And if that horse and cart fall down . . ." All that would ever matter was this passion we feel for each other. "You'll still be the prettiest girl in town." Martha Jane stood up, and I had to leave the room.

I hoped the three of us would be again left alone in the evening, and I was not disappointed. At our prompting, Plumer continued, "One evening, on return from a prospecting trip in the Carson City area, I ran into Walsh, the fellow I so roundly went down to defeat with in the fall of 1857. He had purchased several claims in the Virginia Range of western Nevada from Henry Comstock. Because the gold-laced quartz was almost impossible to separate from the gummy, blue-grey clays of the area, the claims were considered worthless. Unknown to Comstock, this layer of gumbo covered some of the richest silver deposits ever known. In the spring of 1860 Walsh suggested I do a bit of prospecting in the vicinity of Virginia City, Nevada.

"His suggestion proved good. I beat the traffic of the silver-fevered hoards that hit Henness Pass in April by a week and staked several claims that proved good.

"Loathe to leave either my new lady or my Nevada City investments, I maintained my residence there for the next two years. During this time, I made regular trips over the pass to visit my Virginia City claims.

"At Nevada City I became a partner in a silver and gold mine located on Scott's Flat, and in the fall of 1860 I set up the Flora Temple Company to excavate gold in Kelsey Ravine. There we had a head of quartz nearly 15 inches thick and only about 10 feet down.

"All of November I worked with Democrats to form a Douglas and Johnson Club in support of his election for president. Our effort may have been in vain, but I believe the cause was well intended. I know of no man in the club who supported slavery. I needn't tell you, those of the slavery persuasion joined the southern splinter group, nominating Tennessee's John Bell. We feared that Lincoln was too much of a fighter to keep the Union together. Keeping our country united and strong was our purpose. Perhaps even the moderate Douglas could not have mollified the South. There may have been no way to avoid war.

"Had I turned around and taken stock of where I was and where I might be going, I might have avoided further problems with my temper and with the law, but I was on a tear. I had no mind to stop."

I wish I'd met him a few years ago. Then he wouldn't have led such a wild life. But then he wouldn't be as fascinating either.

30 October . . . Sun Again, Snow Melting, Yard Muddy

In that frighteningly direct way she has, Martha Jane asked me what my situation with Mr. Plumer was. I told her true he had not declared his heart, but I knew I loved him with the full strength of mine. Aghast, she exclaimed, "Surely you haven't told him!" And I assured her I had not committed such an indiscretion, that I never would, but if he asked, I would surrender my heart and a promise to become his wife.

This evening the flames in the fireplace seemed especially lively, casting shadows on the walls, making the room seem somehow enchanted. Swift asked if California had always been such a raw and rowdy place and Mr. Plumer answered, "Appears so—on one excuse or another—which ever suits the case." He said the firing on Fort Sumter initiated the latest plethora of dispute, which tended to get out of hand, especially in the pleasure houses. As early as May, he was witness to one such altercation. A couple of men were having some words that led to the death of one by a knife wound.

In February of '61, he was involved in a fracas at the house of Irish Maggie on Pine Street in Nevada City. He was with an acquaintance and they were on a bender (when he says that, I do suspect he is meaning they are raving drunk though one would never believe it of him as he is now). His friend decided they should pay their respects to the house on Pine Street. While his friend was in a room with a woman, another named Muldroon commenced pounding on the door and demanding admittance. When Maggie told him that the woman was with another party and could not see him at the moment, he attempted to kick the door in. Plumer told him to stop. Muldroon commenced swearing at him and calling his mother into the fray. With the butt of his pistol, Mr. Plumer put a gash in his skull. The man was not mortally wounded. The police were not called in. Even so, the *Union* wrote it up, and got it all wrong.

He said, "Late, on a crisp October evening, after a long day's business, I went to Ashmore's to visit my lady. While waiting for her labors to be finished, Bill Riley, a bellicose Secessionist, began spouting rhetoric against the President and the Union. I rose to the bait. Not being able to best me in a verbal fight, he drew a knife and placed it firmly in my skull. I shot him dead. In the jail, a surgeon stitched me back together. The following afternoon, the jailor let my lady in, saying, 'We have no murderer here.' Then he turned on his heel and, leaving both the cell door and the door to the jail wide open, disappeared down the street. We left."

He spent the afternoon in drawing up a power of attorney for a friend and making lists of his holdings and his wishes for their disposition. The "lady" fetched his friend to the house, and they agreed on the terms by which he would sell each of the holdings and planned how they would remain in contact. He slept whilst his friend went out to purchase for him a horse and the "lady" packed for him. On the last day of October he left after dark, technically a fugitive.

My Lord, sometimes listening to Plumer's life becomes exhausting. Tonight he looked so weary, I wished to kiss his dear white forehead, press my lips against the purple scar which peeks from beneath the unruly hair tangled over it, the scar that turns livid when he's cold or tired.

On leaving, he gave me another envelope of clippings. It is a small one, but tonight I am tired. So tired of dreaming foolish dreams. He's only a handsome, polished man who is passing through my life. I'm a fool to think that just because he's the first to take my fancy, he might fancy me.

31 October. . . Woke to a Skiff of Snow

This morning Mr. Cleveland brought in the pail of milk. Having just separated cream from milkings past, he offered to churn it, for which I felt grateful, as I have a lot of knitting I'd like to be getting done. When he'd finished the churning and I'd thanked him, he said, "I'da thought any woman woulda knowed she'd be better served by a man who hauled in the wood and the water and maybe once in a while churned the butter, than one who was only good for talkin' politics an' poetry."

He seemed such a child that moment, I hardly knew how to reply. I said, kindly as I could muster, "Mr. Cleveland, I'm sure you're going to make some woman a good husband." The way he beamed I can only hope he understood that I meant some woman, not me.

After supper cleanup, we played Who's Got the Button with Mary Eliza, and even Bixby and Cleveland seemed entertained. While Martha Jane and I put the children down for the night, Messrs. Vail, Plumer, and Swift engaged in a political discourse, which sent Bixby and Cleveland straight to the peace of their quarters. Again Martha Jane and her husband discreetly retired early, leaving the three musketeers to their adventures.

While prospecting near Carson City, Mr. Plumer had made the acquaintance of a Bill Mayfield. Philosophically they were at opposing ends, he as solidly secesh as Plumer was Union, however he had a reputation as a professional gambler who was a square dealer, and he was a good friend of Plumer's "lady." Therefore, it was with this place of habitation in mind that he made his way over the mountains. In a weakened condition, he reached Mayfield's cabin, where the owner tucked him into bed like a baby.

A man by the name of Blackburn, commonly known as the worst lawbreaker in the Nevada Territory, was the local sheriff. When he got word of Mr. Plumer's altercation and information that he might come to the area, Blackburn boasted he was man enough to capture him. Thus the next day Mayfield and another acquaintance, Jack Harris, placed some boards and a ticking over Harris' rafters, set him up with provisions, helped him into his new quarters, sealed up the ceiling, and left him there to recover.

Sure enough, as Plumer lay recuperating, this Sheriff came looking for him at Mayfield's. Not finding him there, he went on a toot, headed for the St. Nicholas saloon, and interrupted a game, telling Mayfield he was under arrest. Mayfield asked to see his warrant. He didn't have one. Mayfield said, "You can't arrest a man without a warrant," and continued his game. Blackburn replied, "I tell you I can arrest you or anyone else, and I'll arrest you anyhow." As the Sheriff drew his pistol, Mayfield's friends caught the fellow by the arms and started dragging him toward the door, but he broke away and lunged for Mayfield, who drew his knife, stabbed him in the chest and leaving him to die, fled. Soon after, Mayfield was found, tried for murder, and sentenced to hang. Friends helped him leave the jail and, since Blackburn was universally hated, no one was interested in pursuing him.

Nevada City officials did not have a murder case against Plumer and therefore did not want him back, thus, because of this situation, he became a fugitive from a disinterested system. So Mr. Harris opened up the ceiling, and they lived together that winter while Mr. Plumer recuperated and sold off his holdings. During that time, he determined he would do well to return to his home where the world was an ordered and civilized place, where people knew the rules and took the time to live by them.

As for Mayfield, Plumer has been told, although banned from the bars as a troublemaker, Mayfield staid in the area for several months, and as most of the citizenry was glad to be rid of the scoundrel he'd knifed, no one bothered him. No longer able to pursue his trade in Carson City when he ran low on money, Mayfield removed himself to the Idaho Territory.

By late June, Mr. Plumer was ready to leave the country. As he had never seen the interior, he determined to return to the States via the Missouri. He thought to purchase a couple of horses, travel to San Francisco, book passage up the coast in order to visit the gold mines on the Salmon River, then proceed to Fort Benton, there to take the Missouri to St. Louis.

While Mr. Plumer was planning his trip East, Mr. Swift and I were planning our westward trek. Surely it is more than coincidence that pointed us each to the other.

1 November . . . Joseph Swift's Birthday

Mary Eliza and I baked a gingerbread cake and served it topped with great mounds of whipped cream. Martha Jane baked buffalo ribs, potatoes, and squash and served it up with the first sauerkraut of the year. Little Harvey gave Swift his prettiest rock, and Martha Jane and I gave him a pair of wool socks, each having knitted, under his very nose, a single sock. In honor of his birthday, he was given his choice of after-dinner game. Wily fox he is, he chose Proverbs, knowing full well that would drive Bixby and Cleveland early to their quarters.

On finishing our game, we returned to our fire and Mr. Plumer's story. The last week in July found him in Lewiston, Idaho Territory, where he staid at the Luna House. All the talk in Lewiston was about the quality of the diggings in Florence, and the next morning he thought to take a look at them for himself. He found close to 10,000 persons digging, shouting, and fighting over what space they could grab. After a couple of weeks, he determined he'd seen enough and thought to return to the Luna House. He rode back with a small group of companions, including Reeves and Ridgley. They checked into the Luna House, then proceeded to enjoy such entertainments as the town had to offer, not the least of which was a hot bath and a hair cut. On Monday, half the party returned to their claims at Florence. Plumer and Reeves had agreed to travel eastward together since he was heading for Benton and Reeves wanted to try his hand panning Gold Creek. Ridgley took a notion to visit a new Spanish dance hall at Oro Fino, and asked if they'd like to accompany him. They did.

Once at the dance hall, Ridgley and Reeves were soon having words with the proprietor. A table was tipped, breaking some tumblers, and the latter accused them of making a rough house and invited them to leave. Which they promptly did, the proprietor following after to the feeding lot where they had stabled their horses. As they mounted, he fired 11 shots at them from revolvers he held in each hand. Ridgley was shot twice through the leg, as was Plumer's horse. They returned the fire, and in the exchange he was killed. Mr. Plumer said he did not know who killed him, it may have been himself. Ridgley left to stay with friends, and Plumer had to put down his horse and purchase another.

He said, "The only good that came out of my visit to the mines was the acquisition of the good mare Lady Mac."

It was at this point he reached for my hand. Mid-stitch I stopped my knitting and placed my hand in his. "Now the two of you know more about me than any other person in this world." In his voice, I heard a mixture of relief, resignation, and weariness.

"Wait a minute, what about Cleveland?" Swift asked. "Where does he fit in?"

Mr. Plumer sighed audibly. "Yes, Cleveland, my nemesis. I'm too exhausted to go into that tonight. Tomorrow?"

Yet holding my hand, he walked me to the door, and before he left, we just stood there for a moment. I thought I would cry. I ended up with my head against his coat and his arm slipped firmly around me. Into my hair he murmured, "Sleep well, fair woman. Sleep well." Then he was gone, and I was left leaning against the door.

Try as I might, I could not sleep. At last I gave up trying, padded back to the kitchen, lit a candle, and proceeded to read the clippings Mr. Plumer had entrusted to me. According to one article, Plumer's first act, a month and half of recuperation after San Quentin, was to make a citizen's arrest of "Ten Year Smith," an escapee from that same institution.

A reporter to the *Nevada Democrat*, who claimed to have seen quartz samples, reported that Plumer's mine on the Scott's Flat was so rich that hardly a piece could be picked up that did not contain gold.

In a longer piece, the *Democrat* reported the difficulty between Henry Plumer and William Riley when the latter placed a knife in Mr. Plumer's skull and Plumer's reaction resulted in this death, which event Plumer has already apprized me thereof. The paper reported what Mr. Plumer had not: that Riley, who had been living in the vicinity for longer than the past year, "was quarrelsome and dissipative . . ." and was the same man "who'd assailed a citizen of Blue Tent on the Fourth of July for firing a salute. . . . Officials claimed the incident had been an accident. . . . " and, "There is no prospect of his being caught. The circumstances connected to the killing of Riley, as generally understood, would hardly justify Plumer's conviction for murder. But this being the second man he has killed in Nevada, and knowing there was a strong prejudice against him in the county, he doubtless thought it prudent not to risk a trial." They added, "If Plumer shows as much tact in keeping away from the county as he did in leaving the jail, the community will have no particular occasion to deplore his departure, as the cost of an expensive trial would have probably resulted in still leaving him here, a most useless if not dangerous man."

What a terrible thing to have written. In my marrow, I know whatever this man has done, it has been done by one who is honorable, noble, and true.

Sunday 2 November

May Thy will, not mine, be done;
May Thy will and mine be one;
Chase these doubtings from my heart,
Now Thy perfect peace impart.

—*Mary A. S. Barber, 1801–*

In the morning I traded Plumer's envelope for a brief embrace and I said, "I rather strongly disagree with the *Democrat*'s conclusion as to your worth."

He rejoined, "Miss Bryan, you have brought a ray of sunshine into my life."

Would he had said, "Miss Bryan, I love you and want you for my wife." Alas he did not.

At table, he did not look at me with anything approaching emotion. Do I dream?

He talked about his trip through the Bitter Root Mountains. "I have never seen any place more beautiful, nor have I traveled through more rugged country. At one point in the trip, we were literally sliding downhill through heavy timber. My shotgun got snagged in the branches and broke at the grip."

About the 14th or 15th of September they met the Missoula County Auditor and County Commissioner, Messrs. Worden and

Granville Stewart, at Beaver Dam Hill. The talk was all about mining. Mr. Stewart suggested, since they were only going down to Hell Gate and would return to Gold Creek in a few days, they accompany them to Hell Gate, then all could go up the canyon together. And this they did.

While Reeves prospected a bit on Gold Creek, Granville Stuart and another clever fellow mended Plumer's shotgun. They forged four strips of iron about five-eights inches wide and three and a half inches long. Then they set them into the gunstock with one on top and one on the bottom of the grip and screwed them down solid. Plumer avowed, "The stock is stronger now than before I broke it."

Then Reeves went with a couple of miners to the Beaverhead mines, and Plumer continued on to Fort Benton.

After supper, Swift suggested we play Proverbs again, that he might have a second chance to beat us. Unfortunately, he was third man out on 4:1, and Mr. Vail won the last round with 4:26, "Ponder the path of thy feet, and let all thy ways be established."

3 November . . . More Snow and Cold

After laundry, Swift and I came into Mr. Plumer's wrath. We were playing an innocent game of hangman on Mary Eliza's slate when he came in. He came to the table with a smile and a pleasantry for Martha Jane while she served his coffee. For a moment, he watched us in silence. I looked up and saw the color drained from his face. In a firm, flat, grey voice he said, rather gently for the feeling behind the words, "I understand that for you this is just a game. Even so, I wish you'd put it up. I dislike it intensely."

Without a word I put down my chalk, and Swift wiped the slate clean.

"In California, the people were plagued with the fear that Vigilantes would intervene in the proper order of justice," Mr. Plumer explained, "Although none knows better than I the weakness of our system, a better has yet to be devised. The premeditated taking of another's life is serious. Civilized man has an obligation at least to attempt to discern the facts before he chooses to do so. That is what we, as a country, stand for. Every man has a right to a trial and to a judgment by his peers. Even now I believe in that. Frail as our system is, we must remember justice is only an ideal we strive toward, not a concrete concept we own."

With feeling, he asserted, "That 'innocent' game reminds me of the 'innocent' man, heedless of contemplative thought, who would make light of our constitutional guarantees."

The rest of the men came in and the subject was dropped. Yet I felt slapped, and chose to go to bed rather early.

After reviewing this day, I no longer know why I felt so. There's not a state in our nation that hasn't witnessed the horror of those who call themselves "just and vigilant" in the same breath and band together to take lives on circumstantial evidence, without trial, without representation. I have no love for this injustice. Perhaps I'm miffed that I was caught doing something that deep inside I think I should have known was not innocent. Now I regret cutting short any time I might have spent with him.

4 November . . . The Snow Deepens

Wouldn't you know, as soon as she could corner me, Martha Jane began to grill me about what I know of Mr. Plumer's history. While she rolled pie crusts, I kneaded flour into a sponge for making bread and told it to her as best I could, but still I can tell she is mortified. Tonight she staid by the fire knitting and preventing any time alone with him.

I don't know what I looked like to them, but Mr. Plumer, looking as if the world were unchanged, engaged Mr. Vail in a conversation about the status of Indian hostilities now that winter has begun in earnest.

Mr. Vail indicated he viewed the situation much stabilized by the advent of snow. He said, "I'm glad you brought the subject up. We haven't cash to pay you, and we really shouldn't be keeping you on now that the worst is past." I was stunned by his comments, even though I knew what he said was true. Knowing that the boats would not again run till spring, I suppose I was lulled into thinking we'd all be together until then.

Mr. Plumer talked about the possibility of going over to the Beaverhead mines for the duration of the winter. He thought to see if he could do any good for himself in that country.

The very thought of his leaving makes me weep.

5 November . . . Cold

This morning I noticed Mr. Plumer's hands were red and raw and I asked him if he hadn't been wearing his gloves. Mr. Vail said it came from his doctoring one of the ponies in the open. I brought out the jar of hand creme Sadie sent with me when I left their house last spring and gave them each a bit to soothe their hands. Watching me rub my hands together Mr. Plumer said, "You move your hands in the same way both my mother and sister do. I delight in watching them, whether knitting, patting things into place, or smoothing lotion into your skin."

That he would say so private a thing before the ears of so many surprised me. I do believe I blushed, but with pleasure. Martha Jane looked at him with a curious sort of resignation.

In the evening we sat about the fire talking of hopes and dreams. Mr. Vail thinks if the weather would cooperate he could have a successful year at the farm, and he thinks he and Little Dog might be able to work together. Martha wishes there were a village and a church here. Her dream raises a lovely town on the banks of the Sun River. I too dream of civilization: a brick house, with a large lot to hold a garden, fruit trees, and a rolling green for children to play on. Messrs. Plumer and Swift both agreed their dreams include family and a successful business.

After Mr. Vail retired, Mr. Plumer asked me if I objected to all forms of card playing as did Mr. Vail. I replied that I saw no harm so long as one did not place any bet on them, for I do believe that gambling is a fantastic evil. My answer seemed to please him. He said that he would do well never again to place a bet on cards so long as he lived, but he did enjoy a game of Whist now and again and he'd be sore put to forever give it up.

He's such a dear and honest man. How I long to live with him—even in a cabin, so long as it were our own.

6 November . . . Fantastic Day

Last night I woke to a great wind blowing, the likes I've never imagined, and the sound of water running off the roof. I finally rose and went outside. One cannot begin to fathom the phenomenon to which we are witness. The wind is warm—so warm it is melting the snow. It is strange and wonderful and awesome all of one moment. Mr. Vail says he has read of the phenomenon and it is called a "chinook." Chinook. I like the sound of it so, if I ever have a place of my own, I fancy I'll name it Chinook.

6 November . . . Warm as Summer and Smells Like Spring

Not a spot of snow remained on the ground this morning. Mr. Plumer suggested we take a holiday and celebrate the chinook with fishing the river.

Mr. Plumer had with him a cunning bit of fishing gear in the form of a collapsible pole, with all one would need, slipped into the pockets of a piece of felt and rolled into the smallest space you could imagine. Out of it he managed to fix Swift and me up with hooks, sinkers, and line, which he attached to some fairly straight willow branches for poles. He dug up a bunch of worms from under a mound of manure in the cow corral. When we reached the river, he took us to a place where a huge cottonwood had fallen into the water. Then, much to Young Swift's pleasure, he traded him his own good rod. Swift gingerly stepped across rocks until he was out as far the river would allow, then he began casting his line, whipping it forth and back in great arcs. Plumer took me as far out on the tree as we could walk without my coming unbalanced by my skirts. I was then certainly assured I'd done right in leaving off my hoop this morning. He sat me down where a branch, just right for hooking my foot onto, stuck out from the tree—thus I secured myself. He baited our hooks and we dropped them into the water where the tree made a shadow on it.

The sun at my back warmed me through and through. As we sat quietly, I felt I would be happy to spend the rest of my life right there. Too soon I felt a tug on my line. I cried out, "I've got one, I've got one," and I jerked my pole to hook it good, but Plumer had to pull it in.

"You like this?" He sounded smug—acting as if he were some god that brought the fish to me.

"This is not the first time I've fished," I replied. Then he looked so crestfallen that I quickly added, "But it is the first time I've ever latched onto a trout. Or is it the trout latched onto me?" He laughed. His teeth are straight and white and beautiful. He strung it on a stick. Soon we had a half dozen nice fish on our stick and the day was beginning to cool. In the distance Swift looked yet to be hard at it.

Plumer asked, "Miss Bryan, would you allow me to take you fishing again?"

Hardly the question I was hoping for, but yes. "Yes." And many times again yes, I bethought myself.

"Miss Bryan, would you consent to be my wife?"

I could not answer for the swelling that stopped the words in my throat. But, not daring to look at him for the tears in my eyes, I nodded. Then gently he reached out and gently he cupped my chin in his hand and gently he turned my face to his and we staid that way, just looking each at the other. And I, for the first time in my life, I reached out and caressed his cheek, and in the moment before it happened I knew he was going to kiss me.

Next thing I knew, there was Swift singing at the top of his lungs and fairly waltzing down the log toward us. Plunking himself beside us, he blurted, "Say Plumer. You never did tell us what the situation is between you and Cleveland."

"No, I didn't." Plumer swung his leg astraddle the log and pulled me to him so that I was turned in a manner that rested the back of my head against his chest, his chin fair caressing my hair. "First I want to introduce Miss Bryan, my fiancée, the future Mrs. Plumer—to the honorable Mr. Swift."

Swift's grin spread from ear to ear and he gallantly lifted my hands to his lips. "Enchanté, Madam," he murmured. "A most fortunate gentleman is Mr. Plumer and, I assure you, most worthy."

"You've had the pleasure of her hands long enough," interjected Plumer. "Back to Cleveland. Do you recall the story of Sheriff Wright?"

"The dead Sheriff Wright?" interjected Swift.

"That one. We were in the process of going after three men, two of them the Farnsworth brothers."

"They kept breaking out of jail and were mixed up in the Sheriff Wright fiasco," mused Swift.

"Fiasco is right. The man who calls himself Jack Cleveland is in truth John Farnsworth."

"So why didn't you arrest him?" I asked. Plumer did not answer. "You arrested 'Ten Year Smith'!"

"Yes. That was soon after I'd been released from San Quentin. And it did not win me any friends. The Farnsworth brothers left the country after that altercation and John Farnsworth did not return as Jack Cleveland until late in '59. By that time I had no illusions about my popularity, and as I've told you before, I was soon deep into troubles of my own.

"For all I know it is only accident that found the two of us together in Benton. Why he carries a grudge, I do not know, as he never came to trial. All I know is, in spite of his ten-year advantage, he seems to listen to me when he gets drunk and I feel safer having him ride in front or alongside rather than behind. More than that, I do not know he is guilty, only that he was implicated in a gang and wanted for trial in connection with their misdeeds.

"By leaving before the inquest into Riley's death, I too became an outlaw; that the law doesn't want me does not change that. Nor does it change the fact that Cleveland is my enemy and so long as we occupy the same territory I must watch my back."

"Then I hate him," I said. "I must worry for you as long as he lives. And I hate that."

"Please, sweet woman, hate no one for my sake. I can take care of myself. I am wiser and I am faster with the draw than he. Hate's destruction is, by far, more insidious than any bullet. "I pray in all things and ways our love is ever free of it." Mr. Plumer rose and offered me a hand up.

"Cleveland shall be beside himself when he finds out," Swift understated the course. "When will you announce?"

"What is your pleasure, Miss Bryan?"

"Swift's right. I don't know. We've not planned ahead and Martha Jane will be asking a thousand questions. Let's wait."

"My dear, I am not disposed to wait. Now that it is open between the two of us, I do not like to hide from the rest."

"And I do not want to face her questions before we have the answers."

"So state the questions."

"When do you plan this wedding?"

"As soon as I can ride to St. Peter's Mission to fetch the priest to make it legal."

"Oh, no! If I know Sister, she'd as soon as have Satan as a priest. Faith, we're orange Irish you know, not Black. Nothing will do but to wait till the ships return with Reverend Reed.

"All right then. We'll wait till spring. In the meantime I shall go on to the Beaverhead. I need to keep busy. As well you can see, I've about outstayed my usefulness here. As I've mentioned before, I'm of a mind to take a look at what the diggings there have to offer. In the spring I'll be back for my bride."

"Spring seems such a long time."

"I suspect I'll be able to increase our fortunes there. A matter I can not attend to here."

"I shall miss you."

"And I you."

"Is there no way you can stay?"

"I don't think it is wise. If I stay, Mr. Vail will be placed in an awkward position asking Cleveland to move on. Neither Cleveland nor I can endure close quarters much longer. I have worked all my adult life. Idleness does not suit me. If it did, I would not suit you. Shall we announce the deed at supper?"

"I don't think it leaves time for you to apprize Mr. Vail of your intent."

"It can be done."

"Tomorrow's supper will be better."

"Why wait?"

"So that your future bride can make a grand feast in celebration of the announcement."

"So the speckled trout isn't grand enough?"

"Martha Jane will already have supper in the making and tonight it's stew. Good stew to be sure, but stew. Indeed we shall have the trout. Swift can put them to keep in the cold cabin till then."

"And pie?"

"And pie. Especially for you, the pie."

Tonight my lips burn with the kiss. I have touched a man. I have been kissed by the man I touched. I am his betrothed—his beloved.

8 November . . . Winter's Spring Continues

This morning Martha Jane commented, "My, aren't we the cheerful little hausfrau this morning?" Behind her back, Swift grinned at me and winked. "Perhaps, we should send you out fishing more often." I laughed. "What's so funny?" she asked. "Oh nothing," I replied, "this lovely weather must be driving me batty."

I served fried fish, fried potatoes with onions, beets, the hot saleratus biscuits Mr. Plumer professes to prefer over my light loaves of bread, and last, a fine squash pie.

During supper I could not read a thing in the countenances of either Mr. Vail or Mr. Plumer.

After serving the pie Mr. Vail rose and said, "Mr. Plumer has an announcement he wishes to make." Then he sat down and Mr. Plumer stood. "I am pleased to tell you that Miss Bryan has honored me with an acceptance of a proposal to marry." Then he sat down.

Martha Jane, tears glistening on her cheeks, asked when we planned to marry and there followed the expected 21 questions, not the least of which was how he intended to take care of me. He spoke well for himself, saying he was an experienced miner, known for the good luck he had in California and Nevada, he yet had wealth from those endeavors, and he had high hopes for success in the Beaverhead.

At length Mr. Swift stood and said, "I want to extend my congratulations to Mr. Plumer in capturing the fairest maid in the territory, and my best wishes to the woman with the wisdom to accept a most esteemed and loyal suitor."

"Hear. Hear." Much to our surprise, Bixby croaked and raised his coffee cup.

Cleveland then stomped out, slamming the door behind. Before long, from across the palisade yard, we could hear a great deal of cursing and slamming of objects and doors. Plumer stood to go, but Mr. Vail indicated he should stay and went himself to investigate the commotion. He soon put a stop to it and returned.

"Driven batty by lovely weather, my foot," Sister whispered before she went to bed. But she did give me a tired and sisterly smile.

The day has fair exhausted me. I dread seeing Cleveland tomorrow. That man can mean no good for us.

SUNDAY 9 NOVEMBER . . . BRILLIANT DAY

> SAVIOR, AT THY FEET I FALL,
> THOU MY LIFE, MY GOD, MY ALL!
> LET THY HAPPY SERVANT BE
> ONE FOR EVERMORE WITH THEE! AMEN.
>
> —*Mary A. S. Barber, 1801*–

10 NOVEMBER . . . COLD AS IT'S BEEN WARM

What yesterday was standing water in the yard, is today ice and much too cold to melt. All morning Cleveland chopped wood and stomped in and out hauling water and wood. I scrubbed and scrubbed, trying to close him out of my mind. Then he asked, "You knowed he was a jail bird?"

Martha Jane stiffened like she'd turn to stone. I was glad I'd already told her the facts of his life. I thought to myself, "yes I knowed an' I knowed you'd oughtta been one, too, and with better cause." Instead, I said, "Mr. Plumer has discussed his past with us in depth." Cleveland snorted then slammed out of the house.

Martha Jane murmured, "Are you sure you want to have to answer such questions all your life?" And I replied that Cleveland would be the exception, and I had faith that Mr. Plumer would account well for himself and it would not be necessary. "You're sure," she asked, "he's innocent?"

"Martha, there may always be those who will believe that he was that poor dreadful woman's paramour and that he murdered her husband in cold blood, but I've not only listened to the man, I've read the complete reports and I will always know nothing could be further from the truth."

Come evening, I told Mr. Plumer what Cleveland had said and how upsetting to us it was. He assured me it would not happen again.

I finished a sock and snipped the excess snippet of yarn and started to rise to toss it on the fire. Plumer staid me, taking the piece and tying it about my finger. "With this ring I cannot thee wed." His eyes twinkled. "It is not near grand enough. What cut of diamond do you prefer?"

"Diamonds? I am no lover of diamonds. I think they are cold. I think that which represents love should be colorful—well at least warm." I boldly added, "A gold band will serve me well."

He pulled the string off my finger and tossed it in the fire. "A gold band I can promise you, a gold band and the warmth of my love."

He is more charming and more elegant than any man I could ever conjure in dream.

14 November . . . Still Cold

We have spent the week in our regular activities, the men doing chores and mending, mending, mending everything in sight and still no end to it; we women keeping house, playing games with the children and each other, singing childhood songs, and talking, talking, talking late into the night. As ever, Plumer, true to his word, talked to Cleveland, reminding him that should he be inclined to reveal the facts of his life, it would hardly stand up to scrutiny. Cleveland has been mild mannered ever since and will be going to the mines with him.

I have baked biscuits, mince pies, and crackers as well as packed a goodly quantity of dried buffalo meat. He says I've put together for them enough to feed an army. Though I'm sure it's hardly enough for two.

I finished two pair of wool socks, a pair of mittens to wear over riding gloves, and a muffler. This evening I gave them to him. For a moment I thought he would weep, but of course he didn't.

Already, I'm wishing I'd dared to confront my sister and called in the priest, that I might be leaving with him, even if it means riding aback his horse and not knowing where I'd rest my head each night. Mr. Plumer says this is the right way—this way of my first reasoning, when my head was still clear. He says that after this long winter we shall be together forever and that knowledge will give us the strength to endure this trial of separation.

SUNDAY 16 NOVEMBER . . . I CANNOT KNOW THE WEATHER ON GOD'S EARTH WHEN THE SUN IN MY LIFE IS GONE

MY GOD, HOW MANY ARE MY FEARS,
HOW FAST MY FOES INCREASE!
THEIR NUMBER HOW IT MULTIPLIES!
HOW FATAL TO MY PEACE.

—*Allen D. Carden 1792–1859*

At breakfast we all tried to be cheerful. All day I've tried to be cheerful. At last now I do not have to be cheerful.

I cannot believe he is gone. Even the sight of him mounting—with that light spring that lands him instantly upright in the saddle while Lady Mac spins a half circle—seems more a dream than real. I watched him trot through the same gates I watched him enter, not quite six weeks past. When Swift closed the gates behind my Mr. Plumer, I felt cut from a part of me.

Help me to remember it is only cloud that hides him from me, dear God. I pray Thee, keep us through our long winter's night.

In the Loneliness of Winter

SUN RIVER . . . TUESDAY 18 NOVEMBER 1862

I can hardly believe my betrothed is truly gone. The weather holds cold, but not snowing. I imagine him somewhere in the mountains, stiff with long riding and cold. I pray the coughing spell that shook him so last Saturday does not return. And I worry that he might take a chill sleeping close to this frozen ground.

Each morning the pipings of the wee one's voices echo through the cabin, making it feel hollow in the absence of the reassuring resonance in his voice.

I have begun a quilt to cover our wedding bed. From the States I brought a good length of tightly woven, lightweight, deep green wool. I'd thought to make myself a winter dress of it, but the brown merino has yet to be finished (I have several spools of quality ecru crochet thread and plan to make lace cuffs and a collar for it). Then, for years Martha Jane and I have been saving scraps of bright silks and velvet. Altogether we have many shades of blue, purple, and violet and a goodly bit of cream. I have this vision of gay pansies appliquéd in a scatter of clumps across the whole of it and using a pattern of leaves for the quilting stitches. I have made a sketch of the quilt as I envision it.

The men have been hunting geese and I may yet have enough down to make a quilt of it. I have close to four pounds now and am hoping to make it five. This morning I dug out a worn canvas tick from the storeroom and took it apart. Wash day, I'll scrub it up and when it's dry I'll trim the frayed edges and make a casing of it.

This cabin feels so much smaller, in spite of the fact there are fewer occupants inside. Lord, I feel weary.

Sunday 23 November

We are thine, do thou befriend us,
Be the guardian of our way;
Keep thy flock, from sin defend us,
Seek us when we go astray:
Blessed Jesus, Blessed Jesus
Hear, O hear us, when we pray.

—Dorothy A. Thrupp, 1799–1874

A Sunday without my beloved is a day without sun. By now he must have reached Bannack City. I try to imagine it. Too new and too open, I hope, to have acquired the stench of the forts we witnessed on our travels to this land. I wonder if any white women are there, a church, a school?

This afternoon we held a checkers tournament with the children.

After supper I worked on my lace cuffs and visited with Swift. I think he misses Mr. Plumer as much as I. That helps lighten the ache a little.

They say idle hands make for the Devil's work. If so we needn't worry about mine. I've cut all the pansy petals for our quilt.

SUNDAY 30 NOVEMBER

Elizabeth Barrett Browning wrote:

"The first time he kissed me, he but only kissed
The fingers of this hand wherewith I write;
And ever since, it grew more clean and white, . . ."

My hand remembers his first kiss and my heart is warmer for it.

This week the weather has held—cold but tolerable—as have I in his absence. On the one hand, I miss him so, on the other I wonder how I'll ever accomplish all the things I wish before my time of isolation is past.

Last week I put together the down comforter that shall keep us toasty in the worst of weather. I have rolled it up, wrapped it in brown paper, and tucked it into the rafters in my bedroom. Each evening I have worked on the petals for the quilt top. I stitch two pieces of fabric together, turn them inside out, and then press them with a tuck in the center so that the edges curl just slightly so that when I appliqué them to the blocks they will take on a life of their own.

Mary Eliza is becoming quite a reader. She has finished the first *McGuffy's Reader* and I am so proud of her. Little Harvey can write an A, a B, and a C, one letter at a time. His fingers can hardly guide the chalk, so each letter takes up the whole of the slate. Now he can find his name in a sentence written in capital letters by the number of letters in it and the A located in the second position. Young as he is, he seems to have a good grasp of numbers.

SUNDAY 7 DECEMBER

> WHAT CHILD IS THIS, WHO, LAID TO REST,
> ON MARY'S LAP IS SLEEPING?
> WHOM ANGELS GREET WITH ANTHEMS SWEET,
> WHILE SHEPHERDS WATCH ARE KEEPING.
>
> —*William C. Dix, 1837*–

This has always been a favorite of mine and in my mind I'm singing it to my love. Of course, in my mind I have a voice like an angel's.

In the true world, Martha Jane and I have finished sewing the petal pockets, would you believe we put together more than 1,000 pieces? I've stacked them by color in a wooden box. Yesterday I cut the squares on which the flowers will be sewn. At last I am ready to begin this project in earnest. Afternoons, Mary Eliza reads to us while we sew. She is so proud to be a big girl now that she is not required to take a nap.

14 December

> Why lies He in such mean estate
> Where ox and ass are feeding?
> Good Christian, fear, for sinners here
> The silent Word is pleading.
>
> —*William C. Dix, 1837*—

I have finished stitching the petals onto the center of the quilt and have spent the day embroidering the stamens into their centers. I am using French knots to make the tips of the stamens. Martha Jane says I should first finish attaching all the petals before I forge ahead with the fancy stitching. I say that's fine for you. You're a systematic person imbued with a great deal of patience. I'm an impatient forger, who can't wait to see how the finished blossom will look. It's all I want to do, this quilt and those things for our home.

In some blind hope someone will be passing on their way through Bannack to Salt Lake or Walla Walla or any place where letters might be sent on toward their intended destination, I try to write a bit each week to my betrothed.

Saturday 20 December

Today we were surprised by the arrival of our mail in the hands of one Mr. Hermodson hired by Mr. Plumer for the sole purpose of delivering unto us our mail. What a shock! Wonderful shock. The letters from home and the emotions that fill me as I hold those penned by my betrothed are such a treat! What a wonder that letters sent all the way from Ohio and Iowa have reached us, traveling through East Bannack and Salt Lake City as they did. The whole batch of them bare dates that stretch from June through September. Along with the letters came packages, mostly from Mr. Plumer. The children and I wanted to open our presents right then, but the elder Vails' patience and wisdom prevailed. Alas, we will wait until Christmas morning to open them. However, we did allow ourselves the indulgence of nibbling on the dried fruits and nuts he sent. Ah! What a welcome marvel.

We've asked Mr. Hermodson to stay for Christmas. Unfortunately, he says he must be off by first morning's light. He is now abed getting some well-needed sleep before he heads back. We have made use of our time to sign off on the letters we've been writing and to put together a package for Mr. Plumer.

I shall forever keep these letters from him with this rough journal of my time in the wilderness.

East Bannack
Thursday 20 November 1862

My Dearly Betrothed,

Know I have arrived safe and sound—reached Deer Lodge on the 17th. Along the way I stopped at the Stuart's, but found them out, went on to a cabin owned by one Dempsey, and spent the night there. His wife is wrathy and some roughs do hang around, but she manages to keep them in place. When they're hungry, she generously feeds them out of her frying pan; when they don't behave, she whops them up the side of their head with it, or so I've been told. Only spent two nights on the ground.

Came into Bannack City late last night and put up the horses at a fine stable on the end of town. The stableman recommended the Goodrich Hotel, a decent enough place, considering there are estimated to be 400 people attempting to winter over here, all having arrived since late summer and most living in wickiups, tents, and cabins. Fortunate for all, this winter has been mild, and shipments of food and supplies are yet arriving from Salt Lake.

Cleveland put up at the Elkhorn, a bar, run by Cyrus Skinner. The back wall of the Elkhorn is lined with tiers of bunks built right into it.

Ate a late supper of steak, eggs, and biscuits at the Goodrich. A widow Bruckner is cooking for the hotel to keep herself and young daughter together in the absence of a husband. Her biscuits do not compare with yours. Even so, it is not likely she will remain a widow long. Men outnumber women in this place one hundred to one.

Watching her break eggs into the pan brought to mind your lovely slender hands, the quick movement of your fingers flipping yarn over the end of your needle, the movement of your wrist and thumb when flipping open a cracked egg. I miss you.

I know I cannot expect to hear from you, but by happenstance. However, I shall write until such time I discover some pilgrim traveling through your country.

Sunday 23 November

Yesterday, Lady Mac and I took a tour about town. In contrast to the euphony of your Sabbath abode, Bannack City Sundays are cacophonic pandemonium. All week the men work, often in isolation. On Sunday they stop to do their laundry, purchase a cut of meat, cook the bulk of their weekly food, and rejuvenate body and spirit—trading what few books and newspapers can be found in this far outpost as well as with spirits, gambling, visiting their fellow sojourners, and dancing with the fancy women. There is not yet a church, but with about 40 women in town, I'm sure we'll be graced with one in the new year.

Most of the men from Fisk's party, along with a great many from the Salmon diggings as well as the majority of the parties that came up on the steamboats, have located here for the winter. Charlie Reeves says Ridgley has made his way into town and has staked a promising claim. When Reeves first arrived with James Stewart he staked a claim and seems to be doing well. He has set up a gaming table at the Elkhorn owned by Cyrus Skinner, a fellow he knew from the other side. He is living in a tepee. Ah, well! At least the tepees are built to hold back the worst this country has to offer.

There are two bakeries, a brewery, two hotels, two blacksmith shops, a meat market (specializing in wild game), a Chinese restaurant, four saloons, a dance hall, two stables, a saw mill, a bowling alley, and a billiard hall.

People are taking shelter in anything they can pull together. They are living in tents, wickiups, wagons, dugouts, and cabins. Cabins are yet being built, and people are still coming into town. Thus far the winter has been mild. I have no idea how some of them will survive should the winds change. As for food, in September a Mormon freighter brought in ten wagons of supplies, including bacon, beans, and black flour and some produce has come into town from the Bitter Root. The cook at the hotel here has a supply of isinglass eggs and that puts them at top billing as an eatery. Most of the residents have taken Indian custom to heart and jerked some game meat.

In the absence of severe weather, men are yet working their claims. Here, placer gold is found on the banks and bars of Grasshopper Creek. Gold-bearing gravel lies in a thin layer on top of a limestone bedrock no *more than ten to twelve feet above the streambed. I understand that gold at an estimated value of nearly $700,000 has already been taken out.*

SUNDAY 30 NOVEMBER

I saw the Stuart brothers. They've opened a grocery outfit and butcher shop with some of that quality Deer Lodge beef. The butcher shop was just finished yesterday. Now we're beginning to have the look of a real town. Their arrival has added variety to the groceries and goods available in this community.

Ran into that fellow, Langford, who so greatly amused Mr. Vail. Mr. Vail will be tickled to know the fellow has dropped the "of commissary" from his title and simply bills himself as Fisk's second assistant.

Have heard (by way of Salt Lake news) one of the bloodiest battles of the war has been fought at the village of Sharpsburg on the Antietam. McClellan's army of 85,000 Union troops faced Lee's 50,000 Confederates on the 17th of September. Both sides sustained heavy casualties—more than 10,000 each. Lee has retired into Virginia, and President Lincoln has issued a preliminary Emancipation Proclamation.

SUNDAY 7 DECEMBER

I met our illustrious Mr. Langford at the stable Tuesday last. I invited him to join Doc. Biddle, Sam McLean, and me in a game of whist. Over cards Langford told the following story on himself:

"A couple of fellows and I, finding ourselves destitute and in need of employment while prospecting on the Prickley Pear, received intelligence that a company of miners had struck pay dirt on the bottom of a creek in Pike's Peak Gulch, and we were determined to start immediately on a

horseback trip to the new camp. Two miles from the ridge of Mullan's Pass, one of our horses gave out and we could travel no further. We had no choice but to make a camp by the roadside. One of my companions proposed to stand guard till midnight, then I was to relieve him. When it was my turn at watch, I crawled out from under the blankets, which were covered to the depth of five inches with "the beautiful snow," and he fairly burrowed into the warm place I had left.

"Preparatory to an early departure, I gathered in a large heap a number of small, fallen pines and soon had an immense fire. It lighted up the canyon with a lurid gloom and mantled the snow-covered trees with a ghastly radiance. The black smoke of the burning pitch rolled in clouds through the atmosphere, which seemed to be choked with myriad snowflakes. So dense was the storm I could scarcely discern the horses, which stood but a few rods distant.

"About three in the morning the horses began to nicker as if someone was coming. I waded through the snow to my companions and roused them from their slumbers. They looked so ghostly, rising from their snowy coverings to stand half—revealed in the bushes by the light of the blazing pines, that I burst into a fit of laughter.

"Then we heard the counterfeited neigh of a horse a few rods below and of another just above me. I knew then that my worst fears were realized—the dreaded Blackfeet were upon us. We grabbed our guns, rushed to the single picket pin to which we'd tied our horses, and seizing the lariats, pulled them in. A moment afterwards, and from behind the thicket of willows just above our camp, there dashed down the canyon in full gallop, 40 or more of the dreaded Indians."

The tale gets further and further far-fetched as he describes in detail the war paint, dress, and actions of these potential "attackers" who, according to him, already had more than 50 stolen horses, which they were driving through the canyon.

I asked, why they'd camped on the road? He explained that they had no choice, as the canyon was no more than ten rods wide. I did not point out that on a dark night two rods would have been sufficient distance to seclude them in the brush. He had not the wit to realize the fool he was making of himself—building a white man's fire in hostile country, nor what a whiner he sounded—bemoaning the leaving of his bed. So much for our "friend" Langford.

I have been doing a bit of prospecting, finding color wherever I dig, but have yet to find anything worth claiming. The land is rotten with it and I shall find something soon. Most of the men here are placer miners and have no interest in the work entailed in quartz; they skim the easy pickings off the top and sell out at a small price. Come spring, I plan to buy up some good quartz claims and have a blacksmith fabricate machinery for a small stamp mill. This land will be giving up gold for at least the next ten years—possibly as long as twenty.

And bye the bye, Langford's a worse card "shark" than I.

Monday 15 December

As you know by now, I have enlisted Mr. Hermodson into my employ for the purpose of delivering seasons greetings to my beloved and her fine family. As of this writing he will be leaving in two days and, if all bodes well, he will be back with his family before Christmas. He, his wife, and two sons came to Bannack last September with the Salt Lake wagon train and, as of yet, he has not found his load.

For the first time in years, I've spent some time thinking of Christmas, especially those of my youth. The parlor was filled with the pine scent of the boughs Mother and Rebecca placed on the fireplace mantel. During the holidays, Mother would replace our afternoon tea in favor of eggnog—all frothy and laced with nutmeg. And on every Christmas, after midnight vespers, we sat about the decorated tree and sang carols until no one could stay awake. In the morning, after breakfast, we each exchanged presents.

To help ease the ache of missing you, I've been plotting a way to send my season's greetings, blessings, and love to you all. My dearest Electa, there is nothing in this world I can give you that would convey the power of my love and the depth of my devotion to you. And yet, as the rustics say, I must needs try.

Would I were there to hand my gift in person. But soon, soon, this time will be past and I will look into your lovely face, brush aside those wisps of fine hair that always come loose and do so charmingly frame it; I will look into your eyes and tell you myself how deeply I care for you.

Your Devoted Betrothed,
Henry Plumer

EVENING, SATURDAY 20 DECEMBER

I've just finished the notes to be sent with the packets of my scribblings intended for my Betrothed and for my Stateside friends and relatives. Today, I'm more than a little glad I write regularly to all, saving the pieces in expectation of an opportune day, allowing for their departure. Martha Jane and I have also put together a bundle of items especially for Mr. Plumer.

I am so delighted with all the letters and news Mr. Hermodson carried the distance from Bannack to Sun River. I barely glanced through Sadie, Daniel, and Esther's letters. I'll read them in earnest after he's left. I read my darling's letters—feasting on words written in even, neat script. I can imagine no finer gift than the gift of his love. The words he writes are more precious than nuggets of gold. I shall sleep with them under my pillow.

SUNDAY 21 DECEMBER

SO BRING HIM INCENSE, GOLD, AND MYRRH,
COME, PLEASING, KING TO OWN HIM;
THE KING OF KINGS SALVATION BRINGS,
LET LOVING HEARTS ENTHRONE HIM.

—William C. Dix, 1837—

The night is yet black, and the kitchen is filled with smells of breakfast and the steam of the great granite coffee pot. While Mr. Hermodson enjoyed a last cup of coffee before his leaving he told us there were about 25 adult women in Bannack, almost half Mr. Plumer's estimate. He said Mr. Plumer must be taking young girls and Fancy Ladies into account. He tells us that with inclement weather, the social life of Bannack exists only in the saloons, and that every man of them comes in well heeled and with the steady shooting off of guns by the drunks and rowdies, and it's nothing short of miraculous that they have not killed off the bulk of the population. It appears my betrothed has more than Cleveland to be watchful of. On the other hand, he too claims it an up-and-coming town and makes it sound soon to have more stores, a church, and school.

And now that I'm alone in the kitchen with yet another cup of coffee, I am troubled by the differences between Mr. Hermodson's and Mr. Plumer's descriptions of East Bannack. And something more bothers me. On rereading Mr. Plumer's letters, it appears he's quite taken with the prospects of the area—not only taken, but willing to commit to settling there a spell. I had hardly thought about that prospect. I rather thought we'd be heading East, as it was East he was heading when fortune granted our meeting. I hardly know my mind on the issue. Ah well, there is time to be talking with Martha Jane about it and time to be sorting my thoughts on it in my usual fashion with pencil and paper. For now I'll be getting back to the rest of my mail. It seems so strange to be reading responses to that which I've written more than half a year ago.

HORTON'S CROSSING
19 JUNE 1862

Dear Electa,

Your letters of May arrived, so full of adventure it near takes my breath away. The closest I come to excitement is finding a weasel in the chicken house or listening to the call of a sandhill crane. Last week the mercury registered 95 in the shade. At sunrise this day the thermometer indicated eight above the freezing point. I would be happy if God chose a little moderation in our weather. Fortunately, this afternoon finds the mercury climbed to a normal temperature. At the height of heat last week, a mad dog ran through Anamosa. Several men and boys pursued him till he was cornered. They killed him with a shovel. We received word that drafting will not commence till the first of September. As recently as the second of June, Governor Kirkwood reassured the citizens of Iowa that there would be no draft in this state. So much for what he knows! As so many truly able-bodied men have already left Jones County for the good cause, we have grave concerns as to Husband's future. We are of a mind that he join now instead of waiting till they call him up, as the government is paying a $400 bounty to anyone joining now. That would be enough to pay off the rest of our mortgage with Horton, thus clearing the deed on the farm. The crops are in, and it appears that ours are faring well, though many others are worried their wheat will not *head out because of the late cool weather. Father and Jamie D. have faith they can bring the crops in if Jamie does not attend school the autumn term. Well, my dear, the sponge has risen and I must sign off that I might knead our bread.*

Affectionately,
Sadie Bryan

ANAMOSA
20 JUNE 1862

My Dear Electa,

Good news! Good News! Come the end of summer, I shall be heading off to Iowa City. At last my dream shall come true, I shall go to college. As you know, Father has been set against it. But this last time we talked, I pointed out that war changed the climate, and pleaded he reconsider as last year 136 females were enrolled as compared to 116 males.

My sister Hattie's return to the fold with her three wee ones in tow did not set my request to disadvantage. She brings with her horror tales from our sister state Missouri. She claims guerrilla bands rove the state and terrorize the households. She says that when a body hears the thundering of hooves, you cannot know who is coming nor what they might do. And her babe Lulu has scars to show for it. She says, don't be fooled by reports that the guerrilla bands are all secesh. Some are, some aren't. Some are of northern sympathy and more than a few are common ruffians with no care for anything but themselves. Worse yet, no one can know them by their dress, as they all steal off of each other. On a day when her in-laws had gone to town, a band of them came to the house. They held Sister at gunpoint while several ransacked the house. One of the men placed a terrified and screaming Lulu on the kitchen table, and he pulled her dress up exposing her bare belly. Another took a live coal from the fire and held it above her, threatening to drop it on her if someone did not reveal where the hide-ho was. In other words, if some-one didn't fetch up the family treasures. Sister says she screamed and pleaded till the coal in his tongs lost its glow. Still they kept yelling at her to give it up and all the while the babe kept up her screaming. She said, "God is my witness, I had no idea what he was talking about." They dropped the hot coal on her poor babe's flesh. Then the babe stopped screaming. The man fetched another coal and sister thought she would die of terror when a voice of authority called out, "Let it be. We're wasting good time with nothing to be gained." As rapidly as they came they were gone. The child is a bit strange, as yet she does not cry. And poor Sister, she has also to bear the brunt of Father's ire, having married a man who joined the grey.

Yet, I've used Sister's terrible misfortune for my advantage; it serves as example to further my cause; no woman's fate should rest solely on that of her husband's, and the only way to rise above it is to become educated. There, I've given to you my secret and a bit of my shame, knowing that you will understand as no one else ever could and knowing you will love me still.

With Great Love,
Your Friend,
Esther

HORTON'S CROSSING
6 JULY 1862

Dear Sister,

We had a Cracker Jack fourth of July in spite of the reduced numbers attending. Sadie worked, serving food for the M.E. annual fund-raiser for a good portion of the day. But not so long we didn't get to visit with our friends in Anamosa and enjoy the fine brass band they've put together.

News came in that Memphis was taken on the 7th by our gunboats. Nine cheers and a tiger for the Bluff City!

I have joined the 5th and I leave for camp in two weeks. It is a grave decision for me and not come so easy. Should you tire of this great wilderness adventure, please come back. I know Sadie would be heartened by your company. In the event I should not return, your sensible calm presence would go far to steady her. God willing, I shall return and we'll all eat strawberries and cream together.

Your Big Brother,
Daniel

Horton's Crossing
10 September 1862

Dear Electa,

Daniel's been home from camp and gone again. This time he's off to the war. I've hardly had time to think, let alone moon over the missing of him. Father and Jamie D. are swathing hay in the meadow, and I've been putting by the garden and all else I can get my hands on. Fisher's got a good lot of peaches up from Missouri and I've just finished putting four dozen quarts in the cellar. Yesterday a group of young boys came by with a couple of loads of wood. They and Jamie D. held a chopping bee in my honor, and we are now set for the winter. One day a week the boys are going about to each of the "war widow's" houses and fixing them up for the winter. The papers reported that Poindexter, the notorious rebel leader of the Guerrilla bands in Missouri, was caught on August 2nd while riding on the N. Missouri Railroad, 20 miles from Hudson. He has been condemned as a spy and will suffer death. I hear your friend, Esther, has gone to the state college in Iowa City. I'm afraid all that extra education will make her unfit to be any man's wife. Jamie D. misses school and his pals, but is a good sport about it. We are well and able, thus we count our blessings, and hope this finds you and yours healthy and able to work hard.

With Affection,
Sadie

MONDAY 22 DECEMBER

Another wash day, like a million other wash days and yet I keep singing—

I KNOW WHERE I'M GOING,
AND I KNOW YOU'S GOING WITH ME:
I KNOW WHO I LOVE
AND MY DEAR KNOWS WHO I'LL MARRY.
WELL, I HAVE STOCKINGS OF SILK
AND SHOES OF BRIGHT GREEN LEATHER
COMBS TO BUCKLE MY HAIR
AND A RING FOR EVERY FINGER.
FEATHER BEDS ARE SOFT
AND PAINTED ROOMS ARE BONNIE,
BUT I WOULD TRADE THEM ALL
FOR MY HANDSOME, WINSOME JOHNNY.
FAIREST OF THEM ALL
IS MY HANDSOME, WINSOME JOHNNY.

Martha Jane looks at me as if I'm batty, but Mary Eliza joins in with her charming little voice.

I showed Martha Jane Mr. Plumer's letter about his mining plans and asked what she made of it. Martha laughed and said, "I make of it exactly as he states it. He has prospects and plans for this new country. Mining is one of the things he knows and you are about to become the wife of a miner and live in a mining town. At least for as long as it suits him." That's a rather long speech from Sister, but it's certainly to the point. I must have sounded a bit petulant for I said, "Oh, I had so planned to return East." Martha retorted, "Once married you don't have a say in the matter. If you're not satisfied with what might be in the package, you'd best not open it." Of course she's right. I've never fancied a better package and I'm ready to take my chances.

I hope Mr. Hermodson's return trip goes smoothly and the good weather holds. We sent him off with food and Christmas decorations made of walnut shells and bits of velvet, ribbon, and lace.

24 December 1862

Today we celebrated Martha Jane's birthday. When I spanked her, I teased her about being a tad shy a quarter of a century. Unfortunately, I can no longer get a rise out of her as I used to when we were but wee ones ourselves. Against great protest, we insisted she put her feet up and rest for the day. She consented only on condition she be "allowed" to enjoy her knitting.

Evenings I've been working on new night shirts for the children for Christmas and after Sister goes to bed, I've been knitting slippers for her and her husband, so the quilt has suffered. I've been trying to finish a block a day in hopes to have it finished by the end of the year.

Christmas Day 1862

> The first Noel the angel did say,
> was to certain poor shepherds
> in fields as they lay; In fields
> where they lay keeping their sheep,

On a cold winter's night that was so deep.
Noel, Noel, Noel, Noel,
Born is the King of Israel

—*Old English Carol*

Last night we read St. Luke's gospel of the Christ child and sang Christmas Carols. After breakfast we opened the white package of sweets from Gautier's, a delight we have only read about and surely never dreamed we'd ever know. We marveled over each encounter within: marzipan, a crystallized sugar, an almond coated in chocolate and other succulent gems, all mysteriously wrapped in silver paper and tied with gauze ribbon and little nosegays.

Little Harvey is delighted to have a slate of his very own and I shall forever remember the look in Mary Eliza's eyes when she unwrapped her little porcelain doll. She has named her Lola. Not one of us has a clue wherefrom this lavish unchristian name came to her. Perhaps the wrappings themselves suggested it.

Had I been able to open my present in the privacy of my room, they would not have been witness to my tears. After I'd slipped the gilt paper off the ox blood leather jeweler's case with the Galt signature marked in gold on its top, I sat it on the table and just admired the beauty of the container. Everyone was so awed, no one urged me to open it. When I'd adjusted to its simple grandeur, I gently lifted the lid, and there embedded in black velvet lay the square cut emerald set in its lovely plain gold band.

I think I know how Cinderella felt trying on the slipper, when I timidly put my third finger through the ring. It fit perfectly. I marveled, "How in this world was he able to know the size of my finger? How, in this wild country, was he able to come upon such a perfect gift?"

Then Swift recalled for us the evening Mr. Plumer tied the yarn around my finger, and we all laughed about the wool he pulled off my finger and over our eyes. Still, I could swear on it, I was so sure I saw him toss the yarn into the fire after we'd worked it off my finger.

This evening I found a note from him tucked under the velvet platform. And no I did not mind that he'd made the purchase in San Francisco, thinking it might suit the fancy of either his mother or sister. I am amazed that he could find a smith in Bannack with the skill to scale it to my size without blemish. I shall wear this gift with pride and treasure it always. Yet, make no mistake, I do not treasure it more than the words he sent.

New Year's Eve 1862

I have finished piecing our blocks. Martha and I hope to have the whole stitched together before the week is out. As I stitch, the phrase, "With what measure ye mete, it shall be measured to you again," keeps running about my head, but I haven't a notion as to why. Perhaps it is this—each day we have given our all to the life presented us and the rewards have not always been commensurate with the effort, but now, now we are full and are to be fulfilled each in the other. A fine and just reward, I think.

This last day of the year lends cause for reflection on 1862. Twelve months ago I never would have thought to be in this palisade in the center of one vast wilderness—one vast country of strangeness, nor could I have imagined becoming engaged to one such as my betrothed. Above all, I could not have imagined the great joy that fills me as I look forward to our marriage and a new life with my beloved.

SUNDAY 18 JANUARY 1863

> COULD I BE CAST WHERE THOU ART NOT,
> THAT WERE INDEED A DREADFUL LOT:
> BUT REGIONS NONE REMOTE I CALL,
> SECURE OF FINDING GOD IN ALL. AMEN.
>
> —*Madam Guyon, 1648-1717*

Another quiet Sunday. I miss him most on this day of rest. And I do long for our old church, the familiar congregation, and the Sunday company of my youth. I dream of recreating that idyll with him.

Most evenings Mr. Vail reads from Hans Anderson's *Fairy Tales* and puts the little ones to bed while Martha and I stitch, stitch, stitch away the darkness. Some evenings he and Swift do play a game of checkers while we work on.

22 JANUARY

Today we helped Mary Eliza celebrate her 5th birthday. After she'd dressed, I placed a "crown" (made of a twisted velvet circlet with silk pansies sewn to it) upon her head, and we told her she was princess for the day. For breakfast we made pancakes poured into the shapes of animals. All day she had her choice in games and activities as well as her favorite supper, fried porkchop, mashed potatoes, and squash cake. I made a little quilt for her "baby" Lola out of scraps from ours.

The stitching progresses. We are now well past the center with our stitching.

28 JANUARY

Last night I dreamed I was abed the *Emilie* and asleep in the arms of the gently rocking boat. Mr. Plumer came to me, formally dressed—silk tie and a wonderful cape all lined in red. He touched my cheek, bade me farewell, then rode off on Lady Mac. I rose from my bed and called out "Wait! Wait! Do not leave me yet." And then I cried, "Soon. It's too soon for you to be leaving me." Now isn't that a silly dream, from boat to horseback?

As we stitch on and on, a summer quilt is forming in my mind. I have an old cotton spread that has worn thin. I could use it for lining.

12 FEBRUARY

We have finished the top stitching on the quilt. Our joy has been dampened by the event of Young Swift's cutting the palm of his hand while whittling. Mary Jane cleaned the wound with lye soap and slathered it with oil of camphor. Then she took him to the store-room where she had him place his hand against an intricate spider's web, then another and another and another until she had it quite wrapped in the spider's weavings.

She is quite the wonder when it comes to nursing. Swift says it hardly hurts anymore.

16 FEBRUARY

This week I finished our quilt by turning the excess backing to the front, folding under the raw edge, and stitching it down with a chain stitch in a light green. I could hardly bear to put it away, but wrap it up I have, tied neatly in brown paper, and it's ready for the trip to our home.

25 February

Yesterday Father Giorda, a Jesuit from the Mission of St. Peter's, in attempting to ford Sun River, came near being drowned. Iron tossed a rope around him and finally got him to our side of the river, then brought him to the fort. We got the poor man dry and fed him hot broth. He seems an able and kindly person. Over supper he told us he was very grateful to Iron and would hence forth dedicate his life to Iron's people. He has today left for Fort Benton.

I have managed to cut the pieces, front and back, for our summer quilt. The top will be one giant Sunflower made of pieces of varied yellow cotton prints (I think a piece of every such toned garment built in our family is represented here). The center and edges are created of brown cotton prints, and I've cut ribbons of all the colors and added some tans and greens as well, to make strips to be sewn like a ribbon quilt for the backing.

Saturday 28 February

Today is Mr. Vail's birthday. He chooses buffalo hump, baked potatoes, and corn bread soaked in honey for his supper. I gave him a linen hanky I'd embroidered his initials in white thread on.

With a mitten over Martha Jane's unique bandage, Swift is able to work with Mr. Vail at the chores. He continues to mend.

I have sewn all the sunflower petals together and it's rather striking. Martha Jane and Mary Eliza say it's so bright it puts a fire to shame.

Sunday 8 March

> There let it for Thy glory burn
> With inextinguishable blaze,
> And trembling to its source turn,
> In humble prayer and fervent praise. Amen.
>
> —*Charles Wesley, 1707–1788*

Mr. Wesley sings to my heart as much as my spirit.

Finished stitching the border around the sunflower. Yesterday Martha Jane soaked the webbing off Swift's hand in warm water. It has mended nicely, leaving only a red brightness along a line of dead white skin where the knife entered the flesh. Martha Jane trimmed away the excess flesh with her little embroidery scissors.

14 March

This week I stitched together the ribbons for the quilt back. I'd hoped to pin it together for the quilting by today, but alas it will have to wait until tomorrow evening. I think it's the gayest thing I've ever put my hand to.

18 March

Mr. Nelson has ridden in on a chinook from Gold Creek and, on wild warm winds, brings us news from the States and from Mr. Plumer. It is late, Martha is feeding him and keeping the coffee cups full while we come to know the particulars of this welcome messenger. He will spend the night. I, of course, shall burn the midnight oil reading my beloved's words—drinking in the news of him since that fine day in December when last I heard from him.

East Bannack
Christmas Day 1862

My Dearly Betrothed,

Hermodson has returned safe to wife and babe. He told me you were all healthy and in good spirits. I envy him his time with you. I am delighted you are pleased with your presents. Just the sight of your ordered handwriting calms my beating heart. How I long for springtime and the sight of you. I am caressing the finely braided watch fob you created out of Lady Mac's tail hairs. It is the dearest gift. I shall wear it near my heart in honor of my two favorite "ladies."

Now don't you worry about the rowdy elements in town. Most of them frequent the Elkhorn. Whereas I do occasion that establishment, such is rare. I spend most of my time in town close to home—home for now yet being the good Goodrich Hotel. The greater portion of the men are well-behaved and few are contented to be known as bad.

New Year's Day 1863

Dr. and Mrs. Burchett (the Dr. is a dentist and his brother is an attorney) held a grand dance last night in the round bldg. on Yankee Flats—over 100 in attendance. Two fiddlers, Buzz Caven and Lou Smith, provided the music. And everyone had a splendid time, even the Doctor's Sister-in-law, Mrs. Hank Burchett, and their new son seemed to relish the company, and she, in spite of her recent confinement, did waltz to one tune with her Mr.

I think you will be delighted with the women in town. In addition to the Burchett wives, there's Mrs. Biddle (who mentioned she'd met you at the Government Farm when they were camped there with the Fisk train.) Mrs. Biddle asks that I send you her best regards. Both Mrs.

Caven, and the Waddham's young girl, Sarah, have lively minds such as yourself. I think you shall like the company here.

Danced the New Year in, dreaming of you. Next New Year's Eve it will be you in my arms.

Tuesday 7 January 1863

Today several residents of Bannack drafted a petition to Congress requesting that a mail route be established between Fort Benton and Salt Lake via Bannack. Perhaps by the time we are wed, we shall be in close communication with the States.

Reeves has taken to his tepee a Bannack Indian for his woman. Her people are camped across the Grasshopper on Yankee flats.

13 January

Received letters from home dated 15 October last. This is the fastest exchange I've experienced since I left San Francisco. They've had quite a cold snap in Maine. Mother is well, but, according to Rebecca, becoming frail. Rebecca worries that she might slip on the ice. Mother complains that she's kept inside altogether too much for the good of her health. Brother Willmot reports a good year for East Coast agriculture. The crops were bountiful and the hog and poultry prices higher than ever before. He also sold the six-year-old geldings to the army at a good price. He wishes I were there to help with the training, as he could have gotten more for them had they been finished off.

When we've panned out Bannack, perhaps we might relocate to my country. I think you would like it. I know you and Rebecca will take delight in each other's company.

Now if only I could hear from you—

Thursday 15 January

Now it's done. Yesterday morning I shot Jack Cleveland. Today he has died of it.

It has been bitterly cold. After breakfast I joined Ivan Moore, Dr. Biddle, and Corny Bray in front of the big wood stove in the Hotel saloon.

Jeff Perkins, Harry Phleger, and Hank Crawford, the butcher, were sitting on stools facing us and using the bar as a backrest when Cleveland came swaggering in. Since his arrival in Bannack he has taken to drink like a duck to water.

Moore was saying next break in the weather he was heading to see if he could raise some color and asked if I'd like to go with him.

Jack stepped to the bar, slammed down his bag, and demanded a drink. Then turning around, he began braying in a loud voice, "I am chief of this town an' I'll be glad t' fight anybody who says I'm not!"

Crawford slapped him on the back and ordered him a drink.

When no one paid him any mind he took it up again, "I known 'em all. Fact ish, I knowed ever' son — - —— that's come over here from the other side. They're trying to freeze me out, but I'll get some of 'em yet."

According to my companions, Cleveland had been going about town saying, "Plumer's my meat," ever since our arrival in town. I'd always replied, "I'm not looking for trouble, but he knows where to find me if he is." Assuming he'd chosen this day to find me, we became tense.

Instead of continuing his harangue in my direction, he turned to Jeff Perkins. "There you are you son — - ——. I been lookin' for you! You owed me $40."

"I paid you in Fort Hall."

"If you have, ish all right. Filler up again." He downed his drink and slammed the glass to the bar. "Perkins, you dirty . . . you owed me $40 an I'm. . . ."

At that point I interjected, "Leave it alone, Jack. You got your money."

Seeing Jack unloose his pistol and move menacingly toward Jeff, I said, "Now, behave your self, Jack." At that he turned to his drink. We thought the worst had passed.

Defiantly, he turned to us, pulling his gun and saying, "I'm not afraid of any d—— one of you. . . ."

I said, "I'm tired of this," and put a shot to the ceiling.

He placed one in the wall behind me. I put one in him. He fell, then still pointing his gun at me, said, "You wouldn't shoot a man when he were down would ya?" I replied, "No," and started to turn from him when a bullet whistled past my ear and I put two more into him.

Crawford went across the street to his shop and sent his clerk to carry Cleveland to his shop for doctoring.

I stopped by the butcher shop today and asked Crawford how Cleveland was doing. Crawford replied he'd died. Hoping to shed some light on the grudge he held toward me, I asked if he'd said anything. Crawford reported that Cleveland had only said, "Poor Jack has no friends" and "I guess he can stand it." Then he warned me, in the absence of law, some might lynch me for the shooting. I don't think so, partly because Cleveland had few friends beyond a couple of hard-line drinkers and gamblers such as Crawford.

TUESDAY 20 JANUARY

Today Reeves' wife went back to her father (one of the Bannacks camped south of town). I suspect because he treated her unkindly. The story I've been told is, he'd paid for her in blankets and wanted them back. When he went to camp to engage her father he did not agree and they had a tussle, which Reeves lost.

Irritated, Reeves proceeded to retrieve his gun, returned, and shot a round into the tepee, then joined a couple of companions at the Elkhorn where they commenced to drink and nurse a grievance over the fickleness of women and the unfairness of the deal until they worked themselves righteous, crossed the Grasshopper, and fired on the tepees in general. They killed one white, injured two, and killed and injured several Indians. After the fracas, they ran off.

The town, rightfully afraid of Indian reprisal, is in an uproar and out for blood. I've been told Crawford is calling for some of mine as well, though I haven't a clue why. Nevertheless, I've put together provisions and am heading out with a bedroll and Lady Mac till cooler minds prevail.

Your Betrothed,
Henry Plumer

EAST BANNACK
MIDNIGHT 21–22 JANUARY 1863

My Dearest Betrothed,

I am honorably acquitted.

Yesterday Lady Mac and I made our way to Rattlesnake Creek, where the brush is thick and the terrain such as a person could lose himself in it. There I quite by happenstance found myself in company with a trio of Reeves and friends. As dark was falling fast, we decided to camp together for the warmth of it. They said they were planning to quit the country. I thought I'd just dig in for a week or so and then return, as I knew my innocence and had faith that the people would see it that way once the furor calmed down.

Early dawn I spied three riders coming our way. With a promise from my fated companions not to shoot but to let me talk to them, we let them come on until they were close. Then we rose up from the thicket with our guns leveled at them. They said that reinforcements were coming from town. I told them that we would come with—so long as we were given a fair trial. They gave their word on it and I believed them, as they are solid men all. We handed over our guns and retrieved our horses from the gully where we had them hidden.

On our return, a miners' meeting was immediately called. They appointed: Mr. Hoyt, judge of the court; Hank Crawford, sheriff; Copley, attorney for the defense; and Rheem, attorney for the prosecution. That done, the court went immediately into session.

I explained to the court that I left town because I feared that in the excitement caused by the unprovoked attack upon the Indian Village, I might be hanged for the killing of Jack Cleveland and that I'd planned to return as soon as the situation cooled. I told them that my meeting with that trio was but coincidence.

Under oath, Perkins, Phleger, and (would you believe?) Crawford, testified that I was in the process of attempting to break up a conflict that had developed between Cleveland and Perkins and that Cleveland, not I, fired the first shot.

Several witnesses testified that Cleveland had threatened to shoot me on sight. I explained that he had been trailing me and threatening revenge because of the time I arrested him in California. The jury sided with me.

After the sun comes up the other boys shall have their say in court.

Tonight I shall sleep well and dream again of you.

Your Devoted Betrothed,
Henry Plumer

22 January 1863

The local miners are wrought to such a high pitch, that the court has sent up-canyon for unprejudiced jury members for the trial of Reeves and his friends. The entire male population of the mining district is in attendance—so many men that many spill out of the building and stand in the snow.

Last night Rheem promised to serve as prosecuting attorney. This morning he surprised the court by announcing that he had switched over to the defense. Copley agreed to serve the prosecution. Langford, who despite the below zero temperatures, has been attempting to build a sawmill, volunteered for jury duty. After hearing the evidence, the jury's decision was delayed for quite some time. I'm told the delay was caused by Langford's insistence on the death penalty for all three men. Eventually he agreed to a verdict of manslaughter with a punishment of confiscation of property and banishment, but only after the weather had warmed up some. I suspect, if one person could have been pinpointed as responsible for the deaths, the penalty would have been steeper.

Crawford, claiming he has never fired a weapon at a man in his entire life, asked to resign, but was persuaded to stay on. His first assignment is to sell the guns confiscated from the banished prisoners.

I am glad this is now behind us and that justice is more than a pipe dream in this new community.

Good night, Miss Bryan.

23 January

Today I went to Sheriff Crawford to collect my gun. It seems he has sold it along with the others. The miners will have to remedy this at their next meeting.

24 January

Tonight the miners ordered Sheriff Crawford to retrieve all arms and return them to their original owners. He then demanded reimbursement for the expenses of the trial, including the board of the prisoners, as well as the cost of caring for and burying Jack Cleveland. Crawford was understandably unhappy, as this judgment effectively left him personally taking on all the expenses of the trial. The miners' court then authorized him to seize Cleveland's horses in order to recuperate his losses.

26 JANUARY

I hear Crawford has run into trouble again. He went to claim Cleveland's horses and it turns out there was a partner with rights to half of the herd. I'm told Crawford's going about blaming me now. If the man would trade his drinking and gambling for running his shop, we'd all be the better for it. As it is, his clerk is the one that has the good sense.

All I want is my gun back.

27 JANUARY

Tired of hearing about Crawford's grousing, I told his friends to bring him by with my gun, as I was ready to let bygones be bygones. This evening they came over to the Goodrich and I'm pleased to report I have my gun and we shook hands and agreed to end our differences.

29 JANUARY

The last four days, during daylight, the weather has been spring like and I've been engaged in a bit of prospecting. Today I staked our first claim, it commences at the corner of the second cabin near the line of No 15 below Discovery on Jim's Bar running with the front row of cabins 100 feet up and 100 feet back on the level. I've hired three men to work it as soon as the ground permits.

2 February

Today I've officially filed the claim of 29 January in the Bannack records, Central District 1 ledger. This site shows promise, and I expect it is just the beginning of greater things to come. I dream of you and a home.

3 February

So much for truce. Today I met with both Richardson and Ridgley. We're talking of setting up a stamp mill. If we decide to go ahead with it, they'll handle the operating end and I'll bankroll it. While we were there we could hear Crawford, talking loud as Cleveland in his cups, casting aspersions on myself. He seemed startled when I walked up to him. I guess he did not know I had entered the room. I suggested, if he did not care to be friends, we could in the least be to each other unhostile strangers.

5 February

That rascal Crawford has been spreading a damnable rumor about town that I have intentions of courting an Indian woman named Catherine. I swear to God I have never more than tipped my hat and murmured good day to her as we passed on the street. Now I am more than a bit annoyed and I aim to have it out with the scoundrel.

6 February

Today I met Crawford on the street and challenged him to a fist-fight. He refused. I proposed a duel. He called for us to meet at 2 pm at

Peabody's saloon. A fellow the boys all call Deaf Dick agreed to accompany me.

When we arrived at Peabody's, Harry Phleger greeted us cordially, and invited us to have a drink. I declined, saying "I never drink when I have need to use a gun." Then Crawford said in a loud voice, "Well, Dick, you'll drink anyhow." When Deaf Dick retorted, "I would not drink with any coward," Crawford stepped forward to strike him, and I handed my revolver to Dick, who was unarmed. Seeing Dick armed, Crawford handed off his own gun to Phleger, saying, "I suppose I'm going to be shot now." Phleger asked, "by whom?" To which Crawford responded, "Plumer, I suppose." On hearing this, Phleger drew on the lot of us and I wrestled with him in an attempt to get one of the guns. Phleger made tossing me off easy work and then kept the group covered as he and Crawford retreated out the door.

8 February

Rumor has it Crawford was so worried over his ineptness with a gun that, back at his room, he broke down and cried himself to sleep. Poor Phleger was left to keep the watch alone the entire night.

As for my part, I got to thinking about how silly it all is. Crawford's no worse than most of them. He just gets into his cups and can't hold his liquor. I'm feeling sensitive about the Catherine issue because I know how easy gossip can spread. But that's all it is. He may not even know I am engaged to you. I think it will please you to know I'm going to send word suggesting another peace talk.

There's a new fellow in town by the name of George Ives. He just came in from Wisconsin. He's tall, blondly handsome, well horsed, and sits like one of good breeding. Since he is new to the gold fields and green in his knowledge, I've agreed to show him what to look for in the scouting of gold.

3 March

Lord, it seems a long time since I've taken a pen in hand. Alas, Crawford rejected the offer I wrote of in my last letter. Hermodson brought back the message, "He or I must die or leave camp." We did not take him too seriously, thinking it was mostly the liquor talking. But I took to consciously remaining armed at all times.

Two days later as I stood in front of the Goodrich waiting for Ives, one foot resting on a wagon spoke, my shotgun lying across my knee, I was shot with a force that knocked me down. Making a statement unsuitable for either your ears or eyes, I pushed myself up with my left arm, as the right arm was rendered useless. When I stood, I saw Crawford with a double-barreled shotgun, and I yelled, "Fire away you, miserable coward!" And, without further success, he did.

About that time Deaf Dick showed up and we proceeded to Doc Glick's. A ball had entered at the elbow, traveled down the arm, and lodged in the wrist. Doc wanted to remove the arm at the elbow. Said it was the only way he could save my life. I told him I'd rather die than live without it. Truth is, I'd rather be dead than a one-armed groom. So he did a surgery, but could not locate the ball.

The arm swelled to three times its normal size and I spent the next week mostly delirious with a fever. Two weeks ago the fever broke. I am recovering, thanks to the good care of a fellow I hardly knew named Carrhart. Crawford decided to leave town.

9 March

Today I filed a claim by preemption, East of Discovery on the Prospectus Lode Bannack District 2. The mine claimed in January is paying moderately and has kept the three I hired in good employ. I shall hire at least three to work this one.

Richardson and Ridgley have also filed claims on the Dakota and we are talking again about building a stamp mill. I have agreed to put up the money for it in exchange for half the net proceeds.

In spite of all my troubles, the greater portion of the men seem to respect my judgment and for that I am grateful.

12 March

Granville Stuart tells me he is about to make a trip to Gold Creek to get a load of goods from the mercantile there. He has agreed to carry the Vail and Bryan correspondence that's found its way as far as Bannack through Salt Lake City and has been collecting on my desk, to Gold Creek and there find someone to carry it on to you. I pray this finds you well and you will not be disheartened by the news it contains. When weather permits, the work goes on in the mines and is paying reasonably well.

I have been looking for a good location for our cabin. I know how much you love trees, and to that end I have my eye on a spot over on Yankee Flats that yet has vegetation on it.

I have no words for missing you. I can only work and make the best of our separation.

With Devotion Yours,
Henry Plumer

20 March 1863

I am fair overwhelmed by Mr. Plumer's letters. I nearly fainted with the news that he had been shot. I praise my Lord he is recovered. And I wonder that he did not know I would have loved him as much with one arm as with two. It is only for his sake I am grateful the arm has been saved. After Hermodson's tales of the wildness and violence of Bannack, I have worried each day for his safety. Now it feels like the worst has been faced and I can breathe easier. My heart aches as I read his writing, once so fine, now all slant and crabbed. It must be terribly hard to learn to write with one's off hand. How I wish to be near him and how I wish I could have been there to nurse him through his pain.

On rereading my beloved's letters I can see he has staked his future in this place—his future and mine—and that he is trying with all his talk of this person and that to make it comfortably familiar to me. Unfortunately, it sounds a lot like a violent version of the place I left behind—including all the gossips.

Since he's looking for a place to build a cabin, I must remember to make a note to him about how much I like the govt. farm arrangement of a chimney for the cook stove on one end of the house and the fireplace at the other. This arrangement keeps the cabin warmer come winter. At least when I arrive there I shall have a home as well as the advantage of a mate to whom I am well wedded. If I don't stop this scribbling, I won't have time to read the rest of my letters.

HORTON'S CROSSING
11 OCTOBER 1862

Dear Electa,

All the talk around here has been, "Indians, Indians, Indians." They've been on the warpath in Minnesota, and on our northwestern border. I wonder if your Indians are of the same ilk? And I worry for your safety. Last Wednesday was a fine raise-the-flag day for me. All summer I've been making cheeses from our three cows, and that day I sold the whole of them in Anamosa, took the money, and purchased for myself a knitting machine. It's the most fanciful thing (well, perhaps not as fanciful as Asa Bowen's machine for washing and churning that runs on dog power. During the fair, he had little boys running it the entire two days). This is the first time I've done such a thing and I'm so proud of myself. I do believe it will more than pay for itself. Over the summer, I got the wool from our small flock all cleaned and carded and I've commenced to spin it into yarn. Esther's sister, Hattie, gave me a mess of yarrow and I shall use it to dye the yarn. Since Daniel left we've begun sewing together one to two days a week. Neither of us has heard word one from our men since they went to war. The sounds of her children fill the house and yard and make music for us to work by.

Yours,
Sadie

HORTON'S CROSSING
2 NOVEMBER 1862

Dear Electa,

Do you remember Mrs. Lamb? The most dreadful thing has happened. Last Wednesday, she killed herself by taking two or three doses of arsenious acid. She also tried to poison her youngest child, but it was yet alive when found and it was saved. The speculation here is that family troubles were the cause of the act. It is well known that her husband is quite a tippler. But, to think that such a thing can happen in our quiet little community and not but a couple of miles from our farm! On a brighter note, I've cut a couple of clippings from the Anamosa newspaper intended to tickle your funny bone. The weather has been quite mild with just skiffs of snow. Nothing to bother much. I've begun knitting on my machine. What a wonder it is. I'm sending a pair of socks for each of you (and to think, I only had to hand stitch together the heels!). I do hope they fit.

Affectionately,
Sadie

POSERS

President Lincoln has a very dry way of "putting the question." Par example: A clergyman recently gave the President his views of conducting the war and after five minutes drew up to hear what the President had to say. "Perhaps you had better try to run the machine a week," quietly remarked Old Abe.

Another gentleman, after pouring out his vials of wrath upon a Government officer, was surprised to hear the President quietly remark, "Now you are just the man I have been looking for. I want you to give me your address and tell me if you were in my place and had heard all you've been telling, and didn't believe a word of it, what would you do?"

MR. LINCOLN'S ESTIMATE OF THE REBELS

Someone recently asked President Lincoln how many men the rebels had in the field. "Old Abe" looked serious, and replied, "Twelve hundred thousand, according to the best Authority." The interrogator blanched in the face, and ejaculated: "My God!" "Yes, sir, twelve hundred thousand—no doubt of it. You see, our Generals, when they get whipped, say the enemy outnumbers them from three to five to one, and I must believe them. We have four hundred thousand men in the field, and three times four make twelve."

IOWA CITY
5 JANUARY 1863

Dear Electa,

The New Year came with mild weather, moonlit nights, and frozen ground, a marked contrast to Christmas. I went home for Christmas and what a whirl it was. On New Year's Eve there was a numerously attended festival at the Episcopal Church. A table, nearly the length of the interior of the building, was set, cleared off, and replenished five times. On the first day of the New Year, the M.E. Church re-opened its fair. We dropped in the evening and found it in full blast. Next we attended a dance at the Hall of the Fisher House (I beg you, never tell father!). The Hall was as full as it could well be without positive discomfort, and we danced through the mazes in high spirits.

I presume I need not tell you, I've acquired a serious beau. We shared classes in rhetoric and biology last session. He's from Cedar Falls where his father is a lawyer. He plans to become a professor of history. Oh, what I would give for a good long tête-`a-tête with you. What can I say? Father likes him.

With Love,
Esther

HORTON'S CROSSING
10 JANUARY 1863

Dear Electa,

Didn't we have a treat for Christmas? We received word from Husband. He is well, in spite of hard conditions. His was dated December on Sunday the 21st. He says he has received no word from us for over a month (obviously he is not aware this is the first we've heard from him).

He said that the cannons began roaring down the river on the 18th and continued all morning until 2 in the afternoon and have sounded off sporadically since that morning. He says his friend Curtis died here and he helped bury him. They were in Helena, but pulled up stakes and they (along with several other regiments) are headed toward Vicksburg.

May this new year bring us Peace.

With Affection,
Sadie

Sun River
Sunday 21 March 1863

Ready for all Thy perfect will,
My acts of faith and love repeat,
Till death Thy endless mercies seal,
And make the sacrifice complete. Amen.

—*Charles Wesley, 1707–1788*

Mr. Nelson has left for Gold Creek. He carries our messages, and we pray he will reach his destination before Mr. Stuart leaves to return to Bannack.

Yesterday Mr. Vail built two plant bed frames of split log and an oiled paper cover. He filled the bottom with manure and will put the seeds in as soon as the manure cools enough; then he will start our tomatoes and cabbages. We are thankful for the seed we brought with us as our cupboard is near bare.

Martha Jane has taken over the lace making, as I haven't the patience for it. And I, entangled in my thread, become so sour she says life is sweeter if she does it herself.

The summer quilt goes fast. I'm using a long stitch with the aid of an upholsterer's needle to outline the flower petals. I'm near half done with the petal part.

Martha Jane and I have had a difference of opinion. She worries about the troubles Mr. Plumer has found himself in while occupying Bannack. She thinks I should postpone our wedding. I don't believe so, because I know he is not responsible for what has come to him. Mr. Vail says that violence is a part of the mining community and that no one comes away from it without exposure, so she and I have an uneasy truce over the subject.

28 March

I have finished quilting past the Sunflower's center. The center and edges are made of scraps in browns. I have worked the stitching on the center so as to look like the pattern a sunflower's seeds make. The edging is the same, only much larger in spacing.

On the 9th we celebrated the Vail's sixth wedding anniversary.

The children have become pale, listless, and cranky. Nothing seems to suit. Mary Eliza seems dull and has no interest in her reading. Martha Jane and I worry about them. Mr. Vail says it's just the way all children become of a spring season. Outside of that, we are all well. Some days are most spring like, then again comes the snow.

11 April

Children still feeling puny.

Mr. Vail and Swift have turned over the soil in the garden plot and readied it for planting. Martha Jane and I look forward to an excuse to leave the confines of the house.

I've just set a pot of beans to soaking and plan to bake a batch of biscuits and a pie. Our pantry is beginning to look bare, and it will be nigh on two months till we can hope the ships are come to Fort Benton.

Sunday 19 April

GUIDE ME, O THOU GREAT JEHOVAH,
PILGRIM THROUGH THIS BARREN LAND;
I AM WEAK, BUT THOU ART MIGHTY:
HOLD ME WITH THY POWERFUL HAND;
BREAD OF HEAVEN, BREAD OF HEAVEN,
FEED ME TILL I WANT NO MORE,
FEED ME TILL I WANT NO MORE. AMEN.

—*William Williams, 1717–1791*

Our good Iron has returned and brought with him a yearling buffalo. He says the children need raw liver and a piece of that part of the gut the Indians seem to like so much. Martha Jane and I decided we need try something. We reasoned that Major Owen thought it a good tonic for the Indians in springtime and they were not dying of it. Therefore, it might taste nasty, but it probably wouldn't harm us. There being no dandelion greens for a tonic, we worked up courage to give it a try. We diced the stuff into pretty custard cups and added a bit of dried onion, salt, and pepper. Then she, the wee ones, and I sat to treasure our "treat" (we could hardly have gotten the strange food down them had we not joined in the party). As the cows have been dry some time now, we washed it down with a bit of tea. To our amazement, once past the idea of its rawness, it doesn't taste all that bad. Little Harvey wanted more and ate more.

We fed on this at tea time for about five days. I do not think it my imagination the children are back to their old selves, and Martha and I do seem to have our energy restored.

We women have set out the cabbages and planted potatoes, turnips, carrots, beets, peas, lettuces, spinach, and salsify. The children clamored to have a bit of garden of their own and so we staked out two little spaces for them and "helped" them plant, just as they "help" us with the greater garden. Nights are still cold, and the weather seems not to know what it wants; some days it's hot as summer, on others we wake to ice in the buckets and skiff of snow, therefore we thought to wait a bit before planting corn, beans, pumpkins, and squash.

25 April

Would you believe, we no more got the garden in and it commenced to drop six inches of snow? This is certainly the strangest country. Fortunately, we had not set the tomato plants out. I have finished quilting the summer coverlet. When I turned up the backing, I fastened it down with a whip stitch in medium green embroidery thread. I hope it pleases Mr. Plumer as much as it does the children.

9 May

Since the snow in April, we've not seen so much as a drop of rain. It's been unbelievably hot and windy, the wind sucking the moisture right out of the ground. Last week we planted the rest of the garden. We had to irrigate the patch as there is no rain in sight. The winter gave us little snow. Now the Sun River Valley is all parched and burned up and the stock has been driven up into the mountains, there being nothing left for them to eat here. What strange nature it is that gave the farm three floods last year and a desert this year.

Yesterday we celebrated my 21st birthday. Martha Jane's turn to tease. She said, "Now, you are an official old maid." I retorted, "Some things in life are worth the wait."

Saturday 16 May

Iron has been killed. We at the farm are mourning his death. He was so good to us, and we shall be bereft without him. A couple of Johnny Grant's men were hunting near Crown Butte when they found him. They surmise he was killed by Bannacks. They trailed the perpetrators and managed to recapture a couple of horses as well as the saddles, guns, and blankets that belong to the farm equipment.

Each day now finds travelers passing through, heading for Fort Benton to meet the ships. And each time I hear the beat of a horse cantering past, my heart stops, hoping, praying, it will be Mr. Plumer on Lady Mac. And with each passing rider, my heart breaks a little. Fortunately for my poor heart, not many canter past on horses. Most walk or trot on by. In fact, the greater share of the traffic is but oxen plodding past. Somehow I do not visualize my beloved plodding anyplace.

17 May

A Walla Walla express man came in ahead of his train. He brought us a letter from Sadie and told us that Thompson is with them and that he speaks well of us. Sadie has written that Daniel has been wounded at Appomattox. She sent letters dated 3 March via East

Bannack and Walla Walla in hopes that one might make it to us. My heart is heavy with worry for my brother and with the missing of my Betrothed.

21 May

Late Monday afternoon Thompson arrived with several fellow travelers. He seemed very glad to see us, and we urged him to stop with us until the arrival of the boats, which he appears content to do. What, after all, could be worse than to be holed up in Benton waiting for the ships?

Lest he mistake our hospitality, at dinnertime I slipped on my fine ring. While we ate he could hardly keep his eyes off it, but had the good grace to ask no questions in front of his party. Either that, or he did not want them to know he was not privy to all that happens in this household.

Next morning his compatriots left the farm for Fort Benton. No more had they gone, when he came in on the prowl sniffing out the facts of the matter. When he discovered we are betrothed, he immediately began telling tales from the other side about the Oro Fino incident and that he'd heard Mr. Plumer was an escapee from the law. We reassured him his information was slant and that Mr. Plumer was an upright fellow. Even Martha Jane snorted, "Judge not lest ye be judged." That stopped his wagging tongue.

The men pass considerable time and expend a good deal of ammunition in shooting at prairie dogs, which are not what I'd call tasty when secured. Now I wish we'd eaten less and preserved more of the Buffalo our Iron brought in. The thought of greens is but an illusion. Today even a pickle would be a welcome sight. Mr. Vail's last sermon spoke to embracing the lessons God sends us. Somehow I found him less than convincing.

SUNDAY 31 MAY

IF DONE TO OBEY THY LAWS,
EVEN SERVILE LABORS SHINE;
HALLOWED IS TOIL, IF THIS THE CAUSE,
THE MEANEST WORK, DIVINE. AMEN.

—George Herbert, 1593–1632

All week the wagon trains have been crossing Sun River; among others came Johnny Grant's, heading for Benton with 22 empty wagons.

Wednesday we came near to having a tragedy in our midst. An Indian and his squaw came to the farm seeking his other squaw who had left his bed and board. He declared that if he could find her, he would either kill her or else cut off her nose and ears and let her go, as he believed her to be in the company of another man. We truthfully told him that we had not seen her and he kept on his way.

Not long after, the missing woman came in alone. When told that she was pursued, she remained only to take a little food. Martha Jane found her a blanket and provisions, and she struck out to find her people. She was Flathead, and the man looking for her was Blackfeet, so I suspect she may be a runaway slave.

Mr. Vail and Joseph Swift have been hunting enough to furnish meat for the farm and the many visitors, and twice we have been able to get out the government ambulance and take the children for a ride. No matter the diversion, it hardly fits me out to add to the stack of letters I've written to Mr. Plumer in hopes we'd be visited by some pilgrim heading for Bannack. Alas, I now hope to see my Betrothed before I meet a messenger.

This last day of May feels like spring is long past and I'm bereft without my dearly Betrothed.

2 June 1863

Just as Thompson was about to start for Fort Benton, the Walla Walla express man came in from there and reported that nothing had been heard from the boats, so he delayed his journey. Thompson and friends went again to devil the prairie dogs. Bixby, Swift, and Vail returned to working the ditches in an attempt to bring water to the parched crops.

Feeling blue and distraught, I took myself to the garden and buried myself in weeding. Wouldn't you know, I'd no more than gotten myself thoroughly sullied when a horse and rider, dark with the sun behind them, came cantering down the lane. Had I not stood up, the rider would not have thought to stop, so intent was he on arriving at his destination.

Almost before my Betrothed dismounted, I was in his arms. There we stood laughing and crying all at once and Lady Mac blowing and slobbering all over us and neither of us caring.

We almost made it to the palisade before we were espied and lost our companionable privacy.

After greetings all around, Swift took Mr. Plumer to his quarters, but not before he delivered the packet of mail he's collected for us in Bannack, not before we exchanged our letters. I feel all warm inside knowing that he is reading my three-month stack of letters even while I read his—so close to each other—so far apart.

East Bannack
26 March 1863

My Dearly Betrothed,

Your birthday present reminded me of those times when Father would come home from distant places with treasures for each of us. This needle book, with its miniature excerpt from our wedding quilt for a cover, is a delight. I have pierced its blue flannel leaves with my leather, wool, and general sewing needles. What an industrious little marvel you are.

This month the mining districts of Dakota Territory have become part of the newly formed Territory of Idaho. I believe the capital is to be Lewiston as, at present, most of the States people in the new territory reside near the Salmon River mines.

Caven has been appointed sheriff of our Fair Weather Mining District. If he carries out the edicts of the miner's court half as well as he plays the fiddle, we shall stand in good stead.

Ridgely and I have formed a partnership, and I've contracted with a Blacksmith to fabricate a water-powered three stamp mill out of the metal wheel irons and the hardwood stems of some otherwise broken down wagons.

8 April

Apart from the stamp mill, I am now partner in separate claims—one with Ridgley, one with Reeves, and these in addition to another of my own. Our miners are valiantly fighting a soggy muck made by melting and thawing frozen earth, and have piled up a good quantity of ore to be crushed as soon as we have the equipment in place.

The thaw brings another good—we have been able to bury our dead on cemetery hill. While the ground was frozen, those among us victim to the casualties of pneumonia, gripe, typhoid—as well as the few violence killed, were placed in a small stockade (to keep out hungry coyotes and wolves) next to the cemetery.

10 April

This day I have purchased a lot on Yankee Flats. I know how much you like trees and this area yet has aspen and shrubs in it. I have contracted to build a dwelling house, 20 x 30 feet with 10-foot walls and a loft, as well as a back-house, 5 x 7 feet and 8 feet in height at the hip. All measurements to be inside or in the clear. The house is to have four windows, (that is, two on the south and one each on the east and west sides), one door, a cook stove chimney, and a fireplace (to be placed on opposite sides of the building). The whole to be floored and roofed in a substantial manner, the timber to be of the quality afforded at the point selected and the best material practicable. The house is to be built of hewn logs and the buildings to be erected and completed before 25 May 1863. Further, I have ordered a quality cast-iron cook stove (along with the glass for windows) to be brought by freight from Salt Lake City. Our carpenter has contracted with Corny Bray for the flooring and roof timbers, as well as with a fellow over in the Bitter Root for the shakes. As you can see, I have not forgotten your preference for fireplace on the one end, and a chimney at the other. I believe ours will be the first house in Bannack to have wood floors and a shake roof.

George Ives joined James Stuart and a party of 15 who have decided to explore the Yellowstone Valley for prospects of gold.

19 April

Hugh O'Neal, a prizefighter of some renown, brought in his train with a goodly number of emigrants and goods. Thanks to a mild winter, we have had no shortages of goods or food.

28 April

At a miner's meeting of the White District, a day's work has been established at eight hours' labor. And nonresidents shall represent each and every claim, every seventh day.

6 May

Received letters from Mother, Rebecca, and Willmot. They are gladdened to hear of our betrothal and pleased that we are considering the possibility of repairing to the East. They send their love and best wishes for our future together.

8 May

Dearly Betrothed,

Today is a special one because it is your birthday. I wish I could be looking down at your upturned face. I would kiss your nose, then tell you to raise a flag, because today we've hit the "Big" one. In partnership with Richardson, Cross (a Bannack founding father), and Skinner, we've staked a good quartz site on the Dacotah, it's averaging $20,000 to the ton—one of the richest I've ever been in on. We've named her the Gold Bug.

In other good news, in one day's crushing, Ridgley and I have seen as much as $3,800 in neat amalgam in the retort from our Dacotah claim. We are paying our men wages of $5 to $10 dollars a day. Weather permitting, some of our men are working two shifts a day.

Granville Stuart has sold his goods, packed, and returned to Gold Creek. Had I known he was leaving, I'd have sent these letters with him and hoped they would find their way to you sooner than I can deliver them. The community is poorer without those brothers, but I suspect they'll soon be back with wagonloads of goods and their good will.

Happy Birthday My Beloved.

Yours,

Henry Plumer

17 May

Today Carrhart, the man who befriended me after I was shot by Crawford and who in fact nursed me through all those days of delirium, was killed, and several others were injured in a bizarre barroom brawl. His death was the result of a dispute over a card game that ended in gunplay between two young men named Sapp and Banfield. Seems Sapp had accused Banfield of taking a card from the bottom of the deck. In the shooting that followed, one shot struck Carrhart, who was sleeping in a bunk, and in the general melee that followed, Sapp had one finger injured and Banfield was shot in the knee as he tried to crawl out the door. Before Carrhart died, he bequeathed his possessions and a mining claim to me. In turn, I shall see to it my friend is given a decent burial.

18 May

Today I gave the eulogy for my friend. A good number of men were in attendance. I think he would have liked that.

Received news of Rappahannock—understand more than 60,000 were killed and the war is no nearer to an end.

23 May

Today I purchased a lot number 10 on Second Cross Street. In the event you find Bannack to your liking, the lot, being but one block off the main street, would be suitable for a business.

I believe that before fall, Bannack will be second to no other north of Salt Lake. More than 400 houses are already built. The population is, at present, about 1,800, among whom are counted 147 ladies and 64 children. Hardly a day passes without a train arriving. Some estimate that more than 8,000 are on the way and will arrive before the middle of June.

Today a set of governing laws were reported out by the Bannack District Committee and adopted by the people.

24 May

Today was election day in Bannack. The miner's court met, and on motion it was resolved that the offices of Judge, Sheriff, and Coroner be elected by ballot and that the President should appoint judges and tellers of said election. That being done, the polls were then thrown open for two hours. 554 votes were cast, which resulted in the election of Burchett, Judge; Castner, Coroner; and Plumer—Sheriff.

On motion it was unanimously resolved, that the term of these respective offices be for one year unless a territorial organization be declared by the United States Government in the interim and qualified officers elected. The last order of business involved a claim brought before the meeting. The court resolved that the dispute be adjudicated before a legal tribunal. We are becoming quite the civilized city.

25 May

Yesterday Alex Topounce brought his train to town. Among the 600 emigrants was Dick Sapp's wife. Perhaps she'll be cause for him to cool his restless hot heels. Mr. Topounce, the essence of entrepreneur, brought to our city a fine variety of goods and I have fairly purchased enough of them to outfit our house.

26 May

The Bannack District miners refined the mining laws governing the powers and method of trial and establishing claim entitlements; each miner shall have the right to hold one claim and no more on each quartz lode.

27 May

My Dearly Betrothed,

I have appointed my deputies. First, Mr. Dillingham (secretary for the Miner's court), as honorable and capable a man as I have yet to meet. I have entrusted him to head the office in my absence. Also, Smith Ball, Buzz Caven, and Ned Ray (rumored by some to be a bit of a rough, but also one who is a brave man and a good shot). My thinking on Ned is this—as fine as is the character of the rest of the men, if I ever had to go into a dangerous situation, I'd like a marksman with me. Since the deputies only work when assigned, I feel more comfortable knowing I can call on him. Almost as an after-thought, I added Buck Stinson (the itinerant barber at Skinner's Saloon). He's a big, awkward man who seems childlike simple. He came begging to be appointed. At first, I could see no use in him and yet I also saw no harm. There are many day-to-day duties that do not take wit, and he will not grumble about their execution.

Lest you think I'll be serving because of the pay, I must tell you there is no salary, only pecuniary amounts remunerated for services rendered. However, I do believe that each of us must do what we can to further the establishment of order and a civil society. The mining is going well and is in good hands till we return. Our house is nearly finished, and I've promises it will be done before we return.

Now, my Dearest, I must outfit myself, put on the hat of express man, and be off to the Sun River and my Love.

Your Honored Betrothed
Henry Plumer

LATE EVENING

Everyone else is sleeping, and here I am back to my journal. It seems I can't keep my thoughts in my head, but I have to put them down. My heart is filled with pride. By the end of supper, my sheriff, Mr. Plumer, had totally turned Mr. Thompson's head. My Betrothed is so elegant, so charming, handsome, and clever, I cannot but wonder at my good fortune.

Now we have only to wait the arrival of the *Shreveport* and the Rev. Reed. Last year, we arrived at Fort Benton on the 17th. That will be 15 days hence. Mr. Vail, in the capacity of our pastor, will begin the reading of the banns next Sunday, that all will be ready and there will be no need for delay when Rev. Reed arrives. Oh, what a long two weeks this will be.

We hear nothing from Sadie. And Esther wrote on and on about her beau and nothing about her classes nor news of the war. Oh, for shame on her!

SUNDAY 7 JUNE

IF, ON A QUIET SEA,
TOWARD HEAVEN WE CALMLY SAIL
WITH GRATEFUL HEARTS, O GOD, TO THEE,
WE'LL OWN THE FAVORING GALE,
WITH GRATEFUL HEARTS, O GOD, TO THEE,
WE'LL OWN THE FAVORING GALE.

—*Augustus M. Toplady, 1740–1778*

Friday morning, Messrs. Plumer and Swift left for Fort Benton to check on the boats. I don't know which is worse, having my Betrothed here where we are under so many watchful eyes we can hardly have a private conversation, or not here at all. Today the banns were read without him, but we did have a living room of pilgrims in attendance at the service.

8 JUNE

Messrs. Plumer and Swift are back and the news is not good. They bring St. Louis papers saying that the *Shreveport* left that port April 19th and nothing has been heard from her at the fort. The river is low due to a lack of snow in the mountains last winter, to say nothing of the frighteningly dry spring. Many have given up expectation of seeing boats at Fort Benton, and the wagon trains have started for the mouth of the Milk River, 300 miles below.

We speculate the Reverend Reed may have to contract to bring the Indian annuities and the Government Farm supplies cross-country in the same manner. That will take more time, and my Betrothed is impatient to return to his duties in Bannack.

To distract ourselves, we have made plans for a trip to visit the Great Falls of the Missouri, a journey of about 35 distance from the farm. Martha Jane and I will put together the food, Mr. Vail will drive the ambulance, and the rest of the party will ride their mounts. We'll leave the fort in the care of Bixby.

We're more than ready for a diversion to this endless waiting.

Sunday 14 June

But should the surges rise,
And rest delay to come,
Blest be the tempest, kind the storm
Which drives us nearer home,
Blest be the tempest, kind the storm,
Which drives us nearer home.

—*Augustus M. Toplady, 1740–1778*

Tuesday last we made up a party consisting of Martha Jane, Mary Eliza, Harvey, Messrs. Vail, Plumer, Swift, Thompson, Wheeler, and myself.

Wednesday morning, under crisp blue skies we started our adventure, heading east on the Mullan road. By mid-morning we'd cut cross country, following an Indian trail toward our destination. By the time the sun was at its zenith, we were all ready to pause for lunch. The bunch grass, already dried yellow, stretched far as eye could see and summer hardly yet upon us!

My Betrothed and I walked into this sea of grass and sat upon his coat to eat. A breeze came up and the short grasses rippled in it. Mr. Plumer sighed, "This prairie of grass is an inland sea. It is beautiful unto itself and yet it makes me miss my home all the more. Here the smells are different—all hot dust and heavy with sage. How I want to bring you to the smells of brine and fish, inland sea marshes and sand beaches."

I tried to imagine the scene, but my nose has no memory to help me along. When he speaks of home, of sea and farm and village and family, I do so long to go there.

We reached the Horseshoe Falls before dark and built our campfires in a deep ravine so as not to attract the sharp eyes of any roving Indians.

The succeeding day we visited all the falls, saw the "eagle's nest" (I wonder if it's the nest Clark and Lewis wrote of?).

Some of the falls are like graceful flowing lace, but the "Great" falls is a gargantuan cascade of crashing, crushing water, unlike anything I could ever have imagined.

We spent so much time exploring the area that we ended up eating a late supper near a small fire. In the semi-dark my Love wrapped his arm about me and in his close embrace my heart grew as hot as the embers before us. If Martha Jane looked crossly our way, wishing to stay the boldness with which we took advantage of the darkness, I could not see. And that is just as well, I think.

On our return, Plumer, Swift, and Wheeler riding ahead, suddenly turned on the top of a hill and rode toward us who were with the ambulance. Supposing they had discovered Indians, Messrs. Thompson and Vail stopped and loaded their guns. However, it but proved to be a herd of antelope, which they thought Thompson might like to stalk.

When we came in sight of the fort, we saw several horses on the plains, and wondered whether they belonged to enemies or friends.

We found ten Flatheads, on their way to Snake country on a horse-stealing expedition, eating a supper Bixby had fixed. After we finished the meal, they discovered Thompson's telescopic rifle, which much excited their curiosity. Thompson thoroughly enjoyed showing it to them. On seeing a man on horseback a long distance away he rested the gun on the corral fence and after sighting him in, allowed one of the Indians to look through the glass. The Indian liked what he saw so much, he was soon trying to barter for it. We all found the two of them attempting to communicate through gesticulation and pigeon croak amusing.

15 June

Much to my sister's dismay, Mr. Plumer proposes to go to St. Peter's Mission to determine if a priest from that church will marry us. He is adamant, and we cannot wait longer. He has been gone from his new assignment much too long already. At this point, I don't care how the marriage is accomplished. I just want it done and to be on our way.

We are out of fresh meat, tea, and almost everything else needed to keep together life and limb.

16 June

Mr. Plumer has returned, with a commitment from Father Menetrey to marry us on the 20th. It will be a civil ceremony, as his church does not recognize marriages made outside the pale of the Catholic Church. Martha Jane is on a livid rant, "I shiver in anger to think that our baptisms are not considered valid because of some running or lack of running water—that we are considered unclean! What rubbish! I'll take a bath, thank you! And you, Electa! How can you agree to such a thing?"

I tried to mollify her, saying, "I think God will look closer to our hearts and our situation than to the form our vows take."

She retorted it would be better to postpone the marriage than do so.

Needless to say, I'm too cross today to sort anything out, excepting I will be married on the 20th no matter what.

17 June

Today the sun shines again. It has been agreed that Mr. Vail shall marry us on Saturday morning and Father Menetrey shall assist him. Everyone seems satisfied with this arrangement, and Father Menetrey is a willing good sport.

Mr. Little Dog and friends have brought us a fine fresh young male buffalo, thus, we shall have a wedding feast of buffalo hump.

We have spent most of the day taking care of the buffalo. Tomorrow I'll be packing the government ambulance for the trip to Bannack. I keep trying to think of what we will need for the journey and hope to miss nothing.

18 June

The ambulance is packed and I've made up a wonderful bed in it. The tick is of fresh dried grasses and, of course, the feather comforter and the wedding quilt. I have covered it all with a plain sheet so that it will be all new to us on our wedding night and so that it does not pick up dust from the trails we'll be traveling over. We've set up the "kitchen" just inside the boot and will be able to use it open as a table. The ambulance shall be our first abode.

Tomorrow we cook for the wedding.

19 JUNE

All day the kitchen hummed with activity, the men grinding corn and hauling in water and wood, we women cooking up a storm (albeit simple fare); we shall fill the stomachs of all our guests. Wild onion, salt, and pepper filled the house with a most savory fragrance. And we sang and we hummed "Froggie Went a Courting" most of the day, while the children, like the bumblebee, danced underfoot.

This is the last day I shall be Electa Bryan.

Tomorrow I shall become someone new, someone forever bound to another.

A Mountain Summer's Idyll

21 June

We have been traveling since sunup and are now stopped to lunch on the far side of the Dearborn River. While the horses graze and Husband naps, at last I have time again to make a record in my journal.

Early morning on Saturday 20 June 1863 the sun hung on the horizon like a gold medallion on the breast of a sapphire blue sky. I was hardly into my new merino when Joseph Swift, looking tall and graceful in grey foxed buckskins and a festive red and white sash, brought me a lovely bouquet of Bitter Root flowers. He pinned a single blossom to my shoulder. I pinned three more to my hat and the last, but a bud, he threaded into the lapel of my Betrothed's black suit. The soft pink shades of the Bitter Root were charming against the deep somber colors of our attire.

As soon as little Harvey saw Martha Jane and Mary Eliza in their best blue dresses and realized he was about to be stuffed into his starched "go to meeting" white shirt, wouldn't you know he set right off to howling and nothing would do to stop him. He wasn't having anything to do with this strange affair and would prefer no one else did either. Father Menetrey suggested that Thompson act as a substitute for bride's maid, or in this case Matron of honor. Poor Martha was left little choice but to hold the lad through the whole affair.

Behind us, the room was fair stuffed with traveling pilgrims and merchants, Little Dog and his Indians, three half-breeds who'd camped by the river the night before. And, at that, all (excepting Martha Jane and Harvey) were obliged to stand. Father Menetrey opened the ceremony welcoming those gathered and quoted from St. John the story of the wedding feast at Cana. In his closing remarks he said, "May your union, like the miracle of water changed to wine, bless this arid land and help to turn it into paradise."

Mr. Vail, as the Reverend Mr. Vail, then opened his book of services and began the ritual that makes the passage of man and woman into matrimony possible. In somber intonation he began, "Dearly Beloved, we are gathered together here in the sight of God and in the presence of these witnesses, to join this man and this woman in holy matrimony: which is an honorable estate, instituted by God, in the time of man's innocence, signifying unto us the mystical union which exists between Christ and His Church; which holy estate Christ adorned and beautified with his presence, and first miracle that he wrought in Cana of Galilee, and is commended of St. Paul to be honorable among all men: and therefore is not by any to be enterprised, or taken in hand unadvisedly, but reverently, discreetly, advisedly, and in the fear of God.

"Into which holy estate these two persons present come now to be joined."

My hands turned to ice and I could hardly breathe. Affrighted. There's no other word for it. I was afraid, afraid and bewildered by the fear. I'd lived my life that I might come to this day. What a strange thing, this fear. After a long silence, he continued. "Therefore, if any can show any just cause why they may not lawfully be joined together, let him now speak, or else hereafter forever hold his peace." After a longer deafening silence, he continued. "I require and charge you both, (as you will answer at the dreadful day of judgment, when the secrets of all hearts shall be disclosed) that if either of you know any impediment why you may not be lawfully joined together in matrimony, you do now confess it: for be ye well assured, that so many as are coupled together otherwise than God's word doth allow, are not joined together by God, neither is their matrimony lawful."

Mr. Vail's finger followed the text as he read, keeping his place in the book of ceremonies, anchoring himself to the word, to the word that blew through me like some strong wind I was faced into. "William Henry Handy Plumer, wilt thou have this woman to be thy wedded wife, to live together after God's ordinance, in the holy estate of matrimony? Wilt thou love her, comfort her, honor, and keep her, in sickness and in health; and forsaking all other, keep thee only unto her so long as ye both shall live?" I could not look at him. I could not breathe.

He said, "I will." The firm strength in my Beloved's voice stopped the wind, setting me firmly on my heels. And I knew that I, Electa Bryan, would have this man to be my wedded husband, and I would live with him in that holy estate of matrimony, loving him, comforting him, honoring and keeping him, in sickness and in health; I knew that not only was I ready to forsake all others, I was ready to forsake my independence in keeping only unto him, so long as we both shall live.

And I looked directly into his grey watching eyes when I said, "I will."

Father Menetrey gently took my right hand, my dear brother-in-law took my fiancé's hand and the two representatives of God placed our hands each in the other's. In this act was a tacit permission granting us leave to cleave one to the other. I listened in awe to my Beloved's clear, resonant voice as he repeated after Reverend Vail, "I, William Henry Handy Plumer, take thee, Electa Bryan, to be my wedded wife, to have and to hold, from this day forward, for better, for worse, for richer, for poorer, in sickness and in health, to love and to cherish, till death us do part, and thereto I plight thee my faith."

I hardly remember the motions of my response, for I was lost someplace deep inside his eyes. A roar like unto wind filled my head and my heart and Mr. Vail's voice seemed far away. "Oh eternal God, Creator and Preserver of all mankind, Giver of all spiritual grace, the Author of everlasting life: send Thy blessing upon these Thy servants, this man and this woman, whom we bless in Thy name: that as Isaac and Rebecca lived faithfully together, so these persons may surely perform and keep the vow and covenant between them made, and may ever remain in perfect love and peace together, through Jesus Christ our Lord. Amen."

We stood as alone in the eye of a great storm. In some far place I heard the Pastor's voice, ". . . ring is the outward and visible sign of an inward and spiritual bond which unites two loyal hearts in endless love."

The spell was broken when Mr. Plumer turned from me and took from him a golden ring, and as he seated the plain band next to the emerald on my finger, he repeated, "In token and pledges of the vow between us made, with this ring I thee wed. In the Name of the Father, and of the Son, and of the Holy Spirit. Amen."

Yet reading from the book, pastor Vail then placed his hand over ours saying, "Those whom God hath joined together let no man put asunder.

"Forasmuch as William Henry Handy Plumer and Electa Bryan have consented together in holy wedlock, and have witnessed the same before God and this company, and thereto have pledged their faith either to the other and have declared the same by joining of hands and by giving and receiving a ring, I pronounce that they are man and wife together in the name of the Father and of the Son, and of the Holy Ghost. Amen."

Father Menetrey shared with us the biblical precedent for the sacrament of marriage. Mr. Vail delivered a lengthy, but powerful sermon. Having no space available to kneel, we bowed our heads, and Thompson, singing, sent soaring into our hearts the Lord's Prayer. Father Menetery conferred on us his blessing. Then, together, Reverend Vail and Father Menetrey blessed all with the benediction.

Yet holding my hand, my husband then led me through the crowd to the table where Mr. Vail had placed the written contract of our declaration of marriage and we each in turn took the quill and signed our names. After pressing the fresh ink with a clean blotter, Mr. Vail rolled it up and placed it in safe keeping.

At breakfast Harvey took his face from behind his mother's skirts long enough to say, "That new uncle's a bad man. He's goin' take my Auntie 'Lecta away."

I offered him a piece of crisp fat off my portion of buffalo hump. Unable to resist, he climbed upon my lap to eat the succulent tidbit. Soon he was off on a mission to torment his sister.

Thompson enlivened his end of the table telling tall tales at the expense of Joseph Swift. "This morning my roommate," Thompson nodded toward Swift, "having recently traded for a pair of moccasins, he was desirous of donning his new foot gear. Sad to say he soon discovered he was under the necessity of wearing moccasins both of which were made for the same foot." Swift winced. The men at the end of the table had a good laugh. Thompson could not leave it at that. "As you can see, being a leader in Blackfeet fashion, he wears no coat." Under cover of the raucous laughter that ensued, my husband quietly said, "Swift, it's past time we should be leaving. Thank you for your attendance on us as best man."

Beneath the cottonwooded canopy Martha Jane, Mary Eliza, little Harvey, and I exchanged blessings and pledged our love to each other while the men hitched four half-broke ponies to the ambulance and tied Lady Mac behind. Mr. Vail stood holding down the heads of the two lead ponies who were snorting, blowing, and dancing in their impatience to be off. Mr. Plumer had hardly left off assisting me into the ambulance, when Thompson swung open the palisade gates. Mr. Vail stood aside, and we were fairly launched onto the prairie.

Young Swift leapt upon a farm pony and raced to catch up with us before we reached the Sun River landing. On the other side, we traded kisses and hugs and each bade the other a most wrenching farewell.

A year ago green-carpeted bench lands broken only by the cottonwood lined banks of the river welcomed me to this valley. Now, but a year later, prairie grasses dried to dead, yellow grass waved us toward the land swells that mark the foothills of the mountains, toward some future unknown. And our ponies half trotting, half cantering, carried us so swiftly I could hardly hang onto my bonnet and I fairly lost my breath from terror. Mr. Plumer laughed and held me close, saying, "It's good flat land: we'll let them run; it'll get the vinegar out of their systems. I promise, I'll keep you safe." And suddenly the terror was gone and I threw my bonnet into the back of the ambulance and the pins came loosed from my hair and we laughed as though we were half mad.

Long before we reached Crown Butte Creek, the horses settled into a steady walking gait that no longer disturbed the herds of elk, antelope, and deer that claim ownership of this land.

We followed the road down the west side of Crown Butte Creek past Bird Tail Rock, a fan-like cliff. We stopped within sight of the Rock to let the horses graze while we ate a picnic lunch.

There, sun warmed and breathless, amidst tall buttercups and blue flags we feasted like gluttons on the sight of each other. His hair is well trimmed, and the sun brings out hints of red. He says that tho my hair is lighter in color than his it is also highlighted in red by the sun. A light moustache covers his lips and partially hides a comely set of teeth. And his lower lip, I have felt the sweetness of that full lip and I am breathless wanting, waiting, to feel that fullness against my own. But he did not look at me, not that way. He looked at the sky, then me, and said, "My Dearest, we have yet miles to go before this sun sets." With that he was up and in a blink of an eye he had the horses ready and again we were off.

We spent the afternoon and most of the evening crossing into the mountains. Dropping into the basin of Beaver Creek, we stopped for the night near an ice-cold spring. After watering and staking out our tired, hungry horses, my husband built a small fire pit and set it up for an early morning fire. Then he brought up a pail of water and filled our little granite ware coffee pot and set the rest beside the pit. I filled a pot with beans and water and set them to soaking. We both agreed we were exhausted past a desire to eat. Mr. Plumer suggested I make myself ready for bed while he washed up in the spring. Quickly as I could, I washed, then changed into my night dress, and scurried under the covers. My heart beat to a rhythm of terror before the unknown about to visit my body.

While I lie abed awaiting sun set, I wished I'd had the courage to ask my sister how it was that a husband and a wife came together. Once when I was a young girl accompanying Papa to town, two dogs were mating and I asked him what they were doing. He rushed me into a dry goods store, all the while explaining, "They're fighting. Loose dogs are a public menace. They should be shot." Later a cousin told me the dogs were making babies. I shudder to think we shall be that way together. And then he was beside me, sliding under the covers and he was without any clothes excepting his drawers and I froze in shock.

For a time we lay on our backs, neither touching the other, then gently he tucked the sheet between us and turned on his side facing me. "Electa," he whispered. "Do not be afraid. I love you and we have a lifetime before us." Then he wrapped his arm around me and kissed my hair and murmured, "You are my Beloved." Almost immediately his breathing took on the weight of sleep.

My eyes filled with tears of relief, and my body floated deep into the feather ticking. As I rolled onto my side his arm slipped around my waist and I soon joined him in slumber.

This morning I woke, the sun already shining on my face and the smells of smoke, coffee, and frying fish in my nose.

Hopping down from the ambulance, I nearly crushed a lovely Bitter Root beneath my foot. Their pointy rose petals do so shyly hug the ground. Swift chose my wedding flower well, I think.

The sun grew bold while I, in total decadence, sat on a rock in my night dress, drinking coffee and eating fish. After breakfast we stood together brushing our teeth and spitting saleratus powder into the gurgling waters of Beaver Creek.

While he watered and hitched the horses, I dressed and cleaned the dishes. I did not brush my hair until we were across the creek and on our way over some flat country clad in green pines and dried grasses. We must have traveled four miles when we came to the Dearborn, a clear, ice-cold stream 100 feet wide. The waters were not so deep, yet the ponies refused to cross. Mr. Plumer suggested I take the reins and he lead them across on Lady Mac. I told him right then and there that I was no horsewoman. In fact, as much as I loved to watch him handle a horse, I was terrified of the beasts. To which he rejoined, "Well, my Dear, we have ourselves five horses and we have an ambulance that isn't half bad to sleep in. We've food enough to last till I procure more, we have cooking utensils, a gun, some ammunition, and a few tools." In silence he surveyed the country around us. "If you prefer, we could settle here." I had to laugh at my droll man. Wait till I tell Martha Jane and Mary Eliza, I took the reins and my husband led us across.

Well rested, it is time to be off again. I hope the road ahead is not so frightening as the road we leave behind.

25 June

The road we traveled became crooked, and the higher we climbed the colder and colder the weather became, until Mr. Plumer had me wearing two of his wool shirts and a scarf over my head. The road was rutted and the going difficult in the extreme. In one place, we had to make a descent so steep the Mr. had to cut a piece of tree with which to brake the movement of the ambulance so it would not overrun the horses.

Five times we crossed the Little Prickly Pear Creek. At each crossing, magpies cheered us on and the flitting dance of bluebirds, beautiful as flowers, filled us with joy.

The second night out, I set the beans to cook and made corn-bread and coffee while my other half was fishing. It was a good thing he caught fish, because it took two evenings to cook that pot of beans. These last three nights we've been exhausted by the rigors of the road and the cold, so much so that I've come to welcome the comfort and warmth of my beloved's arms. And I do think I shall become accustomed to sleeping thus. When I roll over, he rolls over, and it is such a delicious way to rest.

We are now deep into the mountains. According to Mr. Owen, these ranges are some six thousand feet above sea level, the slopes very steep and the bottoms, filled with robins, camp robbers, crows, white-tailed deer, and a profusion of snow and timber lilies, are but little wider than the streams.

Last night timber wolves woke us with a private serenade. I was so tired, that as soon as I was reassured it was not Indians, I fell back into deep sleep.

This morning as we traversed the edge of a precipice leading to the top of a mountain, I looked down and realized that it was more than 1,000 feet to the bottom and all the way down were rocks, great sharp jagged rocks. And if the wagon should upset, we would be smashed to bits on those rocks long before we rested in foaming stream at the bottom. I started to cry and begged my husband to let me out to walk.

I think he would have allowed me to do so. Unfortunately, there wasn't enough room on the trail to get out of the ambulance.

When the road leveled out, my Beloved said, "You can relax. We are past the worst of our trip."

I love to watch him move. He is slight of build, but sinuous and strong as new wire. Life seems to spring in him, buoying his step, feeding his fingers—some vibration that both soothes his horses and excites something deep within me. I take delight openly watching his neat white teeth cut through his meat, his bread. Oh, fiddlesticks, this romanticizing does not get the evening chores done.

27 JUNE

While I was drying last night's supper pans he came from behind and wrapped his arms about my waist and kissed me at the base of my neck until I thought my knees would buckle. And then he lifted me into the ambulance and there we lay kissing and touching each other until my heart knocked against my chest hard enough to fair bruise my ribs. And we fell asleep that way, all tangled in our day clothes and each other's arms. Now he and Lady Mac are gone. I remember something said about letting me sleep in, giving the ponies a rest—what was it? He and Lady Mac off exploring, not far—not long.

It is now seven days since we left the Sun River Farm. Tonight we are camped near a small stream made gay in its run over red jasper, mica, and rose quartz. The hillside is covered with fir, nut pine, dwarf cedar, and juniper. I think I shall pick a mess of the blue juniper berries that I might use them to add fragrance to my next batch of soap.

29 JUNE

Yesterday we started at noon toward the valley of the Great Prickly Pear. The mountainside was strewn with a tangle of wild roses and currant bushes. And all about, the sweetest little wild canarys dipped and twittered. The road was quite gradual and very good. We supped by a stream of iced crystal water on a mountain covered with fine grass, pine, and fir.

Yesterday, as I rode beside him, I watched his face, his hands, and I wondered why he had not yet made me his wife. I worried that perhaps I wasn't right for him, but when he looked at me I knew it was a foolish thought.

And then, last night he unbuttoned my dress and gently removed it. Last night he asked if I were yet afraid and I said, "No, I am ready." He said he worried he might hurt me—that often the first time hurts. He said he'd stop if I cried out. I thought I'd hurt more if he did not go on and I pulled him to me and I kissed him till my lips did burn and last night I became his wife.

This morning we started early, crossed the valley of Silver Creek and then entered the fork on the Great Prickly Pear. Had a very good road all day, except for the crossing at Silver Creek. Its deep channel and muddy banks made for what Mr. Plumer called, "A dicey proposition."

We are camped near a little creek that winds through a thick grove of alder bushes whose clean bark flashes red among the dark green glossy leaves. I'm told we are but four miles from the dividing ridge. While he and Lady Mac explore a bit of countryside, I stir the fire, and before this sun leaves day behind, I take this moment to catch up on my journal.

A wee chipmunk chatters at me. He has no fear and I flip him a bit of dried corn bread.

30 June

This morning we were up at first light and a blue jay scolded me all through the cooking of breakfast. He and the chipmunk vied to woo the greater portion of crumbs from me.

Mr. Plumer said that men were working some mines but a few miles from here—that both gold and silver could be found in these mountains.

We followed the little creek on which we were encamped some two and one half miles upwards, then took a side hill road (my husband having ascertained last evening, this ascent being the most favorable). By eight o'clock we were on the summit of the Mullan Pass. There, right in the middle of summer, we saw a huge snowbank. We had no choice but to leave off to play in it. The weather was quite warm and it was such a rare delight.

Soon we were descending the west slope, and from that perspective we looked into another range of snowcapped mountains. They were of such splendor, I have no vocabulary to describe them. We lost the view of them as we entered the valley of the Little Blackfoot, which we followed some three miles before we stopped to lunch. We feasted on speckled trout, corn bread, and iced water, then traveled on another six miles, crossing the creek more times than I kept track of.

We are encamped on the north bank of the creek and have the whole evening before us. The hills around us are covered with spruce and pine rather more abundantly than the east face of the mountains. The grass is also thicker. We are now on the Pacific slope and, my husband tells me, within 20 or 30 miles of the Deer Lodge gold mines.

1 July

Starting early, we drove down Little Blackfoot some eight or nine miles, crossing it once; then the road left the valley and wandered over the hills. On each crest we were treated to a sight of the valley of Deer Lodge, as pretty as any English countryside picture. After a long trek over bench lands extending from the east side of the valley and the crossings of several little creeks, we finally reached the Cottonwood. Some ten miles west lay the range of high, snowcapped mountains we first saw yesterday. The setting sun gilded distant mountain peaks and flooded the valley with a most magic light.

We are encamped on the west bank of the creek. The weather is deliciously warm. On our way into this valley we saw a herd of some 500 cattle belonging to Mr. Johnny Grant. We did not see his ranch house, tho I suppose it is nearby.

2 July

The Deer Lodge is a fine prairie valley some four miles wide. Meadowlarks serenaded us and little gophers entertained us, whistling, flipping their tails, and whisking down their holes for the whole of the 15 miles we traveled to Hot Springs Creek.

We nooned at the hot springs. About 15 miles west, the mountains rise (according to Mr. Plumer) some 8,000 feet and are very steep. From here, bands of pine and rock present a variegated aspect deserving the honor of a painter's brush.

We climbed to the top of a red butte, about 12 feet in height and 30 feet in width, where water, too hot to bear the hand, pooled and spilled out to join the creek.

This evening we are camped at the lower end of the valley, pleased with the day's travel, pleased to be in good company, pleased in the joy of living with each other.

3 July

Again we passed the divide. This time it was nothing but a low range of hills. The valley we traveled to the Wisdom River is filled with willow. As we approached the river, we were beset by mosquitoes the likes of which we have not seen since we left Beaver Creek. The trail then led us about eight miles over a broken range of hills, thereby avoiding a canyon off to the right, then dropped back into bottom lands and we decided to call it a day. We are stopped in a lovely patch of pink-tinted white violets. After staking out the horses, my Beloved plucked bunches of them, twined them into my hair, then looked at me, saying, "You are Electa, Goddess of my dreams, guardian of my hopes and my future."

4 July

During the night we could hear the slap of beaver tails and the sudden splash of muskrats as they cavorted in the river. Did they, I wonder, pay us heed?

This morning we crossed the Wisdom River. It is some 150 feet wide with beautiful clear water. My beloved tells me this is the last large river we will cross before we reach Bannack. How different this last crossing was from our first. The horses are now old hats and nothing but great, horrid, green-black horse flies give them fits. And I, like the horses, am no longer a green colt. Now I'm a married matron comfortable in wifehood—satisfied to be in harness with my stable mate.

Today we traveled 30 miles through country scarce of timber and open. We nooned this day after crossing a fine stream, Birch Creek. This evening we are camped on a place named Rattlesnake Creek, a name that does not invite me out for a stroll.

This fourth of July evening, the western horizon is tinged to a blushing pink that lights a bank of clouds. These formations look to me like a city filled with parks and churches and solid public buildings—typifying, at least for me, the ideals of our nation.

This night shall be the last night of our wedding trip. I shall savor it so that I can treasure it like the reading of a wonderful poem.

Bannack: Summer 1863

SUNDAY 5 JULY

> TEACH US, IN EVERY STATE,
> TO MAKE THY WILL OUR OWN;
> AND WHEN THE JOYS OF SENSE DEPART,
> TO LIVE BY FAITH ALONE. AMEN.
>
> —*Augustus M. Toplady, 1740–1778*

On the last leg of our trip we creaked over a tobacco brown road beneath a warm sun. Behind us we left a hovering cloud of alkali dust. Through parched, grey-green sagebrush, across hills unbroken by timber, we rolled until we crested the last hill and stopped. Looking down, I could hear and smell Bannack as well as see it. Below us, the pock-marked earth was covered with a jumble of wickiups, tents, and log structures. From this distance, people (looking small as ants) scurried from place to place, raising dust wherever they moved. Aghast, I hardly knew how I dared react. And I could not help but wonder, what it was I'd been expecting? Surely not a settled Ohio town—all white and trimmed and lovely? No not that, but at least something nearer to civilization—something similar to Anamosa, something not quite trimmed, but perhaps groomed a bit—in the least, a place that surpassed the squalor of Fort Benton.

Looking to my husband for guidance, to my amazement, I saw him observing the scene below with a fascination that was not born of repugnance. I took a deep breath and thought, well, so this is the end of the rainbow, this place where the gold grows. Living here cannot be a forever proposition.

My husband's face was filled with keen interest, benevolence, and pride. This place was his gold mine, his people, his family. Certainly for a time I can indulge him. After all, he is my love and with him in my heart and my arms what more do I truly need?

Smiling, he turned and startled me by earnestly asking, "Well, Mrs. Plumer, what do you think of it?"

Dismayed thoughts stuck in my throat and I croaked, "Trees, where are the trees?"

With pride he directed my sight down the hill to the left. "Over there. That's Yankee Flats." And there, between the bank of Grasshopper Creek and an Indian encampment, were several cabins on either side of a rutted path. Indeed, a mix of shrub and aspen did soften their newness.

Having recovered, I murmured, "It's not quite what I expected, but when I first saw your face, I vowed I'd follow you to the ends of the earth."

He responded with pride. "See the first house on the far right—not the one at the end of the street, that's the Zoller's, but the one next to it? That's our home." He slipped his arm around my waist and snuggled me closer. Indeed, there were a few scrubby shrublike bits of greyed greenery about the cabin. "And over there," he pointed, "that's the new sawmill, and down from it is the stable where I keep Lady Mac. See that largish round building?" He pointed to the left and back across the creek. "That's where the Union League holds its meetings, where the New Year's ball was held." Beyond the roundish building, men bending over shovels, pushing wheelbarrows, and wielding pickaxes were changing the map of the earth. Sounds of metal ringing against rock mingled with their shoutings and their cursings. So this is the sight and sound of the Grasshopper Diggings, I thought. Lord have mercy on us.

In one hand my husband picked up the reins and we trotted into town. "First I'll take you on a tour down our main street and back. Then we'll go home and unload before I stable the horses."

Descending the hill we entered the town at mid point. Mr. Plumer then set our course to the opposite direction from our cabin. We passed another stable, a bakery, a couple of saloons, a meat market, a bowling alley, another hotel, a billiard hall, and a bakery. Between the public places were log homes and at the end of the street, yet another blacksmith shop. I'm told miners' claims and cabins continue on down the gulch for some five miles below. Not far beyond that end of town are two quartz mills; the smaller my husband's, the larger built while he was traveling to Sun River. Mr. Plumer wanted to introduce me to the boys working the stamp mill, but the noise was deafening and I begged not to stay. On our way back through town, the whole length of the journey my good man kept up a patter, the likes of which I've never before heard from him. At the same time he was guiding the horses through long strings of packhorses, donkeys, and mules, gesticulating first to this building, next to that, and would you believe, tipping his hat to half the people on the street.

His chatter did not distract my notice of the loafers that lolled at the doors or slouched in and out of saloons and hurdy-gurdy houses, nor could it cover the sounds of brawling, insults, and oaths emanating from the likes of the Elkhorn. On the street were ladies dressed as if for the queen's ball. Although they did not elicit comment from me, I did notice and I do believe I know what they are about.

"Take note, my dear, we have two public wells where we can draw our table water and look," he pointed to a small low building, "that's a fine Chinese eatery and right next to it is Chrisman's dry goods. My office is in the back of his store and we are taking subscriptions for the buliding of a jail." Prior to crossing the Grasshopper, he nodded toward a rather large single storied structure, "That's the Higgins and Reece establishment and across the street just below the stable is the brewery."

At last we crossed Grasshopper Creek and trotted the ambulance straight up to our door. There, my husband tied the horses to the clump of chokecherries that served as trees in front of our cabin. It is a sweet place—all fresh and clean. And would you believe, there, on the culinary end of the cabin he had installed for me, not one of those little sheet metal stoves—oh no! For me there was the finest cook stove I've yet seen. The Mr. proceeded to demonstrate for me the latest in dampers, how they turned to hold the heat in winter and shunt it past the burners in summer. Further, it has two ovens, one for warming plates and the regular one for baking, as well as a reservoir for water. Above the stove is a drying rack for rags, towels, and the like. On the one side of the stove is a copper boiler for laundry and canning, on the wall behind the stove are hooks holding pans for cooking and washing. I have never seen anything like it. My husband had it special made in Philadelphia by the company that made the stoves for the Union Bakery in San Francisco. In the corner to the left of the stove, just past the window, is a cupboard. In front of it were stacked three wood packing crates that held dishes freighted up from Salt Lake. Mr. Plumer's miners had looked to their delivery in his absence. For a fleeting moment, I regretted not having met them while we were near the stamp mill. In the right hand corner stood a pantry cupboard made out of the packing crates that had served protection for the stove and the pie safe during shipment. Inside I found a basic set of cooking utensils and supplies, right down to flour, salaretus powder, sugar, coffee, tea, salt, pepper, and a tin filled with an assortment of dried fruits. I could hardly keep from starting a batch of biscuits right then and there. A dry sink stands between the stove and the pantry cupboard. A beautiful pie safe stands on the wall opposite the dining table. The table is made of split, hewn log and has benches on either side.

The beds are built into the walls just like those at the government farm. Unlike the pegs on the wall that served at the farm, we have a lovely double-doored armoire for our clothes.

My husband was distressed that the settle and chairs he had ordered had not come. But I assured him I could not have been more pleased and in this manner I have something to look forward to.

He had the ambulance cleared in the time it takes a rattlesnake to strike, then left me in the middle of the mess that he might put up the horses, check in with his deputy Dillingham, and fetch us home a couple of pails of drinking water. I shelved what little was left of the food we'd packed from Sun River, not much left beyond a bit of dried buffalo, some bacon, lard, and a few pounds each of cornmeal and ground oats.

Setting aside our soiled sheets, I covered our tick with the special sheets Martha Jane made crocheted lace edgings for. Spreading our feather quilt over a bunch of currant bushes, I broke in the new carpet beater on it, thereby sending the dust of our trip flying into the air. Finally, I shook out our pansy quilt and topped the bed with it.

I had no more finished organizing my clothes on my side of the armoire, when Mrs. Zoller, my next door neighbor, stopped by to welcome me with gifts of sourdough starter, a pail of milk from her cow, and an invitation to come to coffee after we'd settled in. She then took me down to the creek and showed me where the men had dug out a settling pond and lined it with rock so that we could acquire, without a great deal of trouble, clear water for washing and cleaning from the much disturbed and roily waters of the Grasshopper. This summer she is teaching a group of subscription students from eight to three, four days a week. I do think I shall very much like her.

As soon as Mrs. Zoller left, I wrapped myself in an apron and, wondering what on earth was keeping the Mr. so long, mixed a sponge for bread. The corner pantry is cleverly made; the bottom is built out of the stove crate and is just the right size to work as a mixing table, then the carpenter took the pie safe crate, which is quite narrow in comparison, and placed it on top. He made shelves for the whole out of the tops. It will be very attractive after I make curtains for it.

The bread begun, I betook myself to fetch the water for tomorrow's laundry. Near the settling pond I found the Grasshopper richly mantled in tender green watercress and I bethought myself to cut a mess with which to make a pot of watercress soup soon as my water was in. By the time my husband returned, I had worked a good deal of irritation into the kneading of our bread. While I put the soup together, I had well rehearsed a good speech against such abandonment of one's wife on the first day of introduction into a new town and a raw and dirty town at that. I'd finished hauling in wood and lit a fire before I heard his footsteps. To be sure, I turned, ready to allow him a piece of my mind. But as soon as I saw his face I stopped. "Oh, my Darling, my Beloved, what has come to pass that makes you so pale?"

He poured one bucket of the good well water into the reservoir and set the other on the floor next to the stove. "Electa, I hardly know where to begin." I gasped at the familiarity of my name on his tongue in the full light of day and not after dark when it came to my ears more like a dream than real.

"My best deputy, Dillingham, has been shot dead."

"How?"

"I have before me two stories. Deputy Stinson, who, as I've said before, is a bit weak of mind, tells one, and a man I met on the street, whom I hardly know, tells another. Since I left this city, there has been an exodus to a new set of mines 70 miles distant. There, a new city, Varina, has sprung up on a creek called the Stinking Water."

Thank God for an exodus, I'm thinking, how much more dreadful this miserable excuse for a town would be if one multiplied its sins.

"I need to get to the matter of the situation." Having stated the obvious, his color returned and he noticed the work I'd been up too.

"My dear, I hardly expected you to cook this day. I thought we'd take supper at the Chinese restaurant."

"Ah, my darling, you did not mention it earlier, neither did you mention any particulars about our neighbors; more to the point, I have had the pleasure of meeting Mrs. Zoller." Having said that, I could not but throw my arms about his neck and kiss him full on the lips. "She is lovely, our home is lovely, I am feeling lovely all over."

"Dear-heart, you are lovely all over. To be sure, so lovely I'd like to show you to the town."

"Ah, but Mrs. Zoller brought me sourdough starter and a fine fresh pail of milk and I cannot resist trying out my new stove. Surely the town and the Chinese supper can wait?" I asked more than stated. "Besides tomorrow I must do laundry. That's a day I'd truly appreciate a supper out."

"Then we must be off to town for more provisions."

Dreading another sight of the town proper I suggested we first unpack our dishes. Like a father indulging a child, he nodded assent and fetched a small pry bar from a box near the door. Soon, he was as caught up in the project as I. We unpacked a twelve-place setting of fine china in a blue willow pattern and a fine set of glasses. When we prized open the last crate, we found it filled with silverware and a Sheffield plate water pitcher. Now the floor was littered with packing materials and large, sturdy, wooden boxes. We put the largest two into immediate service; one we placed near the foot of the bed for a blanket chest (all it needs are hinges to make it good as any) and the other near the stove to hold kindling. Like children, we ran to the back house, against which the kindling had been stacked, and filled our firewood box to overflowing. By this time my dough was ready for shaping and the dishes needed washing. For a moment I thought to use the work at hand as an excuse against accompanying him to the mercantile. On second thought, I knew he truly needed me to go with him.

At the meat shop we collected beautiful steaks of beef, at the mercantile, carrots, potatoes, onions, a bolt of muslin for curtains, hinges for converting the packing boxes into chests, and two men, John Bartelson and Cyrus Gilbert, who had volunteered to carry home our parcels.

The foot bridge across the Grasshopper to Yankee Flats is made of a great split cottonwood, the halves anchored side by side. The three of us followed Mr. Plumer across, looking, I'm sure, like the children who followed the Pied Piper of Hamlin Town.

The Messrs. Bartelson and Gilbert had come together from Minnesota by way of Salt Lake City to join a couple of partners in working a claim on the Grasshopper near Marysville. Traveling with the O'Neal Train, they reached Bannack on the 19th of April.

While I cooked supper and washed dishes, they sat down to the table to fill our Sheriff in on the six weeks he'd lost fetching "his bride."

It seems a group of five or six men headed by Wm. Fairweather that had planned to go with James Stuart's party to explore the

Yellowstone, was delayed in leaving with them by the prospect of having naught but shanks-mare to travel on. By the time they procured enough flesh of the four-legged persuasion they missed their rendezvous with the Stuart group on the Stinking Water Creek, and in the missing, they found instead a great bonanza in gold!

During the first week in June, when the Fairweather party returned to Bannack for supplies, word soon leaked and the stampede to the new diggings was on.

Gilbert said, "None of our crew went, as we ain't got no complaints about our operations here on the Grasshopper, but almost every one of the 600 that come with the Pikes Peak Wagon Train on the 24th of May joined in the stampede. . . . "

Bartelson interrupted. "There were two, maybe three, trains of people what come last spring an' went over in that stampede."

"Somethin' like that. Within a week of staking their claims, they done staked the city of Varina and held two miner's meetings."

"An acquaintance of ours, Hamilton, the same that's been freighting between Bannack and Salt Lake this winter past—Ham, the same that brought in your fancy stove—were sent over by Bill Carter of Fort Bridger with a large assortment of goods, groceries, and supplies. Last week he comes by and spends a couple of days with us afore heading back to Salt Lake. Anyways, this here Hamilton reported that at the second meeting mining regulations were adopted, Doctor Steel was elected president and G. E. Bissel was elected judge. Doc. Steel appointed someone sheriff, but he quit after a week, and they didn't remember who it was. Afterwards, he appointed Dick Todd, and Todd is still in the position of acting sheriff for Varina City. Only the name has already been changed to Virginia City by Judge Bissel, as that was as close as the good man could make his pen come to putting Jefferson Davis' wife's name to paper. They report that a number of folks continue to call it Varina anyway.

"On the 29th of June the Virginia City miners' court met to settle a claim dispute. The courtroom was a wickiup that stood on the creek bank at the foot of Wallace Street. The tent was barely large enough to hold judge, clerk, plaintiff, defendant, attorneys, and deputies Dillingham and Gallagher.

"Gallagher?" My husband asked, obviously puzzled.

"Yeah, Gallagher."

"Who's Gallagher?"

"Oh, that's right, you wouldn'ta knowed him, cause when he come through you was already gone," replied Bartelson. "Jack Gallagher come into Bannack on that last train what started in Denver, but I think he jined 'em at Fort Bridger. Musta come in one, maybe two days afore the stampede to Varina were on. Dillingham thought to jine 'em in hopes of making his bundle there. So Dillingham appointed Ned Ray to take his place here in Bannack and headed out."

"Because their womens weren't keen on the idea, none of the other deputies were interested in going over," interjected Gilbert.

Bartelson continued, "It's my understanding that Sheriff Todd appointed him and Gallagher deputies over there. Anyways, they was on hand and helped with the trial."

Bartelson and Gilbert took turns telling the tale. "Hamilton espied the goings on by peeping through gaps in the wickiup brush. He told us Ed Richardson were asittin' at Judge William Steele's elbow makin' notes, when deputy Buck Stinson and his old friend Hays Lyons come in and whispered in Richardson's ear. Nobody knowed what the tarnation Stinson and Richardson was doing in town, but then nobody were wondering about it neither. Richardson looked at Dillingham and indicated with a jerk of his head he should leave the wickiup with them. Outside, not far from the tent, Lyons cursed at Dillingham and demanded, 'Take back those lies.' As hands moved toward revolver butts, Richardson cried, 'Don't shoot! Don't shoot!' Then all Ned breaked loose and nobody could tell for sure exactly what happened, but for certain Dillingham were dead with one shot in the thigh, and another in the chest."

"Deputy Gallagher disarmed Stinson, Lyons, and Richardson and turned them over to sheriff Todd who ordered 'em bound. Five of Todd's men, headed by Beidler, as bloodthirsty a little rat as ever come up from the bottoms of a back-house, was guards for the men."

"Ham, ah-Hamilton done heard Beidler braggin, 'We held the prisoners in a log cabin near Dorris' store. Having no handcuffs, we secured the sons a—', 'scuse me ma'am, 'with chains and padlocks. We ironed one bastard—', 'scuse me ma'am, but that's what he done said, 'when the balance bucked and said they would die before we should put chains on them. I told them ass—', 'scuse me ma'am, but I gotta tell it like I were told it, 'it was a good day to die.' The captain of the guard said: 'Pull down on them boys!' And Biedler went on, saying, 'Bout that time the sons a—', 'scuse me ma'am, you should not be hearing this, '—choose chains over lead. You can bet we took our pleasure chaining up those a—', 'scuse the language, ma'am, but it weren't mine, it were Beidler's."

"Bout this time, we're thinking poor Dick Todd has got hisself surrounded with a greater mess of bad characters than Bannack's Sheriff."

"That night Lyons said he were the one what done it. He shot Dillingham, and they should let the others go. The court decided to try all three of them the following morning anyways."

"Your partner Richardson talked them into separate hearings and made his own plea before the court and the people. Being, as well you knowed, a bright, handsome young fellow and a capital talker, he had no trouble convincing the jury he was in the clear. Several fellers told the jury, he called to the others not to shoot, and deputy Gallagher swore Forbes' gun were never fired."

"Lyons may have said he were the one who shot Dillingham, but it appeared that Stinson's gun had also been fired, so by a fair vote of the people, Stinson and Lyons were sentenced to death. They told Dick Sapp and Beidler to build a scaffold and dig the graves. But when they come to put 'em in the wagon and haul 'em to their hangin', a big crowd, near on 2,000 excited miners, and a few weeping women what got 'em so stirred up an' agitated, Sheriff Todd was got to let 'em vote on to hangin' or settin' 'em free. This time the miners turned the jury's verdict back on itself and every man of 'em was on the free."

"Richardson, rode away and we ain't seen him since. Gallagher kept his job, don't know where Lyons skedaddled to, and, as you already knowed, Stinson come back to Bannack."

My husband rested his elbows on the table, spread his hands over his eyes, and rubbed as if to remove a great curtain. "The Gold Bug. Are our men, guess it's my men now, are they still working the mine?"

"You betcha! Those fellows are still goin' strong. They knowed you. They knowed you'd make it good with them."

"And Ridgley?"

"Well he ain't shot nobody and the weather's holding fine, the men are working steady at them diggings."

"Reeves?"

"Skedaddled bout a week after you made your departure."

"You remember Banfield?"

"Shot in the knee the day Carrhart died?"

"The same. Anyways he's dead now. He were beyond doctorin' and it got infected bad. Died from the poison in it."

They no more than finished supper before they were off. My husband, declaring a need to talk with his foreman at the Gold Bug, was close on their heels. I finished cleaning the kitchen and sat to write. This has been the longest day of my marriage. It's almost midnight, time to trim the wick and go to bed. I trust my housemate knows his way home.

6 July

'Tis afternoon, the clothes are drying on the gooseberry bushes and I have dried apple pies cooling on the table. Last evening, I'd hardly finished my prayers before husband returned, took me in his arms, and kissed all my petty irritations away. He says the mines are doing well and he will set aside Richardson's portion against a time when he may make his whereabouts known again.

I wondered aloud that a man should just take off like that. Husband said, "He's young. He's found himself in trouble before and found facing it down a sometimes hard and unjust thing. If he came here to start afresh, he left as soon as the waters muddied."

I wondered if husband would have to spend time at Virginia City. He thought only occasionally, in as much as it is 60 to 70 miles away and over there they have sheriff Todd to take care of their needs.

For "dessert" my husband handed me a packet—three letters from Sadie, one from Esther, and one from Martha Jane. A fellow on horseback, passing through Bannack about the first of July, left the latter at Chrisman's for us. We must have crossed near each other about the 30th of June. Of course Sadie's was posted near six months ago.

Horton's Crossing
7 February 1863

Dear Electa,

I do believe this has been the coldest week of the season. Monday last the mercury was sixteen below. This morning it has already risen to the zero mark. Perhaps this spells the end of the worst of it. Last week I engaged Mr. Saums to deliver his fine Coteswold ram to our small flock of ewes on Saturday next. I first saw the beast at the Anamosa fair. He is all of 250 lbs. and yielded a fine, light-colored ten-lb. fleece. I think Daniel would be pleased with my decision. President Lincoln has issued a final Emancipation Proclamation. That should deliver unto the Union ranks those who felt he was going too easy on the moral issues of slavery. Jamie D. is writing a paper on sheep husbandry for his class in English and Father is teaching him to play his mandolin. We are all fit here and hope it is the same with you.

With Affection,
Sadie

Horton's Crossing
2 March 1863

Dear Sisters,

I post this letter through both Walla Walla and East Bannack in hopes that one of them will reach its desired destination. I have just received word Husband has been wounded at Vicksburg. I have no other details. Pray for him. Pray for us.

Sadie

Horton's Crossing
16 May

Dear Sisters,

Husband is home. And we hardly know whether to laugh or to weep. He is but a shadow of his former self and is wracked with cough. I'm certain if I can but keep him alive long enough, if I can get a bit of flesh on him, he will live. His wounds, over four months old, are not yet healed. The slowness in the healing comes from the poor food he's been maintained on—the poor food and the cold weather and that cough. He will not speak of the war. Oh, the dreadful war! On the ninth of March Anamosa High started spring session without Jamie D. And what a good thing that has turned out to be. He and father have the crops in; unfortunately the weather has been more cool than desirable for their growing. We've had a fire in the kitchen all week as the mercury has been down as low as six degrees above the freezing point and rain has fallen early in the week—enough that there will be no danger of drought in the month to come.

God be with you.
With Affection,
Sadie

Sun River
26 June 1863

Dear Sister,

On the afternoon of your wedding, a messenger from Benton arrived with news that the Shreveport *would probably reach Benton the next day. Mr. Vail immediately started for Benton, intending to ride through the night, it being easier and the danger from Indians being lessened. Report came to us that all the horses at St. Peter's mission had been stolen, and the men speculate that those three half breeds who camped at the farm the night before the ceremony may be the thieves.*

Upon Mr. Vail's return from Benton he reported that the Shreveport *had reached a point about 200 miles below Benton (Cow Island) and had unloaded her freight on the riverbank and returned to St. Louis. The passengers put on shore by the* Shreveport *were coming into Benton on foot, many used up by their experiences. Provisions were very scarce at Benton, and none could be supplied until the teams came in from Cow Island. We pray for a speedy arrival of our provisions and for safe passage for Reverend Reed.*

The Missouri shows the effect of there being no rain in the country since September last. Nick Wall, who had come from St. Louis by way of Salt Lake, arrived on his way to Benton and informed Mr. Thompson that he had left several letters for him at Bannack City. Mr. Wheeler returned from Benton, being discouraged by reports of Indian atrocities from descending the Missouri by Mackinaw boat. He plans to make his way to the States overland by way of Bannack and Salt Lake to St. Louis. He has agreed to bring our letters to you. Bixby plans to travel with him and try his hand at panning gold.

Now we are out of coffee, tea, sugar, wheat flour, and salaretus. The garden has thrown up some radishes and the other day I did find a patch of wild onions to savor the wild meat. I've been serving up lambs quarters in any way I can think of and have been experimenting with wild greens besides lambs quarters. I guess it could be worse, we could be out of salt. The other day Harvey said, "I miss my Aunt 'lecta. 'Specially, I miss her good ginger cookies." He speaks for all of us. We all miss Aunt Electa, her ginger cookies and more—so much more.

In spite of our hardships we are well. We remember you every day in our prayers and we miss you very much.

Your sister,
Martha Jane

Martha Jane, dear sister, you and the Sun River could be on the other side of the earth, for all my heart can fathom the distance, we're so far apart, so different, and yet our loneliness is so much the same.

7 JULY

Last evening I ate foreign food for the first time. These Chinese are very small and the ceiling to their place is very low. They cook everything in a great huge cast iron cross between a fry pan and a cauldron using but a small hot fire beneath it. We were served small bowls of steaming rice and sliced pork with a sauce of raisins and spices I could not identify and chicken with nuts, celery, onions, and many little dishes of delights I've never before tasted. These foods are eaten by them with two sticks held between the fingers of one hand; a feat my darling has mastered, but I think I shall starve before I should.

It was dark before we left the eatery and thus, when my beloved led me across the foot bridge, our path was lit by shooting stars.

Before daylight he was coughing in a most frightful way, but wouldn't you know, he was off at the crack of dawn with naught but a bowl of porridge and a cup of coffee between himself and his belt.

He returned for lunch and we ate buttered bread, warmed steak, fried onions, chopped watercress, and dried apple pie. In spite of the night coughing, he seems well today and his appetite is good.

In my pleasure serving him, I forgot to mention we have need of a spot for keeping milk, butter, and eggs cool.

8 July

Today my husband learned that, while he was fetching his bride, the territory of Idaho had divided the land east of the mountains into separate administrations. I cannot see that this makes a whit of difference to anyone, but he seems to think it's important. He also thinks he needs go to Virginia City to see for himself how the mines there fare. I asked him to put it off as long as possible. I'm terrified of being left alone, but more terrified of riding a horse and the ambulance is already on its way back to Sun River Farm.

This morning I cut curtains for all the windows and the cupboards. The muslin is so plain, I'm yet wondering if I should brighten them with fancy work.

I met Mrs. Zoller at the settling pond, and she invited me in for coffee. She has covered her ceiling with muslin, which lightens the room considerably. But then she has a sod roof and but one window, so she truly needs the covering. She says Mrs. Biddle and Mrs. Arnold have covered their walls with printed calico and that looks quite inviting.

I don't know how she manages the teaching with the cooking, cleaning, and the laundry, but she does have Emma, and Emma's almost grown. At that, she's up before five each morning and the light yet shines from their window when I put ours out.

SUNDAY 12 JULY

HE LIVES, TO BLESS ME WITH HIS LOVE;
HE LIVES, TO PLEAD FOR ME ABOVE;
HE LIVES, MY HUNGRY SOUL TO FEED;
HE LIVES, TO HELP IN TIME OF NEED.

—*Samuel Medley, 1738–1799*

Friday last, Mr. Plumer, responding to some request from Sheriff Todd, left for the Stinking Water. And in his absence I have been taken with some kind of sickness. I have this metallic taste in my mouth and I keep wanting something in my stomach, but I can't find one item I can keep down. Even the smells of cooking leave me faint headed. All in all, with the way I'm feeling, I'd be just as glad he's gone if it weren't for all the frightening night sounds. I lie awake shivering and wishing I could fit under the bed. All night I listen to sounds, real or imagined, I know not. When the noise of revelry and fighting is not obvious, I hear footfalls outside the window, hoof-beats on the road, or the Indians. Between the night revelers in the town and the Indians, this place never goes to sleep! Yet, when I am nestled in my love's arms, I do not hear a thing.

Yesterday, when Mrs. Zoller came over for coffee, I couldn't even eat the gingerbread she brought. And wouldn't you know, she gave me a "cat who just swallowed a mouse" kind of look and I asked, "What?" and she just started to laugh as if there were some kind of joke going round. I just hate it when I can fairly see people thinking, but haven't a clue what it's all about. After she left, an Indian woman with a papoose on her back and a little girl in tow passed between our houses on her way back from getting water at the creek. The girl was about our Mary Eliza's age and such a darling little thing. I invited them in and fed them the gingerbread I couldn't eat and offered them milk they did not want and tea they did drink. At least food has no language barriers.

I have been appliquéing ivy leaves and embroidering vines on the cupboard curtains. The green cotton thread I've been using has a variegated pattern and the overall effect is pleasing in a quiet way.

I'm beginning to feel much better. I think the rest has helped me overcome the sickness. If I make potato soup and biscuits, supper will be ready when my husband returns or, should he be delayed till the morrow, it will keep.

13 July

My Beloved crossed the bridge in time for supper. His trip went well, but it has taken its toll on his constitution and he hopes not to make another in the near future.

The dear man brought for me some lovely wild flowers, lupines and sweet rockets, roots and all, wrapped in wet burlap. Tomorrow we will plant them and if I keep them wet perhaps they'll take hold by the side of the cabin. If they take, how lovely they will be all purple and blue peeking through the bunch grass.

Husband says that in the long run he believes he will do as well in Bannack as those mining on the Stinking Water. I'm glad for that as, at this juncture, I haven't the courage to move again.

At Nevada City, another site near Virginia City, he related the strangest happenstance, "Strolling down the street I saw George Ives, and while we were talking, a couple of his acquaintances came by. He asked us if we knew each other as we were both residents of Bannack. We had not met so he introduced us saying, 'Mr. Plumer, I'd like you to meet Mr. and Mrs. Dalton.' After a polite exchange, the Mr. said, 'Oh. Henry Plumer, we knowed of you when we was farming near your father, Amos, in Wisconsin. You was borned in Maine.' I replied, It's true I was born in Maine, but my father is not Amos, and I've never been to Wisconsin. Then they started asking about this neighbor and that and about events of which I have not one clue. And when we parted they said, 'Goodby Mr. Plumer,' and the Mr. winked."

We had a good laugh at the silliness of people with a notion stuck in their heads.

This morning while making breakfast, I became ill all over again. Mr. Plumer wanted me to go straight way back to bed, but I just couldn't let the washing go, so I remained standing. He insisted on bringing in the laundry water and extra wood before he left. He says in the future he'll have the Chinaman pick it up and take care of it. We've had that argument before. I think I should do it. He thinks that I shouldn't do what doesn't have to be done. If he had his way, we'd eat out every night, too. Then what would that make me? His fancy lady? He says that after the children come they shall be all I need worry about. I wanted to stamp my foot and shout, "What on earth do you think I'm about, some glorified brood mare?"

15 July

A chilling dream filled my night. In the dream, flies, knocking against the kerosene chimney, woke me with their ping, ping, pinging against it. Blotting and blocking the flame they made flickering shadows against the wall and on the wall they turned into giant moths, dancing shadows, circling round and round the room. Dark grey shadows bled bright red at the edges, then to a deep old blood red in their entirety. The flickering shadows paused as if in hesitation, then began to hum and turn black to red, black to red, black to bright red, and the bright red shadows turned into a baby curled in the palm of my hand and I screamed and I woke.

Husband asked me what was wrong and I could only reply I'd beheld a nightmare. He held me in his arms and rocked me back to sleep.

16 July

Well isn't this a red letter day? At noon Husband came home in a wagon carrying our parlor furniture with him. It came in with the extra dust of a good-sized train from Salt Lake. Oh my! Isn't this living in comfort?

18 July

I cannot believe I am so dumb. This afternoon I told Mrs. Zoller how sick I've been and wondered if she thought I needed to see a doctor.

She immediately came over and put her arm about me saying, "Oh, my dear little friend, you don't know, do you?"

I think my mouth dropped. "So that's what the sickness is!" I exclaimed, there being no doubt as to the meaning of her question.

"Have you missed your time?"

I nodded. "A week ago. It should have come a week ago." Then stricken, I clamped my hand over my mouth, "Oh dear Lord! Don't tell anyone, please don't tell anyone. I could not look them in the eye, knowing how it is with me."

The dear woman assured me my confidence was safe with her. And she wrote me out a recipe for a salaretus cracker she swears by for keeping that awful frothy metallic taste down.

Now I must tell my Beloved. I should be eager to do so, because I know how happy he will be. But I just feel out of sorts and I don't know why.

SUNDAY 19 JULY

HE LIVES, AND GRANTS ME DAILY BREATH;
HE LIVES, AND I SHALL CONQUER DEATH;
HE LIVES, MY MANSION TO PREPARE;
HE LIVES, TO BRING ME SAFELY THERE.

—*Samuel Medley, 1738–1799*

20 JULY

My good man has confided in me—on promise that I not disclose the latest good fortune until he has a working crew in place—that he has staked another good mine. It's west of the Discovery on the Bevin Lode.

I was planning to tell him about my condition, but it just didn't come out right. In fact it just didn't come out at all.

22 July

Today Mrs. Zoller asked if the Mr. weren't about to burst his buttons over my good news. I'm not good at lying, so I confided to her that I hadn't told him yet; that I knew he would be delighted, so I didn't know what was stopping me—I guessed something was wrong with me.

She told me nothing was wrong with me, beyond my size, and that was not wrong, just could be a problem when my time came, as if I didn't know that already. She said it was usual for a woman to become weepy and illogical in her thinking for the duration.

I don't know if I feel better or worse for talking with her, but I can hardly talk about these things with the Mr., even if he were home long enough to do so. Seems whenever he has a free moment, he's off recruiting money for a new jail. At this moment he's at another miner's meeting; each week there are at least two, each of a different district, to be sure. Today he files his claim by preemption, west of the Discovery.

25 July

What a marvelous raise the flag day it has been. Young Swift came from Sun River carrying a letter from Sister and bringing sunshine into my life by his good graces. He arrived in Bannack with Mr. Thompson, but as Thompson has business in town, he found our cabin on his own. Unfortunately, my husband is about the city today.

It's such a shame they could not find their way to take supper with us. Yesterday Mr. Plumer brought home a fine roast, which I already had in the oven. It makes the kitchen hot, but I can't complain so very much, as the heat has long left the house before morning.

Sun River
5 July 1863

Dear Electa,

On the 3rd, the first of the Shreveport *passengers reached the farm and were loud in their disappointment in the captain of that boat.*

Out of materials left from broken government vehicles, Mr. Thompson has built a chariot-like rig with a seat in its construction. Mr. Vail has dubbed it a "go-devil." He lent it and his horse, who has become accustomed to the strange rig, to Mr. Vail for a trip to Fort Benton. The odd vehicle saved the trouble and expense of a packhorse. He said it was much easier than riding astride.

There he learned that our goods and the Indian's annuities have been dumped on the banks of the Milk River. Rev. Reed hotfooted it back to Iowa without making any arrangement for the transfer of either the Indian annuities or the gvt. farm provisions, and the Crows have confiscated most everything. In the wake of Mr. Reed's dastardly execution of his duties we have given up all expectation of funds to pay Mr. Swift for his year's services. Therefore, Mr. Vail has come to an agreement with him that he shall take from the farm stock, at appraisal, for the amount due to him.

Yesterday Mr. Vail got out the fort cannon and fired a national salute, but we had no fireworks.

Thompson and Swift plan to leave for Bannack tomorrow.

We have gotten a few necessities from Johnny Grant's last train, so life is not quite so grim. The garden is producing a scant amount, with a great labor in bringing water into it. Perhaps, before the ground freezes, we, too, must leave. Husband is of a mind to join you in Bannack in hopes he can find employment there, (not, I hope, before I've harvested what little we have been able to raise in the garden). But I so want to be with you and we've seen such hard times that I hardly know I much care. If it be God's will, we shall be in each other's company soon.

'Tis late and I must be closing.

Affectionately,
Martha Jane

To think we put our lives in the hands of such a wretch as our Reverend Reed has turned out to be. To think it is in part a failing in my observations, my naivete if one must allow, that set us into such a situation. I am beside myself.

Swift and I commiserated over the dissolution of our trust in the Reverend. I could spit nails. I would have never believed a man of the cloth would prove a coward and a shirker to boot.

Fortunately, Swift managed to sell his six oxen at Johnny Grant's. There Thompson found a number of letters, including one from his brother in St. Louis, with information that he had sent six tons of goods by the *Shreveport* for him. They continued to Bannack to decide on a location for business, either here or at the newly discovered mines.

According to Swift, Thompson has been informed that he has letters awaiting his arrival at the Stinking Water, and they feel their star will soon fade if they're not off. I don't think Swift was here much over an hour. Having entered into business with Thompson, he dared not dally for fear of causing his partner distress.

I feel as if I could have told Swift about my condition. I think that's some kind of sin—to feel more comfortable with a near stranger than one's husband. But my feelings and thoughts are more like dark shadows than anything real, and I surmise, feelings are truly what I want to talk about. And my love is so grounded in his perception of real, I feel shy floundering before him. Swift is more a dreamer.

I think I'll put this heat to good use by making some of those crackers Mrs. Zoller suggested for me.

SUNDAY 26 JULY

HE LIVES, ALL GLORY TO HIS NAME;
HE LIVES, MY SAVIOR, STILL THE SAME;
WHAT JOY THE BLEST ASSURANCE GIVES:
I KNOW THAT MY REDEEMER LIVES! AMEN.

—*Samuel Medley, 1738–1799*

Thanks to Mrs. Zoller's crackers in my stomach, I have found a way for getting on with this infirmity, and that's a blessing I have needs to thank her for.

27 JULY

This morning the event my sister warned me of did indeed occur and I feel very shaky all over from it. Mrs. Zoller, her daughter Emma, Mrs. Dalton, her all too handsome daughter Matilda, and I went gooseberry picking. Emma and Matilda were working in a patch of berries below us. They were so busy chattering away at each other they did not notice us working our way down hill toward them. As we neared the girls, Matilda was saying, "Aren't you afraid of living so close to the Plumer's? She seems a dear and I've heard nothing but good of her, but him! I've heard he's a murderer that broke out of San Quentin and murdered another in doing so."

Dear Emma, bless her. She retorted hotly, "Rubbish! Rubbish and nonsense, that's just the idle gossip of a kind of people who are more entertained by it than by the truth."

At that moment, Matilda looked up, saw us, and her face flushed with her embarrassment. Wanting to ease the situation I said to them. "Thank you, Emma, for your noble defense." Turning to Matilda, I asked, "Do you, for one thoughtful moment, believe a God fearing woman such as I would marry a murderer? Having met and visited with me, do you, for one thoughtful moment, believe I could be duped by some handsome slick talking suitor?" The poor girl stuttered an apology. I almost felt sorry for her, but not for her red-faced mother. She's only passing on the gossip of her elders I'm sure, never the less, it's a hard thing to bear; this malignant maligning of my beloved.

Mrs. Dalton tried to apologize for the girl's behavior and I stopped her saying, "'Tis a hard and wild country. I'm certainly glad I do not have the responsibility of rearing children in this wild place."

I do not think it wise to tell my husband about this. He will know how much it upsets me and that will be unduly bothersome for him. Besides, they're the same ignorant couple who couldn't understand that Mr. Plumer was not the son of one Amos. Hardly of a caliber worth losing sleep over. No, better to keep busy. Next thing, I'll bake a gooseberry pie.

Noon today my Dearest arrived bearing a paper of trout along with the bucket of fresh drinking water from the town well. I'm thinking, fresh hot biscuits, fried potatoes, fish, and a pie on the supper table will make for a good time to talk about our expanding family.

27 July

Again I managed to keep my thoughts to myself. And indeed it was not hard as Mr. Plumer had a miner's meeting to attend and he ended up taking a late supper of over-cooked fish.

The Miner's Court of Bannack District directed a writ of execution to be issued by Judge Burchett in a suit by Moses Burris against John Ault. Ault is to turn over to Sheriff Plumer either monies or goods and chattels to cover the judgment against him in favor of Burris by August 3rd. If he doesn't comply with the order, the sheriff is to seize his property and sell it to the highest bidder, after properly advertising it of course.

According to Mrs. Zoller, who got her information from Mrs. Castner, who has a sister in Little Falls, Minnesota (the town where Ault has left his wife), Ault has all but abandoned his wife. He neither writes nor sends her money and the poor woman is about destitute.

29 July

Last night, after supper, I told my Beloved I was, well we were, on a path toward a larger family. I couldn't help but tell him I was scared. He said he thought a trip to the doctor was in order. He said his mother always had a doctor. He said Dr. Glick was as good as could be had in Bannack and he'd take me to him.

We talked a bit about the possibility of Martha Jane's imminent arrival. He thinks that would be good for me. I didn't really say it, but I'm not so sure. I do so truly enjoy running the household my way for a change, and she can be so bossy.

Would you believe he did not know I'd been sick? How can that be? I suppose leaving so early in the morning he never noticed, and usually by noon I am in control of the nausea. Now knowing, he expressed his sympathy and joy, not so much in words, but in the way he held me and the glow in his eyes. He says I needn't get up to serve him, being as he sleeps so little, it's no bother to him.

This morning he not only bid me stay abed, but brought me breakfast. I did not have the heart to tell him the very thought of food made me sicker, but sent him off to work with a smile and when I did arise I tossed it into the yard for the birds.

At noon he reported that Captain Higgins had arrived bringing States papers, letters, and a package from home. He said Vicksburg has been taken after a 47-day siege. If the Union forces can take Port Hudson, they will control the Mississippi River Valley.

His brother Willmot's letter is dated the 24th of May. He reports all is well in Maine. The crops are in and the weather favorable to date. The horse trade is holding steady, and he's working up another group of six year olds for the cavalry.

His mother sent us a sterling silver slice for a wedding present. I felt the fool not knowing the utensil was built for serving fish. Nevertheless, my ignorance hardly detracted from the beauty of the piece.

When I hear him talk of home I try to visualize a life there. He working with his brother, me with his mother and sister. I see candle light reflected in the polished wood paneling and lace curtains and fresh flowers on the table. I see us stitching and darning in the evening light. I see us walking on sand and can almost hear the waves breaking, but I cannot for the life of me smell it, as does my husband.

30 July

Mrs. Zoller and I have organized the respectable women of the town to help raise funds for the new jail. The last couple of days we have been baking pies. We have talked Mr. Plumer into auctioning them off to the highest bidder. Much to my dismay, he plans to hold it on

Sunday, that being the day the greater portion of the population is in town. Perhaps I'll see a bit more of him after the funds are gathered for the new jail.

Sunday 2 August

> I worship Thee, most gracious God,
> And all Thy ways adore;
> And every day I live,
> I seem to love Thee more.
>
> —*Frederick W. Faber, 1814*—

The auction went well, with all the business wives contributing pies. We were only fifty dollars short the moneys needed to have the jail built. Not to be out done, Madam Hall contributed the balance from her establishment. She said, "As a business woman, I just haven't time to bake pies. Nevertheless, I do want to contribute my share." Considering its source, I didn't think we should accept the money. Mr. Plumer said it was good money earned by honest, legal employment; therefore, we should not look a gift horse in the mouth.

3 August

Mr. Plumer stopped home with a letter from Sadie, then spent the better part of the day settling the Burris/Ault affair. As it came to pass, he had to hold an auction after all. Now Burris owns a quarter interest in Claim No. 9 West on the Dakota Lode.

Sadie tells me my dear brother is putting on some flesh, but is not the same man we knew. And she is beside herself, wondering what more she can do. I don't believe she's gotten my letters. She doesn't make any mention of my marriage, and even stressed as she is, I cannot believe she wouldn't say something if she knew. May God grant her the strength of stone, as it looks as if she's going to need it.

I spent the afternoon in writing letters to my family and in composing my first letter to Mrs. Plumer.

4 August

Mr. Plumer took me to see Dr. Glick today. He bade remove my hoops and lie on a miserable high bench. Once there, he proceeded to poke and prod my stomach in an altogether too familiar way, all the while, talking to husband as if I wasn't there. "When was she last visited by the female complaint?" He asked, as if Husband would know. "Does it normally come at regular intervals?" He continued to prod my stomach pressing wrinkles into my dress in the process. "Is there much pain?" To each question the Mr. would look to me and I would either nod yes or no, and in this way we continued as if I were some pumpkin. Then he had the gall to say, "Tiny as she is, you ought never have gotten her in a family way. I've seen women a damn sight bigger 'an her die abirthin'."

Husband asked him if he would take care of me during my confinement. He said he'd do what he could, but if I were his, he'd send me east to a doctor who was more familiar with the female side of medicine. Last one he delivered was to a fourteen year old, bigger than I, and he lost both of them. Of course, he added, he hadn't been called in until time for birthing was long past and the poor thing was nearly dead of blood loss by the time he was summoned. I have never been so humiliated. No wonder Martha Jane was so adamant in her refusal to see a doctor.

Long into evening husband and I talked about whether I should go east or stay, neither wanting to leave the other. We both agree the babe and I would be better served by going east. And, much as I wanted to resist the idea, even I have to admit it makes no sense for Husband to abandon his mines so long as they are producing such a fine return. He says at the rate they are being worked they will be finished by next fall. If we save the better share of our monies, by then we should enjoy enough to set up and furnish both a fine house and a business wherever we chose to locate.

That makes good sense, but I think we can manage on less, and he will be a success in any business venture in which he chooses to engage himself.

5 AUGUST

Again last night I dreamed of moths—giant moths banging themselves so hard against the chimney I thought they'd kill themselves and then I became the flame inside and I flickered and flinched each time they hit the glass. Then the glass cracked and I ineffectively tried to keep them out by placing my hands against the glass. Soon it was all smudged and grimy with soot in the cracks and handprints all over the glass. In frustration I struck out, breaking the glass and cutting my hands. The moths were then gone and my hands were bleeding. When I looked down at my hands, there I beheld a bloody, dead bird.

6 AUGUST

After I set the laundry to drying, I spent the morning composing a letter to Martha Jane. I told her everything. Well, I did not tell her how I felt about her bossing me always, but I did allude to the rest and I did ask for her advice. I do wish she and the little ones were here, perhaps not living in the same house, but at least in the same city. And when I answered Sadie's letter, I did not exactly state my condition, but I did tell her that the best doctor on this frontier was a drunk and I mentioned my desire to be near a competent doctor. This whole affair is a worrisome bother. The mails are anything but regular and the stages have no schedule. They seem to run when some fellow takes a notion to make a trip from Salt Lake to Bannack or Bannack to Fort Benton and that never until he has a full coach of travelers with desire to make the trip. I'm told that it's a much better situation this year than last. Evidently, last year no coaches were running.

SUNDAY 9 AUGUST

> WHEN OBSTACLES AND TRIALS SEEM
> LIKE PRISON WALLS TO BE,
> I DO THE LITTLE I CAN DO,
> AND LEAVE THE REST TO THEE.
>
> —*Frederick W. Faber, 1814–*

This afternoon I packed a picnic lunch. Then Husband and I walked upstream along the Grasshopper till we were out of range of the town's noise and had found a quiet and shady spot. There, on the banks of the creek, we spread a cloth and sat in the quiet to eat. For the moment it was like our wedding trip—filled with earth's most beautiful gifts of blue sky and green leaf and flitting bird and with the wonder of each other. For the moment I didn't even particularly mind the infernal flies and mosquitoes.

10 August

Mr. Plumer, sheriff, in response to miner's court orders, spent the better part of the day advertising and selling goods to settle a judgment. Mr. Plumer, husband, came home at noon to share a meal, then rubbed his wife's stiff shoulders before he returned to the work at hand. Today I feel like a petted kitten.

13 August 1863

Didn't yesterday end up in a mess! A few days ago D.S. Payne, U.S. Marshal of Idaho Territory, came from Lewiston. His business has been to estimate the population, its resources, and to redistrict the eastern portion of the territory so they might establish election precincts. The newly appointed U.S. Marshal is urging citizens to organize and promote the establishment of suitable counties and send representatives to the first legislature from the communities of Hell Gate, Benton, and the gold camps. He is also looking to establish a U.S. Marshal's office in this new eastern district. For some time there has been a Union League in Bannack, and Mr. Plumer is one of their members. I can hardly believe it, when they came looking for someone to support for the Marshal's office, without so much as a by-your-leave from me, he tossed his hat in the ring; worse they unanimously elected him! I'm so angry I could spit nails. Here we've been talking about leaving this hellish place and I've been dreaming of the East Coast, or home, or even southern California (now that the gold is gone and a civilization could be possible), but what does he do? He goes on building ties to this godforsaken place.

He said it was his understanding I would only be going east for the duration of my confinement and would return in the springtime. He added that I led him to believe I accepted the wisdom of remaining in the gold fields so long as the claims panned out. And I said it was my understanding he'd said the claims would be finished within a year, possibly two at best, therefore he would be able to follow within a reasonable time. Then he yelled at me. I have never heard him yell at anyone or anything, but he yelled at me. He yelled, "Are you daft, woman? Do you really believe I'd consent to being apart from you for two years? And the child—the child wouldn't even know me!"

For a moment I thought he was going to swear. But he did not. He pointed out that my sister and her family might be coming to town and that might change the way we viewed things. He thinks I should rely on her advice as to whether I should return east for the duration, she, having been through this, she, being the wise, the steady, the sensible one. Sensible, ha! She's the one who married a nineteen-year-old school teacher. I'm the one who waited for the real thing to come my way!

In the end, I promised I'd consult with my sister before making any decisions; he promised he would not accept the office should he be appointed and, in the event we decide I truly must go east for my confinement, he will sell out his properties here and join the child and me in the States come next fall.

I just know if I return after traveling east, we'll never get free of this place. Already I am filled with some strange dread of it, as if it shall become a nightmare that will haunt my dreams the rest of my life. Last week I told Mrs. Zoller that I felt as if the dust, the curses, and the continuous insect hum of this place would follow me forever. She said it was just my delicate condition, and that after my confinement I'd hardly even remember the strange moods and ideas that do now come over me. I hope she's right.

I write at this good table, beneath the fine light of a good kerosene lamp, inside the snug house my husband has provided for me. Husband is out on his evening rounds doing his part in making this town a better place. I've been so angry I have not written of the lemons he brought me yesterday. They came in on the latest train from Salt Lake City and came at a dear cost I'm sure. Their scent fills the air with sweetness and reprimands my churlish behavior. Dear God, forgive me.

14 August

This morning Husband settled some business between a couple of miners. Come lunchtime, my Love brought me a great bouquet of moss-flowers with a scent and a blossom like sweet-William, and in it were also bluer and glossier forget-me-nots than I've ever seen before. I filled the blue willow serving bowl with them and at the edges some of the flowers trailed all the way down to the table. I set the whole of the arrangement in the center of the table on a white linen runner where it charmed both myself and my husband. He said I, as do his mother and Rebecca, have the knack for dressing a room most beautifully.

I spent the day frying chicken and making potato salad and pies, three oatmeal and one lemon, for a social to be held tomorrow in honor of the completion of the new jail.

Sunday 16 August

I have no cares, O blessed Will,
For all my cares are Thine;
I live in triumph,
Lord, for Thou hast made
Thy triumphs mine.

—Frederick W. Faber, 1814–

What a crowd there was at the social! I felt most overwhelmed. As usual I never know how to make small talk. Mrs. Zoller thought I'd enjoy Deputy Stinson's wife as she is somewhat religious. Unfortunately, that's all we have in common. She, like her husband, are secesh, so what was there to exchange after God bless?

The very thought of talking to Mrs. Hall makes my knees bend, though much to my surprise I had a delightful conversation with her, what would one call him? Not husband. Lover? No, too lewd. Perhaps paramour. At any rate, he's an intelligent fellow, an engineer who shares my political persuasion. I don't know where he derived his reputation as a rough; in demeanor he is anything but. Perhaps it comes from his liaison with Mrs. Hall. What a strange combination!

And Mrs. Cavan, in spite of her youth, is so vivacious I wilt before her. Mrs. Burchett, for all I've met her before, is still in the political league with the Stinsons. Mrs. Arnold is pleasant enough, but she doesn't read. I should talk, I haven't read a word outside the covers of my Bible since my wedding. Truth is, I have only my Bible and the Sonnets from the Portuguese with me. Truth is, I do enjoy watching and listening to other people more than actually talking with them. Truth is, I had a good time.

The new jail is sturdy enough to hold the orneriest prisoner. Mr. Plumer's tidy little office in the back of Chrisman's store is within sight of the jail and, should the need arise, Chrisman has a good safe available for holding anything of value.

Mr. Chrisman treated me with the gentlest of respect. Best of all, he enjoyed my lemon meringue pie almost as much as my husband does.

18 August

Yesterday morning I picked wild gooseberries, service berries, and choke cherries with the Zoller family. I'm about thoroughly tuckered out with putting it all by, but don't I feel smug having lined the cupboard shelves with all those jams and syrups? It's a pity everything comes ripe at the same time.

I've saved out enough gooseberries for making pies tomorrow. And the bank on the opposite side of the Creek is covered with little blue, yellow, and white violet-like flowers. I think I should like some of them for Sunday's table.

19 August

What a shame it is for some folks that life's events never seem to fall right side up. When Bixby left the farm he came this way, selling his take from the farm and borrowing more to set himself up to work a claim. In the execution of a court judgment against our former laborer, Mr. Plumer had to sell at auction his goods as well as his interest in his claim. I've been told Bixby leaves town with but little more than an old broken down mule and the clothes on his back. Not a very fine accounting of nearly a year's labor, but better than most carry out on departure from this "Eldorado." Poor silent Bixby exited the town without leaving behind so much as a footprint.

In other business, the court sent my husband out to arrest Peter Horen, who has been charged with murder. Soon as he brought the man in, they held a trial, found him guilty, and ordered husband to have a gallows erected. Thus, the good man had to arrange for a gallows to be built. Mr. Horen asked if Mr. Plumer would act as power of attorney for him and they had to go through all that attendant rigmarole. I asked if Mr. Plumer thought him guilty. He replied it was not his duty to judge—only to see the law was carried out and that the accused had a fair trial. He said the trial was fair.

I told Husband I was grateful, now, that jail had been finished and I told him how I shudder to think I might have had to put up a convicted killer under my roof. He gave me such a weary look, then replied, "One of the deputies would have taken care of him." By the time supper ended he was so tired, for a moment, I thought he would call on one of his deputies to go about his regular evening round. Alas, he did not, and I burn the wick waiting for his return.

How can I subject this child who wakes to life within my sheltering body to this harsh reality? What imprint will the likes of hangings, loose talk, and looser women make on his presence? Truly, how far could the presence of my sister go to mitigate these circumstances? I see no way for us to remain in this place and be healthy.

20 August

Neither the Zollers nor myself joined the crowd in climbing the hill to the gallows. Mr. Zoller remained at his establishment while his clerks took a "holiday" to watch the hanging. Mrs. Zoller, her girls, and I held a prayer vigil for the soul of the condemned and for the souls of those who are led into temptation. Of course Husband, as sheriff, had no choice in the matter.

21 August

This afternoon the sum of Peter Horen's life was gathered, advertised, weighed, and by the accounting of one Henry Howland, was found to be worth $205. For that amount Mr. Howland took possession of an undivided one third interest in two mining claims below Stapleton Bar, one third interest in a claim on Grimms Bar, one third interest in one cabin, one wheelbarrow, eight sluices, and some mining tools.

SUNDAY 23 AUGUST 1863

> HE ALWAYS WINS WHO SIDES WITH GOD;
> TO HIM NO CHANCE IS LOST.
> GOD'S WILL IS SWEETEST TO HIM WHEN
> IT TRIUMPHS AT HIS COST.
>
> —*Frederick W. Faber, 1814*–

The Mr. is again at a miner's meeting and while there he will tally the record of Horen's existence.

I try to read Elizabeth Browning and I wonder if she had children. I think not.

When I close my eyes, the specter of Horen's gallows is imprinted there. I need to leave this place, lest I go mad.

Mrs. Zoller says I will not be so sick after quickening. But that will not be until, in the least, another month has passed; equal to forever, by my calculations.

24 AUGUST

Husband brought me the finest piece of calico with which to make myself a dress. Scattered, in bunches and singles, all across it are lovely blue forget-me-nots, and the background is a rich brown. I am too tired after the laundry to do anything with it today, but tomorrow is another tale.

26 AUGUST

Today we have received letters from both Martha Jane and Joe Swift. Each delivered by a different messenger. They are as welcome to us as the sun shining in these crisp blue, blue skies. My dear husband gave me Swift's letter to read while he washed for lunch.

FORT BENTON
19 AUGUST 1863

Dear Mr. and Mrs. Plumer,

It is with pleasure I remember my few moments at your house in Bannack. When I return, I do hope we shall again play a good game of charades. Some of my fondest memories are of the time we all spent together last fall on the Sun River.

After leaving Bannack we camped that night on the Rattlesnake, I suspect on the same ranch Plumer has an interest in. The night after found us at Beaverhead Rock, and we rode into the new mines the next day. There must be at least 2,000 people, some gathered into three towns, others strung out here and there along the Stinking Water. All things considered, we concluded we'd get a better bargain on a building in Bannack than over here. In the end, we'd do as well setting up shop over there. I, of course, had the added incentive of reunion with you.

We kept one horse and traded the most of our possessions for three yoke of cattle and a wagon, and next day we set out for the Milk River to recover our goods. We were told that a shorter route could be had by keeping to the east side of the mountains. There was one hitch, no wagon had ever been taken over this trail.

We kept to the east side of the mountains all the way. After crossing a bridge over the Stinking Water we followed down river till we forded the Jefferson, then we struck up a creek. At the head of this creek we ran our wagon into a canyon so narrow that we were forced to unyoke our cattle, drive them out by the side of the wagon, and then draw it out backward until we could turn around. We finally found a very steep hill over which we took our wagon, but had to attach two pair of cattle behind the wagon to hold it back as we descended the far side. We were glad enough to make camp when, following down a little stream, we came out on a rich bottom, the same which Thompson followed when they made their discovery last fall.

At the crossing of this stream we met four men on horseback. They had come from the Milk River, having been left there by the steamer, and were heading for the Stinking Water.

Our trail led us to the top of the divide, which we crossed. Soon, following down a little creek, we ran into a nest of beaver dams. The sides of the mountain were so steep that we saw no way of taking a wagon along them. The bottomland was overflowed by reason of the succession of dams. After much head scratching, we cut a long pole and fastened it across the wagon. By way of one holding the end of the pole while the other drove the oxen, we kept the wagon from over turning. A hard day's work brought us to Prickly Pear Creek.

In the morning we found the camp of some miners Thompson knew. I wanted to forge on, but Thompson insisted on trading yarns with his pals for three long days.

Late in the evening, after leaving the camp, we came upon Silver Creek and the Mullan Road. In the night, one Warren Witcher came into our camp. Next morning, Thompson tied his pony to Witcher's wagon and rode off, Witcher's mules stepping out smartly.

Three days later, I caught up with Thompson at the government farm. Witcher had gone on with his team to Benton; Thompson pleaded poor health and, after a brief visit with the Vails, I, too, pushed on for Benton. When I reached the fort, Witcher's goods had arrived. I helped load his wagon and a friend of his, who plans to ride out this afternoon, promises to deliver my letter as soon as he reaches Bannack.

Tomorrow I'll start the team toward Cow Island to facilitate the retrieval of our goods.

Until we meet again I remain
Affectionately Yours,
Joseph Swift

After reading Swift's letter, I traded it for the yet unopened one I'd been saving, my sister's letter.

SUN RIVER
21 AUGUST 1863

Dearest Sister,

Yesterday, we received your letter of the 6th. Because of the nature of your concerns and the need to post this response as quickly as possible, I shall be brief. I have talked your "situation" over with Mr. Vail and we think you had best return to Iowa. You know Sadie and Daniel will welcome you and will see that you have the best care. We believe it is the better answer to your problem.

I don't believe anyone has ever told you the circumstance of Mother's death. As you know she, like you, was quite small. She died with her fourth child. I did not know this until I was told by sister Sarah, some-time after I married. I do not think this in itself is cause for alarm. After all, she did successfully give birth three times before she was called. Even so, it is not wise to take chances. Under the circumstances, even I would seek a reputable doctor's help.

I cannot tell you how I wish I were with you. Do you remember how I used to hold you when you were but eight years old and mother so recently gone? I held you then and I'd hold you again if only I could.

We have sent word to Agent Reed asking permission to leave his employ as we have neither received last year's wages, nor provisions for the year to come. As you well know, due to this year's extreme drought there is no river traffic—no reasonable way we can return our whole family to the States. Therefore, as soon as we receive word from the Reverend, we will repair to Bannack for the winter. At that, we cannot be there till early in September.

My dearest, know how much we love you and know you are in our every prayer.

Your Devoted Sister,
Martha Jane

P.S. Mr. Thompson was here for three days before heading for Benton and plans to return on the morrow. This letter is going off today with a fellow heading straight for the Grasshopper. I just want you to know we haven't whispered a word of anything to Thompson. He's a dear in many ways, but as you well know, he's such an old gossip.

Loving you, Martha Jane

I handed the letter to my husband. He read the letter, and for a second time I saw him weep. When at last he looked up he said, "Then you must go. I can bear to be without you for a circumscribed time, not a lifetime."

We left our lunch uneaten.

27 AUGUST

Today I packed my clothes, that I might be ready for the next stage traveling east. We are allowed to carry up to 25 pounds of luggage on board the stage. I will take a small trunk, tho' God knows I've not enough personals to fill even that. I suspect what I'll be carrying will be 5 pounds of clothing and 20 pounds of gold. We've heard rumors of road agents that frequent the trail between Bannack and Salt Lake; therefore, Husband will be carrying the rest in his saddle bags, this being a perfect occasion for transporting our gold out. We shall exchange it for notes in Salt Lake. Best of all, my beloved shall ride alongside the coach as far as Salt Lake. I am surprised at myself. I'm beginning to wonder if, perhaps, I'm becoming an addict to adventure.

28 August

The new dress is almost finished. It has a square neck and bell shaped sleeves. Husband says he'll buy me a sun parasol and a bonnet to match, when we reach Salt Lake.

30 August 1863

> Plenteous grace with Thee is found,
> Grace to cover all my sin;
> Let the healing streams abound;
> Make and keep me pure within.
> Thou of life the Fountain art,
> Freely let me take of Thee:
> Spring Thou up within my heart,
> Rise to all eternity. Amen.
>
> —*Charles Wesley, 1707–1788*

This day we savored sweet, walking arm and arm above the town, beyond its sound and dust. How precious time becomes when the morrow looms a dark unknown.

31 August

We have word that the Salt Lake Stage is due in Bannack on Sept. 3rd. When Husband came home with the news, I hardly knew whether to laugh or to cry. I snapped at him, "I suppose that makes you happy doesn't it?"

He was so shocked. "Wife!" he said, "Dear woman, you know I've never wanted you to go."

I can't believe I said that. I don't know what's wrong with me. All I can do is weep. I do not want to live in this godforsaken town. I do not want to raise children here. I do not want to be alone. I do not want to leave this country without seeing my dear sister—without kissing my dear little ones one more time. I am distraught, and haven't an idea how to smooth it out.

This afternoon I took my sewing to Mrs. Zoller's and, while sewing the last of the buttons on my new dress, I told her of our plans. I could not bear for her to know about my earlier irrational outburst. But I did ask her to tell anyone who might ask that I've gone to visit relatives, which, to be sure, is hardly a stretch of the truth.

She has insisted on our taking supper with them tomorrow and says she shall miss me terribly. By the tear in her eye, I do believe her. I told her my sister would be arriving soon and she would enjoy her company as much as mine.

Mrs. Zoller has been my only friend here. I am the more to blame for that. If I were to remain, I should have cultivated the friendship of more women. But staying was never a piece of my vision for our future.

1 September

When my good husband came in to lunch he was most beside himself. He began talking before his lunch was placed before him. It seems this morning Thompson came limping into town on shank's mare. I'm not just sure why he was afoot, but Mr. Plumer is greatly disgusted with the fool. Over lunch he related Thompson's story. After a long lament on the rigors and the loneliness of the trail, the poor quality of the feed along the trail, the high price of corn at Benton, and his fears of the Indians who he says "are quite ugly along the route," Thompson launched into a long story of the wonderful men he met at Cottonwood who took him in and cosseted him for the duration of the trip to Bannack.

"Thompson claims the shopkeeper at the Cottonwood store told him it was not safe to travel alone and turned him toward a party of 12, camped a mile or so below, who were waiting to find a guide to take them to Bannack. He said this shopkeeper told him they seemed to be nice fellows and were from Lewiston, or some place on the west side.

"Their spokesman informed him that one of their men had a lame back and could not ride. Thompson offered to exchange with the party and let him ride in his cart whilst Thompson would ride the fellow's horse. After a short conference, they fell in with his proposition and invited him to stay with them until the next morning and then make a start. Finding his own company wanting, he was only too glad to oblige. He said, 'They treated me like royalty, neither permitting me to cook nor even take care of my horse.'

"'Lucky you.' I replied contemptuously. I'm thinking, when one man woos another that blatantly he's up to no good.

"Taking no notice of my shortness, he continued gaily, 'What a small world this is. I have been traveling these past four days in the company of your close friends, a Yale man, Dr. Howard, and his companion, James Romaine.'

"In California, I spent a good deal of time putting the companions of those men in prison. They belong to the lowest order of cutthroats and robbers in existence! Hell will be to pay now! I told

Thompson as much and I also let him know they were no friends of mine. I said he need not associate with them any more than he chose."

Would you believe, he tried to argue with Husband? Like a petulant child, Thompson said, "But they claimed close friendship with you and they are of such agreeable manners and a Yale graduate in their midst! They are such educated men."

My dear man ranted, "Yale! Educated! Educated by the ease of working gullible Thompsons! Sometimes I think there are people who will believe anything if somewhere in their tiny minds they think the teller has something they might gain."

My husband tends toward the disposition of a stoic, thus, I have never before heard him rage against a fellow man. I placed my hands on his shoulders to give him comfort and pleaded, "do eat your lunch."

"My dear woman," he said, patting my hand with his. "I am almost glad you are leaving this place. You are right in your assessment of this country as uncivilized, but you have no idea how much further civilization can degringolade when men become so full of themselves they do not know their limitations—perhaps, cannot know they have need of limitation. These are the men who enable evil to win the balance for the day."

"Ah, my Beloved," I answered, "it is only for the day." And, I continued lightly, "our tomorrows will be lived in more settled places."

Idyll's End

7 SEPTEMBER 1863

We are stopped for the night at a road house near the Snake River. A great number of pilgrims are camped here, waiting for the ferry to cross. Husband has gone to see who's about, I to work on my journal.

Since leaving Bannack, I've spent five God-awful days jostled and jounced by this open-air, springless "stagecoach." And all the while I've been unable to keep a thing down, excepting the salaretus biscuit and tea, and, of the tea, none but the tea we've brought from home. I have no idea what goes into the swill that goes by that name at these fledgling coachline eateries.

We've been traveling through spectacular country, mountain meadows crisscrossed by wooded groves of cottonwood and aspen, red rocks, and snowcapped mountains. Often the trail tracks near rushing crystal waters with names like Black Tail Deer Creek, Little Sage Creek, Red Rock Creek, Dindsy's Springs, Dry Creek, Camas

Creek, and Market Lake (so named because there are so many wild water fowls here that everyone who stops is assured of fresh meat.) The lake is fed from some underground cracks in the lava beds.

The Fire River is the source of the Snake River's head. It's a deep swift river, with a treacherous under-current and flows between craggy bluffs, but its waters are clear, cold, and pure and contain many mountain trout. Here at the Snake are camped numerous freight trains heading for East Bannack, the Idaho gold mines, the Oregon coast, as well as trains coming down from the mines to pick up provisions for the winter trade. The country we've traveled through has been as spectacular as the coach has been miserable. It's a lousy time to be traveling light headed.

This is our fifth night sheltered in a road house. There are five of us on the "coach" and of course the driver. All seven of us have been sleeping on bare dirt floors at the station houses. At least each night there's been a warm fire and my Beloved's arms. Thus far, the stations have been little more than hovels and the food nothing to write home about—the best spread for bread or biscuit has been bacon grease. We've come about 150 miles, and the finest thing on this trip comes each time we stop. Mr. Plumer dismounts, takes my hand, and assists me down. In the process, I always end up in his arms, my head resting in the hollow of his chest, the indentation between his shoulder and his clavicle seems to have been created with the shape of my head in mind. I do wish he would return. Supper's being served and, though I can't partake, I sorely hope he will not miss it.

The morning of the 2nd, on our way home from the stage station where we'd gone to purchase my ticket, we met Thompson. Mr. Plumer was into a conversation with one of the miners when Thompson came at me, hands outstretched and gushing like an old woman, "Ah, my dear, dear Electa, how are you?" He squeezed my faintly proffered fingers much too tight and the question begged no answer. "I suppose your faithful husband has apprized you of the band of cutthroats I so innocently led into town yesterday? Lucky me, he showed me how to prepare for the worst and to protect myself. I never should have told them I had a large shipment on its way into town. Your friend, my faithful young helper, Joseph Swift, has gone to the Milk River to meet with the packers with whom I have contracted with to deliver my goods here."

"When I last talked to Mr. Swift," I interjected testily, "I was put under the impression that the two of you were in partnership?"

"Technically, that would be correct. But surely you are aware, we're operating primarily on my good credit and very little cash from him." Changing the subject he asked, "Have you heard from your sister?" He awaited no reply. "The poor, poor woman. In the absence of the steamers, they are indeed in dire straits. Mr. Vail and I were able to keep the farm in game while I was there, but how long can one subsist on game? I'm sure they're on their way as we speak. But as they say, 'Tis an art that needs practice, of that there's no doubt, but 'tis worth it, this fine art of doing without.' At any rate, I'm sure you can look forward to her company soon."

I blurted, "I doubt that." I was so irritated with his smug, know-it-all attitude that I nearly stamped my foot.

"Oh, yes, yes, yes, my dear. I just saw her. I took my 'Go-devil' from there on the 22nd, was at Dearborn the 23rd, Morgan's Ranch the 24th, and Little Blackfoot on the 25th, having crossed the Rockies the 11th time. Fancy that? Eleven times in the span of one year. She says they'll be arriving in Bannack yet this month. So you see my dear, you shall indeed see her soon."

"Oh, no, no, no, my dear. We've just purchased my stage ticket east. I plan to leave tomorrow to visit relatives in Iowa. Mr. Plumer's so busy these days with his duties as sheriff, his mines and all, fall seems a good time for me to go. He plans to come after me later." Dumbfounded, Thompson staid rooted while I nudged the Mr.

"Husband," I said teasingly, "Do you plan to escort me home, or are we to stand about the street jawing all morning?" Husband and I had a good giggle thinking on the dumb shock that decorated Thompson's face.

Waiting for my husband, I am reminded of the many times I've kept an eye out, waiting to see him, face turned toward home, striding across the Yankee Flat bridge. Here, wagon trains are backed up for miles and waiting to cross the river on the ferry. I cannot look at these pilgrims and not see in them their future: The women, bent over fireplaces that don't draw, trying to keep house in hovels with packed dirt floors, trying to survive the endless drudgery. And the men . . . the last time I crossed the Yankee Flat bridge I thought, I shall never again either see rough clad men with long hair and flowing beards digging for bedrock, bending over barrow loads of earth, heaving pay dirt into sluice boxes, nor shall I ever again have to endure the sounds of their cursing, the dust of their working, or the smells of their unwashed living. It seems a long time past, we last crossed that bridge; even so, unwilled, unwilling, I am reminded of it again.

Yonder comes my husband. A better thing to attend to than this journal.

Would you believe? Here we are in the midst of nowhere yet Mr. Plumer returned saying, "We've been invited to take supper with one of the families awaiting a ferry to cross the Snake. I suspect the family is rather well off, having with them a serving girl and several 'lesser' family members to help turn their cross-country trek into something more like an outing. The patriarch, Mr. Edgerton, has recently been appointed Idaho Territory's Supreme Court Justice."

"Mr. Edgerton!" I exclaimed! "Mr. Sidney Edgerton?"

"You know him?"

"Personally, no. But I hardly think there could be two. If he's from Ohio, he's an old Free Soiler turned Republican, and on that ticket elected Representative to Congress by merit of his claim to fame as having been the prosecuting attorney in the shortest murder trial ever held in the States, having tried, sentenced, and hung a man in a matter of hours and that on circumstantial evidence alone. I can but wonder what kind of chicanery he used to convince a man like Lincoln to appoint him to any office, let alone that of Supreme Court Justice."

"Politics makes for strange bedfellows. Probably lost his bid for reelection and Lincoln rewarded him for his support."

"God be praised he's heading for Lewiston, not Bannack. You can not trust those stiff-necked legal men from Ohio. I fear them more than I fear a stray bullet from your fellow miners."

"That aside, I'd still like to find out what makes him tick. Besides, his young daughter, Mattie, saw you alight from the coach and desires to meet you."

"You know I am discomforted to be with those I find disagreeable, and I am most travel weary. Please send my regards if you must, but tell them true, I am indisposed."

"I wish you could find it in you to come. I'll not tarry late."

"Do watch your back, my love, and this time next year will find us a whole family living in a civilized country."

If I thought I felt weary before, now I know, 'twas but a trifling thing.

8 September

After leaving the Snake River we managed to make jig time. At Lander's Crossing we were treated to a good tea and bread with real butter. We stopped for the night on the far side of the Bear River, having taken the ferry across. Yesterday was the first day of the trip I've been served food I could keep down. We reached Salt Lake City mid-morning and found a fine hotel with every comfort one could ask for. We've washed away the grime from our travels and sent out our laundry. While Mr. Plumer exchanges gold for notes, I am taking tea in our room, which looks out over a nicely planned town square. What a joy it is to be in a nearly civilized place. What a joy it is to be forever off that miserable coach.

Salt Lake City is a bit raw, but laid out so fine and graced by the sight of women and children on the streets as one would in any normal, respectable town. And what a joy to see the women in fine summer garb pulled over a full compliment of petticoats and hoops, as opposed to the homely calico of the frontier! Since our arrival, I have feasted my eyes on matrons in nankeen dresses with full waists, short puffed sleeves, low necks, and 22 buttons up the back, as well as young girls in numerous petticoats and pantalets reaching to their ankles. Even the young lads are scrubbed and combed like gentlemen. And yet I keep having this disturbing thought that something is unfinished. No. Missing. The trees perhaps? No. I close my eyes and on my lids scenes of the old line girls in their gaudy dress stroll up and down the Bannack boardwalk, clatter along on horseback, sitting sidewise as if glued to their mounts. Through a window, I catch a glimpse of a fancy lady lounging in a diaphanous dressing gown, making smoke-rings in the air. What kind of bedevilment, I wonder, brings these crude scenes to mind?

This afternoon we plan to do a bit of shopping, purchase my ticket, and send a telegram to Daniel. And won't they be surprised to hear I'm coming?

Our pending separation fills me with anxiety. I hardly know how I am to tear myself from this dashing husband, but I remind myself that in good part my pleasure is come from our distance from Bannack, its noise, its filth and not least the demands it puts on my husband. For the sake of our children, I must not weaken, I must not turn back now. Dear God make me strong and help me cherish each moment.

ECHO CANYON . . . 9 PM, 9 SEPTEMBER 1863

It is a good thing the coach left on time. Had we been together another moment, I'm afraid my resolve would have altogether broken down. As it is, I've too much of his parting image foremost in my mind, it's thankful I was to be wearing a veil to hide my tears.

This Concord Coach is a marvel of comfort and we are making good time. The stations are 10 to 15 miles apart, according to convenience to water, etc. A relay of well-groomed horses is already harnessed and waiting when we arrive. It takes but a few minutes to make the exchange and unload passengers, cargo, and mail, and the drivers are changed every 25 to 30 miles. Most get out to stretch and some purchase a bite to eat and either coffee or tea, at least at the home stations. Most of the stations between leave much to be desired. After we left off a couple of passengers at Kimball's, I had room enough to take out my crochet hook and yarn. I have begun a blanket for the next family member and there was yet room to work when another passenger joined us at Weaver.

We are stopped at a beautiful place for supper, Echo Canyon. Truth is, my fellow passengers are eating supper, I'm staying with tea, fruit, and some crackers from the tin we put together yesterday. We are to have a change of drivers at this place. This is one of the home stations I mentioned earlier.

I have not yet had occasion to use my new parasol, but I'm putting the cunning pencil and pad Husband presented to me on parting to good use. When I am not actively using it, I am admiring the apple blossoms embossed on its protective silver cover and the linkage of the silver chain that secures the two together.

Fort Bridger. . . 5 am, 10 September 1863

Last night the rhythm of the movement of the coach became such that I was well able to sleep. Some passengers got off to spend the night on the dirt floor of the Quaking Aspen Springs station. Even though I can certainly afford such, I feel safer in the coach and fully intend to remain here till I reach Omaha. Here at the fort are many trains backed up waiting to show their papers and take an oath of allegiance. We are stopped for breakfast and to change drivers. The coffee here smells good, not like the bitter chicory served up at some of the stops. So if I've a mind to have some and I rather think I do, I'd better say good-bye and hand my letters over to the man in charge.

Rock Springs . . . 9 pm, 10 September 1863

Thus far the only other passengers have been male. We traded two civilians for two military at Fort Bridger. Their conversation is quite boring, all military strategy and who should have done what, or not done such and such, as the case may be. I keep behind my veil and pay attention to my crocheting, thus they hardly know I'm rocking along in the same coach.

The station here at Rock Springs has walls of stone with loopholes every 12 feet. It is 60 feet long and 25 feet wide. All in all it's quite charming and the food smells wonderful. They're serving roast elk, potatoes, vegetables, real butter, and fresh milk. At last, I have an appetite to dine.

I've made a good beginning on the blanket and am quite able to sleep, while the coach lumbers along, with the knowledge that even in slumber I'm making progress.

I wonder where Husband is on his way back to Bannack and do hope the snows have not reached the mountain passes yet.

Time I close that I might stretch and board. I try to be one of the first on so that I may regain my niche at the far corner on the back seat of the coach.

DUCK LAKE . . . 9 PM, 11 SEPTEMBER 1863

Some of the men slept on top of the coach last night. Just stretched out prone, strapped themselves down, and proceeded into the land of nod. A bit too chilly for my taste, even if I were a man. But it did give me room to curl up on the bench with my pillow and my comforter. Would you believe they're still at it? The military men, that is, talking military strategy even at the table. The facts I glean from their chatter seem thus: About the 25th of June, Jeb Stuart's cavalry began a raid on the rear of the Union Army. By the 28th, Meade replaced Hooker as commander of the Potomac Army. On the last day of June, Buford led the Union cavalry into Gettysburg. The next day, part of Heth's infantry division of Northern Virginia clashed with Buford's cavalry. Mid-morning Reynolds' unit arrived to stop the Confederate advance, and he was killed in the conflict. Early that same afternoon, Ewell's corps and General Lee arrived and broke the Union lines. What Union forces were left retreated through the town to the cemetery.

One of the men (I believe he's one of those captured Confederate soldiers allowed to go free on condition they "protect the frontier") felt the South could have won the war right then and there if Ewell had followed Lee's orders to attack the cemetery, as it is situated on a hill. The next morning Longstreet attacked the Union on the left of the Cemetery and they fought until dark, when Ewell's corps and later Stuart's cavalry and Pickett's infantry division joined in the assault. All the next day they fought with great losses on both sides, but the general consensus of the men at the table is that the South was winning. On the morning of the 3rd of July, the 12th Union Corps attacked and retook trenches on one of the hills, and in the afternoon the Cavalry blocked Stuart's advance toward the Union rear. All afternoon the Union held off an attack at its center and eventually repulsed the Confederate army. On the 4th, the Confederates retreated to Virginia. That same day, Vicksburg surrendered to Ulysses Grant's Army. I'd say hooray for the Union victory if the men didn't feel so sure that the end is nowhere in sight and that each side will fight unto its death.

It's a good thing I had no mind to eat in this place, as it's already time to fold up and board.

Sage Creek . . . Noon, 12 September 1863

The stage driver invited me to ride atop from Pine Grove (our last stop) to Sage Creek. It made for a pleasant change and gave me good cause to use my new sun parasol. The world does look brighter and wider from the top. It is a 10-mile jog, and we made it in little more than one hour.

Earlier, the men continued their "discussion" and I discerned that in mid-July there were draft riots in New York City. I'm not sure how they were put down, nor quite what the issue of contention was. As de Tocqueville says, American soldiers are the best paid and fed servicemen in the world.

Most of this country is as dry and dreary looking as Bannack. And no place has invited me to stay.

Fort Halleck . . . 9 pm

A telegram from Sadie awaited me at the fort. She said, "Looking forward to your arrival. Post us as to the date. Will pick you up at Fisher House." I will telegraph back when I reach Council Bluffs. We are yet on schedule.

Our soldiers also reported that on the 14th of July, the Confederates re-crossed the Potomac to Virginia and on July 18th, a Union assault on Fort Wagner in South Carolina was spearheaded by 54th Massachusetts infantry. Black soldiers were used, and the Rebs were repulsed with heavy losses. Even the Copperheads on board praised the bravery and skill of the black soldiers.

Virginia Dale . . . 1 pm 13 September 1863

I staid on the coach and slept through the breakfast stop. Can you believe I even sleep through the driver's blaring on his horn for the two minutes or so he takes to wake up the station boys and have his teams on the ready. I believe I can now claim fame to being a seasoned traveler since I am at present so steady, as to fear neither Indians nor strangers we come upon along the road.

Sometime in the morning we switched to mules, as the road has become quite sandy in places and I'm told the mules, though not quite so fast, have more endurance for it.

We are "Nooning" and changing drivers late today and everyone is quite weary.

The road from Elk Mountain past Medicine Bow had my fellow passengers complaining. Indeed the road is almost as bad as anything I've seen—nothing but rocks, and large ones at that. I mustn't complain, at least this stage has fine springs and that is more than I could say about the first leg of my journey. Now the sandbed is more comfortable for us, but not for the poor beasts that do our work.

At Fort Halleck, I heard that last summer 34 mules valued at $68,000 were taken by Indians. That sounds a bit inflated to me, but I suppose when the government is reimbursing, the loss becomes most dear.

Am about halfway finished with the blanket. It makes my time spent in travel seem productive.

Big Bend . . . 1 pm 14 September 1863

Took tea at Childs this morning at 5. Took most of the time at the station untangling my hair and washing up. They had a nice little room for such and, in spite of the dirt floors and lack of real windows, it was kept up quite nicely. The buildings at this station are rectangular and frame built with vertical timber siding.

This morning the men were talking about the elections they had voted in and the whole process sounded disgusting to me. One of the men said that "his" party was sopping the opposition as they came through the lines with sponges of blood, and the other laughed and said he remembered an election where the Pug Uglies stood on either side of the entrance to the polling booth and interrogated the voters as to their party preference. If they were not satisfied they made them run a gauntlet of awls four to five inches long and sharp. I do not for the life of me find it amusing and, for the moment, I'm thankful that as a woman I do not have to endure such nastiness.

KELLY'S . . . 5 AM 15 SEPTEMBER 1863

Last night's supper at Freemont's Orchard put an end to the men's infernal singing of their anti dried–apple pie song. We were served our choice of either fresh stewed pears or fresh apple pie. A fine end to a great meal of roast Buffalo, sweet corn, snap beans, sliced tomatoes, new potatoes, fresh biscuits, and real coffee. Even so, as I fell into sleep the words of the song kept rattling about my brain and continue to do so.

> ABHOR! DETEST! DESPISE!
> ABOMINATE DRIED-APPLE PIES;
> I LIKE GOOD BREAD; I LIKE GOOD MEAT,
> OR ANYTHING THAT'S GOOD TO EAT;
> BUT OF ALL POOR GRUB BENEATH THE SKIES
> THE POOREST IS DRIED-APPLE PIES.
> GIVE ME A TOOTHACHE OR SORE EYES
> IN PREFERENCE TO SUCH KIND OF PIES.
>
> THE FARMER TAKES HIS GNARLIEST FRUIT,
> 'TIS WORMY, BITTER, AND HARD TO BOOT;
> THEY LEAVE THE HULLS TO MAKE US COUGH,
> AND DON'T TAKE HALF THE PEELINGS OFF;
> THEN ON A DIRTY CORD THEY'RE STRUNG,
> AND FROM SOME CHAMBER WINDOW HUNG:
> AND HERE THEY SERVE A ROOST FOR FLIES
> UNTIL THEY'RE READY TO MAKE PIES.
> TREAD ON MY CORNS, OR TELL ME LIES,
> BUT DON'T PASS TO ME DRIED-APPLE PIES.

There! Perhaps I now have the infernal thing out of my mind.

Frémont Springs . . . 5 am 16 September 1863

Mid-morning yesterday, at Dennisons, I was able to replenish my supply of fruit and crackers.

And last night at Julesburg we were treated to a fine turkey supper with mashed potatoes, squash, pickled beets, cucumbers in sour cream, and real bread.

According to the proprietor, about three weeks ago a fellow and his two sons came by driving a flock of over 500 turkeys. They said they had purchased the birds in Iowa and Missouri and were aiming for Denver. Their wagon was loaded with shelled corn and drawn by a team of six. The birds grazed on grasshoppers as they traveled during the day, and at night they roosted all over the wagon and on the ground around it. The boys said they had an easy time driving them so long as the wind was favorable, but when it came from the west, it was almost impossible. The proprietor purchased a dozen of them and has those left fenced behind the stable.

The buildings here are nearly square in shape. They're built of cedar logs and have roofs made of poles, brush, hay, and earth. When we build our home I do believe I'd like it to be of either brick or stone and two stories high. And of course a coach house for the buggy, horse, and milch cow. I dream of trees with great girth and a big garden and chickens. Perhaps I dream too much.

I am so tired this morning I think I shall have no trouble going back to sleep. After the fine supper last night I staid up much too long crocheting by candle light and listening to the gentlemen while away the miles with their singing.

Fort Kearny . . . 7 am 17 September 1863

Came into Willow Island a little before nine and took supper.

Last evening the sun set the richest red I've ever seen. The air was cool and still and we watched a great flock of blue herons flying overhead. Their cry haunted my dreams, and in the night when I woke I was reminded of the soft trills and stops a young brave breathed through his courting flute one evening on the Sun River.

We arrived at the fort at five this morning. My coach went on to Atchison, and the one from Saint Mary's is not due in till seven so must wait. I've had plenty of time to wash up and unknot my hair. I spent a portion of yesterday letting out the seams in the waist of my lovely new dress. To think I've only worn it twice and already it doesn't fit! I want to be wearing it when brother comes to fetch me.

All is going as well as can be expected on a trip of this sort.

EAGLE ISLAND . . . 7 AM
18 SEPTEMBER 1863

Supper at Grand Island last evening. Tea and crackers for breakfast. I've a mind to finish letting out my dress today if I have room to work on it in the coach. We are scheduled to arrive at Omaha tomorrow. 'Tis been a much faster, if more uncomfortable, trip back than the one into the wilderness.

LEWIS, IOWA . . . 20 SEPTEMBER 1863

By the time we came into Omaha, wasn't I tired, grubby, and out of sorts? Originally I had planned to stop over there, but I took it into my head that nothing would do but that I find myself a bed on the other side of the Missouri. Thus, I did not so much as stop for tea come lunch time, but got myself and all my earthly belongings ferried across the river and safely ensconced at the Pacific House. While making arrangements for the last leg of my journey, I received a telegram from Sadie. "Pleased you're coming home. Will fetch you home from Anamosa. Send word of arrival date." I sent word back, "Meet me at Fisher House on the 24th." Actually, I plan to be there on the 23rd. But first, I do want to freshen up, finish my dress, and indulge in a good night's sleep. And I can't begin to capture in pencil what a wonder fresh clothes, bathing, and a good night's rest can do to putting a fresh face on the world. I took tea in my room before day break and watched the sun come up on the city. I still think Council Bluffs is the jewel of prairie cities. Before I repaired to my room last night I made arrangements with the Western Stage Company to take me through to Anamosa. They picked me up at the door of the Hotel and shall leave me off at that of Fisher House. We are stopped for lunch and I am taking my usual tea, which is just as well as the food looks old and greasy. I yet cannot keep down much besides tea and crackers prior to the evening meal. And sometimes even that will not sit well.

After we crossed the river the scenery immediately changed. Gone the rattlesnakes and soap weed, soaring eagles, and prickly pear, in its place are trees and sweet water streams, charming houses and cultivated gardens. And green, so much green, I'd forgotten how much I'd missed it!

Yesterday, a light rain fell, not enough to soften the road, just enough to settle the dust, and isn't this a pleasant trip? This company changes its horses nigh on every 12 miles and the horses then return to their home stable. The men make the change in jig time, about six minutes, so there's hardly time to leave the coach.

Lewis sits on the east side of the East Nishnabotna River and it's a charming cluster of neat clapboard houses.

ADAIR . . . EVENING

Supper here is strictly fried, fried, fried—eggs, potatoes, ham, and liver. The latter looks like shoe leather. I'll subsist on tea and writing, thank you.

For the first time on this trip I shared the coach seat with another woman. This woman of great girth boarded at Lewis Atlantic and is traveling to Desmoines where she is going to visit a daughter who is married to a carriage maker for this Western Stage Company. She tells me that Desmoines is the headquarters for the company and that they do a good business building coaches.

She warns me that a body can count on poor fare in any establishment that lays out pies, cakes, and preserves. I almost laughed aloud thinking, "Lady if you only knew the places I've been and the food I've seen."

We have been traveling through the prettiest country. It's fair, flat, and broken by lovely stands of trees with stretches of corduroy road over the sloughs and bridges over the larger streams. Every few miles the country seems to have been civilized with a lovely cluster of buildings, and in spite of goodly stretches of unclaimed land, much is under proper cultivation. Nevertheless, she claims that the charming view the countryside offers up to us is deceiving. In fact, with most of the men gone to war, there is a great deal of treachery and lawlessness going about this fair place. She says that Morgans' Raiders have instigated a spate of horse thieveries and robberies. Then vigilante groups, as lawless as the criminals, get together and hang someone for the crime. She says some Iowans are pleased to get their law dispensed on the cheap, others wonder if they dare speak out for fear they will be next on the hanging list. She asked if I'd heard of the terrible tragedy over in Bertram Township July last. Of course I had not, but I was sure certain I was about to become enlightened. It seems a terrible man met his death at the hands of his sons. Amid much sighing and wheezing, this woman took great pleasure in the telling of the tale, which I find so frightfully compelling I must write it out.

On a June Saturday, about noon, one Mr. John S. Hollar returned to his house. He had been engaged nearly all the forenoon in driving out some unruly cattle from his cornfield and was in quite an enraged state over the affair. When he came into the house, he found that his wife and one of the children had gone out blackberrying. He turned his anger to the task of making known just what he would do to them when they returned. He then ordered his two sons, one about 15 the other 17, to go to one of the neighbors to bind wheat. The boys, out of fear as to what he would do to their mother, refused to leave, and an awful storm of wrath poured out of the man. He seized his axe and told them that he would split them open if they did not go. One tried to escape through the house, but was met at the back door by his father who made a pass at him with the axe, but missed him. He then took back through the house, snatching the shotgun as he went, whereupon he was met at the door by his enraged parent yet wielding the axe. The boy fired upon him, yet did no damage beyond tearing the shirt. The father then took the gun away from him and twice tried to shoot him, but the gun failed to go off. At this juncture, the older boy came to the rescue, and the father turned upon him. A scuffle ensued for possession of the gun, during which it was broken, the boy getting the breach and the father the barrel. By a well directed blow, the boy knocked him down with the breach, but the father rose to his feet and was about to strike with the barrel, when the boy wrested it from his grasp and struck him a blow over the head that broke in his skull and killed him almost instantly. A coroner's inquest was held over the body and returned a verdict of not guilty on account of the children acting in self-defense.

I kept thinking on the poor mother, who'd chosen such a man. How horrified and shamed she must be, not only to have committed to such a one, but now have to live surrounded by a community aware of her folly, to say nothing of the impact such an event must have on the children. When I tried to express my thoughts, she shrugged and spat out bitterly, "In time you, too, will come to understand that all women's lives come to naught but sorrow." Although I suspect she takes more than a mite of pleasure in telling the tales and tends to exaggerate, still her words are disturbing and I'll be glad to be shut of her.

DESMOINES CITY . . . 21 SEPTEMBER 1863

We are breakfasting at the Desmoines House and doesn't it all look good? I've a mind to partake of their servings of fresh milk, warm biscuits, and warm dipped eggs, and I've no mind to rush the project. This is the first breakfast I've had a desire for in what seems the longest of times.

NEWTON . . . 2 PM

The coach driver suggested I'd be best served if I would forgo lunch at Lamb's Grove in favor of the new eatery in Newton. The hall has been freshly whitewashed and is newly refurbished. The table was adorned with tumblers of radishes, dishes of lettuce, sliced boiled eggs, filberts, and almonds. That, along with tea and fresh buttered rolls, was all the lunch I needed. The men on the coach did pitch into beef, boiled mutton, chopped buttered potatoes, fried ham, and hot coffee. We have been rolling over hills in a countryside less wooded than that we came through yesterday. Even so, the grasses wave in a perfect sea of beauty, and there is not a cloud to be seen in the sky.

EVENING

The evening is splendid. We have just passed a group of turkeys, and deer abound, feeding in the dusk in a countryside that looks more like a park painting than any live landscape. I ate my last supper of this trip in the little village of Victor at a fine place, the Way Side Inn. Indeed it was a pleasant stop on a pleasant leg of my journey. The roads have been blessedly free of dust since Council Bluffs, in spite of a brisk wind today. This evening we crossed Big Bear Creek 13 times in the 13 miles between Victor and Marengo.

The crowd on board says the place to eat in Cedar Rapids is the Greene's Hotel. For the most part, food and accommodations have gotten progressively better and better the further east we've come, even so, tomorrow comes not a moment too soon.

ANAMOSA, FISHER HOUSE . . . 13 SEPTEMBER 1863

We left Cedar Rapids traveling in fine style behind a lively span of spanking dapple greys. Oh, my! How Mr. Plumer would have delighted in them! I was delivered to Fisher House by 1 pm. I've sent my laundry out, bathed, and am taking tea in my room. Tomorrow Daniel will gather me up for the trip to the farm. To be sure, I may hardly know how to sleep on solid ground. Nevertheless, I'm ready to chance it. I am stitching together my waist. Had so wanted to do it on the coach, but it was quite impossible. Crocheting is one thing, wielding a needle quite another. I thought myself to post a letter to Husband before I lay myself down, but that bed with its high feather comforter trumpets like a swan inviting me to cast myself into its loft.

Sadie's Waltz

HORTON'S CROSSING . . . 24 SEPTEMBER 1863

Well wasn't I surprised to be met, not by my brother—but his wife! I could hardly believe my eyes. Her father had bought a buggy off a man who was leaving for the war, and when he came to live with her he gave her the rig. She purchased a little Morgan mare, all on her own, after determining the mare was bred back to her brother Vermont Morgan, a descendant of the great Gifford Morgan. She hitches up the mare just like a man and drives as well as any coachman I've ridden with and with a far greater gentility. I trust my husband would be impressed.

She is so changed from the woman I knew just two years past, I hardly know what to make of her. When I expressed my amazement, she snorted, "Electa, the day will come when you, too, shall have no choice but to take up the reins and drive your own mare." I bethought myself, I'd been doing just that most of my life. I was just surprised to see Sadie take the reins like that. To understand my position, a body would have to have known the old Sadie. I'd swear, she did not so much as plan a meal without consulting my brother. She'd say things like, "It's a lovely day out." Then she'd turn to him in a voice that questioned her own wisdom to ask, "Isn't it a lovely day?"

Before we left town, we paid a visit to Skinner's and there I purchased two full bolts of flannel. I fully intend to put Sadie's machine to good use whilst my condition confines me to the farm.

We arrived at the house by noon, but I have not seen Jamie D. or Sadie's father, as they are harvesting the corn. They took a lunch to the fields and will keep at it till the sun goes down. Sadie says they had a killing frost on the fourth. It killed any tobacco and corn planted in the low lands. Fortunately for them, they do not raise tobacco. They've cut the injured crop over in the creek bottom and dried it for fodder. Fortunately, they planted the greater share of their corn on high ground and it headed out nicely even with the frosty nights. 'Tis the field they're yet working.

Of brother, what can I say? He is as changed as his wife. He is drawn and pale and so weak he cannot stand. He will not have the doctor to the house. He has it in his head that if Father had not run up such a debt to the doctors in the years preceding his death, he and James would not have had to sell the farm. Sadie says she's talked till she's blue in the face. She even asked Dr. Martin out, but when he came she says her husband cursed him and bid him on no uncertain terms to leave. He takes no interest in the activities around him and will not so much as look at a newspaper. Sadie believes we should leave him alone, but for feeding and such. I think he will die if we don't pester some life into him. And pester him I shall. After all, I am his little sister!

I am writing from a perch beneath a great box elder tree looking at the building Horton built in '55 above the banks of the Buffalo River in the hopes of cornering a market from those choosing to make this the place of their crossing. The house is clad in white sandstone transported from the quarry at Stone City. It is lovely. From where I sit, I can see the reflections of maples and buckeyes in its long narrow windows, and the sun on the white stone makes it fair glitter. A large vine climbs over the porch by the parlor door, and in summertime it is filled with yellow roses. Alas, like the katydid and the smell of new mown hay, they are long past their season. I can not refrain from favorably comparing this lovely homestead with the crued quarters we lived in on the Sun River and in Bannack.

Inside, the walls are made of planed wood, painted white, and the trim is of unpainted hard oak as are the upstairs floors. The house is L shaped. Both the parlor and the kitchen have doors opening onto a porch, which is situated on the northeast portion of the house. One day Sadie hopes to screen it in. Downstairs there is also a back entryway with a small pump inside, as well as a pantry and a small library. Upstairs there are three bedrooms, one of which Grandpa and Jamie D. share.

The sun is now low in the sky and is trading its warmth for the painting of wide, breathtaking bands of pink and gold above earth's edge. I am reminded of the one I left behind, and doesn't that bring useless tears to my eyes?

25 September

The morning air is brisk and there's ice on the water. Grandpa and Jamie D. are mowing hay. Reluctantly, Sadie has agreed to help me move Daniel to the kitchen for a spell this morning. A bed has been stationed especially for him in the library, so as to lighten the burden of nursing him, thus it is not a far stretch we're taking him. I plan to pull the rockers close to the fire and read the papers to Daniel (skipping the political parts for now, of course).

26 SEPTEMBER

Faith, yesterday was certainly a disaster. It is so shameful I can hardly bring myself to speak of it. But, of course I must, lest I hold it inside where it will fester. Brother Daniel and I were comfortably ensconced before the fire, and I picked up an old paper dated Aug. 21st of this year. I thought I was doing well as I trod lightly through the print, not reporting that the news of Vicksburg's fall on reaching London drove U.S. Government stocks up 70 percent and Rebel stocks down 20 percent and reporting on such items as the arrival of peaches at Skinners, the usual ads for sewing machines, harvesters, and social events, including the works of the M.E. ladies aid. Daniel had closed his eyes, and I noticed he occasionally nodded—that is until I reached the report of a Cotillion held at the Fisher House. The man's body jerked, and he began shouting. "Cursed waltzing women! Jezebels! Disgraceful! Waltzing jezebels! Satan's hand upon your breast—turned and twirled into shameless, wanton wenches! Have ye no mind? Decent women hide what's beneath their skirts! Oh shame, shame, shame! Turning twirling dervishes of sin!"

Sadie came in, and together we managed to get him back in his bed. By this time he was ranting about the guns, stopping the guns, exhorting us to silence the guns. His face was tinged red with a fever, which Sadie says comes to him both in night sweats and whenever she tries to move him. She says it is canceled only by the placing of shaved ice wrapped in a cloth over his flesh, which we proceeded to do. Just as she predicted, he calmed. Then I asked to see his wounds. His legs from the knees to the groin have been shredded and are now covered with red and purple knots and welts. In the right groin there is a bulge that looks to me like some poorly mended fistula. It is the size of the palm of my hand. I must have pulled back from the sight, for Sadie said, "You have no idea how much improved these wounds are. When he came home, the scars were all of them still raw, some of them proud, and none would keep a scab. When I tried to bathe them, the scabs would slip right off. I talked to the doctor, and he suggested I bathe them in an iodine solution and feed him raw onions every day and I have been faithful in it. As you can see, it has paid well, the wounds are healed."

On rereading the words I've written, I no longer know what I thought was so shameful about the event. Of course Brother was not his usual self. A fever can bring delirium to anyone. I'm suspecting the moving, the feeding, and the fire aggravated it. What bothers me is this nagging question—where does this fever come from? If we can solve this mystery, I think we can bring him back to health. As it is, I do believe he is only with us by the grace of God and the ministrations of Sadie.

Sunday 27 September

> We are Thine, do Thou befriend us,
> Be the guardian of our way;
> Keep Thy flock, from sin defend us,
> Seek us when we go astray:
> Blessed Jesus, Blessed Jesus!
> Hear, O hear us, when we pray,
> Blessed Jesus, Blessed Jesus!
> Hear, O hear us, when we pray.
>
> —*Dorothy A. Thrupp, 1779–1847*

Today Sadie, Grandpa, and Jamie D. went to church, leaving me to tend Brother. When I was a child we attended both morning and afternoon services on Sunday. Of course, since the church was located on the corner of our farm, that was not much of a hardship. I well remember sitting on the hard pews, swinging my legs, which were too short to reach the floor, my mother slipping me peppermint drops in summertime and horehound lozenges in winter.

This morning I bathed Daniel in cool water and fed him iced tea and toast for breakfast. I chose to read to him (not without a bit of trepidation) from the book of Psalms. Daniel said nothing of yesterday. I do not believe he is aware of what happened!

Yesterday, while walking in the wood near the creek, I found a lively bunch of bittersweet, which I've put together with some dried hops for a centerpiece. I do wish my husband were here to see it! It's just the sort of thing that would brighten his day. I have a large piece of fresh beef roasting in the oven, along with squashes, onions and potatoes, and a yeast bread, rising to be put to bake as soon as the folks return.

The harvest is in and Sadie's larder is full. What a joy to go to the basement and smell the crocks of apples, winter pears, carrots, potatoes, pickles, kraut, and corned beef, to see the walls lined with bottles and jars of syrups, jams, jellies, tomatoes, and every kind of jewel-toned preserve you can imagine. On the floor among the crocks are jugs of apple cider and vinegar, and from the rafters she has hung onions, hay beans, leather britches, and canvas bags filled with every sort of edible one can find to dry. The back wall of her pantry is lined with tightly sealed bins of nuts, flour, sugar, tea, and all the seasonings and spices anyone could ask for. On one wall a counter for mixing stretches its length and shelves below hold the churn and the larger pots, while above are hooks for the rest of the cooking wares. On the other side are floor to ceiling shelves that hold the household dishes and linens. Whatever we decide upon when we build a house, I do want a pantry just such as this one.

Wednesday next we plan to butcher some hogs and render out the lard. Grandpa and Jamie D. drove the greater share of hogs to market on Thursday and yesterday we cleaned out the smoke house and have it ready for the new guests.

2 October

A sudden change of weather has occurred this week, which necessitated the addition of wrappers, long drawers, and warm coats to our apparel. But it didn't cause us to slow down in our butchering. And, oh my, doesn't the hickory smoke smell like riches? We've larded a great crock of chops, hung the salami from the attic rafters to dry, and Grandpa says we should have bacon for Sunday breakfast.

The *Anamosa Eureka* reports from an Indiana newspaper, dated the 28th of September, that a battle at Chickamunga was fought on the 19th and 20th. The Union sent 65,000 soldiers into the fray and yet was repulsed.

The weather does not bode well for Brother, and I feel helpless to do anything but bring hot rocks wrapped in towels to warm his bed.

Sunday 4 October

> Thou hast promised to receive us,
> Poor and sinful tho' we be;
> Thou hast mercy to relieve us,
> Grace to cleanse, and power to free:
> Blessed Jesus, Blessed Jesus!
> We will early turn to Thee,
> Blessed Jesus, Blessed Jesus!
> We will early turn to Thee.
>
> —*Dorothy A. Thrupp, 1779–1847*

After services, Sadie's sister Rose and family came for a visit. After dinner, Grandpa got out his mandolin and accompanied a house full of warblers. Then Jamie D. took the instrument in hand and showed us what he could do with it. Hard to believe the lad picked the thing up but a year ago. Soon even the little girls were singing. I am mouth-agape amazed. Grandpa laughs and says 'tis but a family thing. It must be. I can hardly remember any words to the tunes, let alone the melodies.

Later, while the men went out to tend to chores and the sisters chatted, I read fairy tales and Mother Goose to the girls. Wasn't that a treat? And didn't it make me long to hold our own in my arms?

'Tis hard to believe I have not had one moment of the morning sickness since the day I came to brother's house? Last week Dr. Martin stopped by. Husband will be pleased to know he will be attending when the time comes. He promises to come as soon as called, and to stay until the babe is born. With Sadie in attendance he examined me at the house. Oh, my, it is wonderful to be with a civilized doctor. He was so gentle as well as delicate of speech. He says that to be small is only part of the issue. What really counts is how small a woman's interior is and that is not always determined by her exterior. I am much comforted by his visit.

8 October

Early in the week I had a most disturbing dream. In the dream, I was chopping raw liver to feed to my brother. But instead of feeding it to him in a normal fashion I kept trying to spoon it into the fistula in his groin but I could not get it in. Then the wound opened and he began to vomit. And I kept saying, "Good, this is good!" On waking I could but wonder, "What on earth?" That might have been the end of it, but I could not return to sleep and my mind kept coming back to that fistula until I came to the conclusion that it need be opened up. In the morning I proposed the same to Daniel and Sadie. Sadie thought it a dreadful idea and did not believe I could hold steady to the task. Daniel thought it a better idea than that of calling on the doctor. So I cleaned his razor in a bit of Sadie's "medicinal" Brandy and then proceeded to pour a teacup full down his throat. And then didn't the fun begin? I sliced an X across the membrane covering the mess—sliced straight through the "skin" that Sadie was sure represented a healing and I believed with equal fervor was holding in a body poison. I expected to unleash a fountain of fluid. That did not happen. Instead I unleashed an unholy smell fair strong enough to make a stout man gag. The putrid smell emanated from a soft, slimy substance that was certainly neither fat nor flesh. I tried to scrape it out with the razor but it eluded me, slipping around my blade and keeping itself together in a most tenacious fashion. It seemed to me I was going to either have to slice into good clean flesh and lift the mess out or find a way to dissolve the substance. I peeled back the membrane and trimmed it back to the healthy flesh then poured a bit of the brandy on it. The brandy did nothing but run off the side, so I poured another teacup full, added three drops of laudanum to it, and had Daniel drink that while I pondered the problem. That I needed to separate this viscous matter from his body seemed obvious, the question being only how—to burn or to cut? As to the option of cutting, these were my thoughts. If I cut into good flesh I will release blood. If the blood flows, I will not be able to see what I am doing. Thus I rejected that idea. Then I wondered, if I am to burn it, what is the best method to use? I rejected items such as hot pokers and lid lifters as too unwieldy. I thought for a moment of heating the razor to red hot and using that. It might have worked, but it's handle is wood and I wasn't sure of two things, whether the wood would catch fire from the heated metal and whether the blade would maintain the heat needed till the operation was done. I thought of using lye or full strength iodine to clean the wound, but rejected that idea on the grounds that I did not know how I'd keep it from eating at the good flesh after using up the poor. This is what I did—I broke a batch of live, glowing coals into manageable sized pieces, extracted, and carried them to the bedroom in a covered iron frypan. Using Sadie's sugar tongs, I began to burn the wound clean one coal at a time, tossing each spent coal into a pie tin. And didn't that fill the house with a stench so powerful I nearly lost Sadie? I started the process at the outer edges and worked lightly over the top of the mess. Daniel was long out of this world, so I felt no need to hurry the task. That worked well to my advantage; for after burning a good layer of the matter off, I found some pulsing vessel which looked to have a stout covering and which I felt certain I must not damage. I then continued working away the foul stuff until there was no spot remaining outside of that remaining near the vessel. Then I had Sadie bring me tweezers from her sewing cabinet and clean it in the brandy. With my left hand I prized the smaller tweezer under the vessel and pulled up on it. It felt very strong and elastic in my hand, and I firmly held it up and quickly slipped a hot but somewhat cooled coal over it, thus cleaning this last bit without damaging it, while insuring that every speck of the cavity's flesh was cauterized. I asked Sadie to make up the iodine solution just as Doctor instructed her, and I swabbed the area around the now-gaping hole with it. Last I dressed the wound with clean gauze.

Sadie can hardly believe I did such a thing, but she was there.

Today the wound yet weeps, but Daniel is joking. He says, "If the Lass don't kill you, she'll cure you sure." And his face is no longer ghastly, chalky white.

Tomorrow is Sadie's go to town to check the mail day. So I'd better finish my letter to Husband before I close my desk.

9 October

Now isn't this a red letter day? Sadie brings me my first batch of letters from the territories.

East Bannack
15 September 1863

Dear Wife,

We came into Bannack late night before last, one spent horse and rider. By measure of the cinch, Lady Mac lost about 50 pounds and I dropped a couple myself.

Last Sunday your sister and family came into town. They found the house without a hitch and were settled in when I returned. Yesterday I sold it to them for $500, which is about what it cost me last spring. Later this day we will record the deed. Your sister has invited Thompson and Swift (who has returned with the bulk of their goods) to take board with them. And I, of course, continue to bunk and board here. We curtained the spare bedroom so Mary Eliza could have a "room" to herself and I "allowed" Harvey the upper bunk, as it was his first pick.

It is good they arrived before I. The cheer of family and good home cooking will ease the pain of our separation.

I'll write more when I'm rested.

Your Devoted Husband,
Henry Plumer

East Bannack
Sunday 12 September 1863

Dear Sister,

'Tis sorry we did not arrive in Bannack in time to say a warm and personal goodbye to you, and when we read your parting letter we were all reduced to tears.

The house is all we could have hoped for. It is wonderful to come into it all fresh and clean. Nothing like what you and I faced when we crossed the Sun River threshold. Mary Eliza and Harvey have drawn pictures for you, which as you can see I've enclosed.

In spite of the rumors we hear of road robberies and murdering Indians, we saw none of them on our trip down from the government farm. For that matter, we've met no one who even knows personally any victim of such.

Before we'd unloaded, Mrs. Zoller brought us a sour cream raisin pie and a bucket of milk. What a fine introduction to a new home!

By the time you read this, you will be by the safety of our brother's fire.

For now, it's time to finish moving in.

With Love and Longing,
Martha Jane

East Bannack
4 September

Dear Mrs. Plumer,

Bannack loses what little charm and civility it had for me when I witness your empty house. I hope your trip went well, and I hope your return to the States accomplishes all you are hoping for. If it weren't for the war, I could envy you. Alas, I am alone, left with the necessity of bringing a bit of civilization to this new country of my husband's choosing.

With Affection,
Your Friend,
Mrs. Zoller

I read and read my letters till I'm afraid I'll wear the ink off them. This night I'll sleep with Husband's under my pillow.

Sunday 11 October 1863

Early let us seek Thy favor,
Early let us do Thy will;
Blessed Lord and only Saviour,
With Thy love our bosoms fill:
Blessed Jesus, Blessed Jesus!
Thou hast loved us, love us still,
Blessed Jesus, Blessed Jesus!
Thou hast loved us, love us still. Amen.

—*Dorothy A. Thrupp, 1779–1847*

After dinner Daniel joined us in the parlor, where we spent the afternoon playing dominoes and eating warm gingerbread with whipped cream on it, and didn't it cause me to remember those wonderful days with Husband on the Sun River? As precious as that memory is the movement I felt the babe make this day. Already, the memory of the quickening of my heart and quickening of our babe cannot be separated. I did not know how much more real this new creature would become with its tap, tap, tapping on the inside of my skin, like some ageless message being tap, tap, tapped into my soul.

Oh Mr. Plumer, how I wish you were here.

Sunday 18 October 1863

Jesus, Lover of my soul,
Let me to Thy bosom fly,
While the nearer waters roll,
While the tempest still is high:
Hide me, O my Saviour, hide,
Till the storm of life is past;
Safe into the haven guide;
O receive my soul at last! Amen.

—*Charles Wesley, 1707–1788*

22 October

I have finished the items I wanted to send to Husband and to Martha's family and took time this morning to write. We spent the whole of yesterday making soap. Both hand soap and laundry soap. The last time Sadie was in town she purchased a new supply of kerosene. I'd forgotten what great a difference a cup of kerosene added to a batch of regular soap makes. When it starts to set, she stirs it so that it does not set up in bars and she keeps it in a newspaper-lined barrel. In this manner we do not have to shave it before commencing the laundry.

Daniel improves and is up each day and gaining strength steadily. It's been some time since we've had to bathe him, except for what we call his "last wound." He yet disdains the newspaper, saying he's heard more than anyone ever wanted to know of war, and he's sure certain we'll keep him abreast of anything worth knowing outside of that arena.

FRIDAY 23 OCTOBER

Sadie picked up a letter from Husband today. Pleased as I am to hear from him, I fear the frontier has just become more dangerous. It's a shame we seem to be exporting, for the most part, the least desirable members of both the Northern and Southern persuasions.

EAST BANNACK
20 SEPTEMBER 1863

Dear Wife,

Received your letters written on the "trail." I am so proud of your pluck. A lesser woman could have never found the fortitude to do what you have done. A lesser woman would not have had the courage to take command of her destiny. And you make the trip sound like an everyday undertaking. Your letters are a treasure to me. I shall keep them safe for the time when our children will want to know how it was in the old days.

You'd never guess who blew into town a couple of days ago, so I'll tell you straight off, Edgerton and circus. On the day he came in, I was in the process of disposing the Higgins and Reece store front building, the one that's been vacant since the Alder Gulch stampede, in a sheriff's sale. He bought it. His nephew, Sanders, rented half of old man Jakes' house. Sanders follows his Uncle about, mimicking the "wise" mans' rhetoric as if he hadn't a mind of his own and Edgerton disdains to acknowledge him. Thought you'd like to know what you're missing in new neighbors. No one seems to know why they didn't go on to Lewiston as sent, some think he didn't know any better, others speculate he's looking for a short way to riches.

The Indian hostilities have cooled rather than heated, and the expected war has not developed. After all the worry about an Indian uprising, it seems they've simmered down and there are none in sight.

All is well. Our mines are still producing, though I think I'll sell two of them as I've been offered the kind of money only a fool would refuse. The quartz mill is yet operating at full speed. I spent a couple of days scouting prospects over in Virginia City, but turned up nothing to impress.

Well, Wife, it's time I turned in. I hope all goes well with your new situation. I'm sure I'll rest easier after I receive word you are in the safety of your brother's home.

Your Husband,
Henry Plumer

Sunday 25 October

Other refuge have I none;
Hangs my helpless soul on Thee;
Leave, ah! leave me not alone,
Still support and comfort me:
All my trust on Thee is stayed,
All my help from Thee I bring;
Cover my defenseless head
With the shadow of thy wing.

—*Charles Wesley*, 1717–1788

29 October

Yesterday was cloudy and rainy with a great amount of rain and lightning in the evening. It was a good day to sew. I made a couple of flannel dusters for wearing about the house and finished five dozen diapers all on the machine.

In spite of the stiffness this current weather is making of his joints, Daniel is milking one of the cows, feeding the chickens, and looking for eggs (good thing Sadie has put a goodly number into isinglass, as a fresh egg is becoming a rare thing, what with the molting and short days). The work he's doing is woman's work to some. Others I'm sure would find argument in that presumption. At any rate, he's glad to make himself useful. He even started to churn the butter this morning (reminding me or our friend Thompson—I'd call that case in point) but tired before the job was done.

I read in the paper where our local editor writes a hateful piece against Mr. Mahony of Dubuque, calling him every evil thing not excluding devil's apprentice. I, too, thought him one with a tail and horns till recently when I discovered a piece Mahony had written. It turns out he's a peace Democrat like my husband and doesn't hold with secesh nonsense anymore than does he. I notice that the *Anamosa Eureka* yet carries ads for Mahony's paper. I suppose Mahony does the same for Anamosa. I suppose he roasts our editor as harshly in return. I don't see the point of this willful vilification, and the hateful rhetoric upsets me, so I too am about ready to dispense with reading the rag.

31 October

Wasn't I disappointed when the mail came with letters from Sister and Mrs. Zoller and none from Husband? We have witnessed our first light snow and I'm wondering if he's deep in the white stuff, or if the ground is brown and blown free?

The Anamosa newspaper reports that on the 14th the Cedar County Sheriff made a descent upon two whiskey shops in Mechanicsville and seized about 100 gallons of different kinds of liquors.

The two proprietors of these "hell holes" were arrested and brought to Judge Betts, who fined one of them $20, and the other $40, besides costs. They paid their fines and went their way, glad to get off so easily. Their school fund is now richer by $60. The captured liquors remained, and will be disposed of according to law. If the law keeps up with these types, in jig time Iowa will become as civilized as any north eastern state.

Sunday 1 November

Thou, O Christ, art all I want;
More than all in Thee I find:
Rise the fallen, cheer the faint,
Heal the sick, and lead the blind.
Just and holy is Thy Name,
I am all unrighteousness;
False and full of sin I am.
Thou art full of truth and grace.

—Charles Wesley, 1707–1788

6 November

The evenings are long, but we fill them reading and stitching posies on babe's layette. The slight fall of snow last week disappeared in a day or two, and we have had mild weather since. I read that the Confederate dollar is now only worth ten cents on the dollar, that they are starving in many places, and that their railroads are nearly worn out. If such is the case, surely the end of this terrible war cannot be far from hand.

The other day I asked Brother about his views as to ladies waltzing. He shrugged his shoulders and said, "About the same as my views as to men dancing."

"And?"

"And what?"

"And what pray tell is that?"

"If you must know, I can find no harm in it. Not every church finds it a sin, and I've met many a reasonable man who did not find it so. In fact, dear Sister, I've been known to be guilty of waltzing my fair Sadie about the room a time or two." On seeing some expression of shock on my face, everyone burst into laughter. In defense of my shocked countenance, the brother I thought I knew would never pass such negative judgment on the persons who were dancing. It simply never occurred to me he would be a dancer. I repeated his expressed sentiments while he was delirious. Now wasn't it his turn to be shocked, and mine to join in the gaiety?

EVENING

Wouldn't you know, the first time I miss posting my letters I receive a batch and don't I feel guilty?

EAST BANNACK
14 OCTOBER 1863

Dear Wife,

I rest easier knowing you are safe. I am disheartened by the slow progress in your brother's recovery. However, if there are two nurses in this world that can turn the tide in the man's favor, I'm sure they are you and your sister-in-law.

Today another miner empowered me to dispose his interest in his quartz claims as he is ready to quit the country.

Early morning I carried out Judge Burchett's directive and sold the Frontiers Ranch Claim on Horse Prairie for the sum of $3,670.

After lunch William Hunter came into town and offered two half interests in quartz claims by Virginia City, one on the Ottowa Lode and the other on the same Lode West of Discovery for the sum of $1,000. That may seem dear, but both claims are rotten with gold and will not play out in the next season. If nothing else, I can turn a profit on them come next spring. Many are leaving before winter sets in.

Well Wife, I think we're doing all right for ourselves here. By the end of next summer we shall have a fine nest egg to show for it.

Your Husband,
Henry Plumer

LATE EVENING

Well, didn't I enjoy my dear Husband's letters and those from Martha Jane, Mary Eliza, and Little Harvey? The wee ones send such sweet sentiments. It's glad I am that the family is snug together and in good health.

I also received a letter from Brother James. He reports weather in Ohio much the same as what we're witnessing here in Iowa, that they are all well, and that Cornelia is ahead of her class and shall graduate early, that is, the end of spring session.

And now it's past time I said my prayers and went to bed.

7 NOVEMBER

The weather is yet mild—today is cloudy and muddy. Sadie and I made a great crock of mincemeat yesterday. For preserving it, Sadie purchased five gallons of Brandy at Fisher's. And doesn't our cellar smell heady?

Our men are planning to get the icehouses ready to fill as soon as the creek is frozen deep enough to make the cutting of it a worthwhile proposition.

I'm feeling a bit light headed and am of a thought to put myself down for a nap.

3 December

Sadie brought me Husband's letter of 24 October. I have been so sick so long—glad as I am I can neither write nor comment on them until I am stronger.

East Bannack
24 October 1863

Dear Wife,

Your description of your brother's home was such I can fair see it. I've always been partial to English Tudor myself. What would you think of that style of home?

I am tickled there is a "Skinner's" in Anamosa, as you know Skinner runs the Elk Horn here in Bannack—I'd hardly be likely to meet you there.

On the 12th day of March last, a 125-foot creek claim, No 2 above the large pine tree, sold for $250. It didn't get recorded until today. I can just hear you say, "And wasn't that a mess to straighten out?" At the end of a long trying day, I find comfort in the memory of your sweet voice and your emphatic declarative questions.

Dear Wife, the days seem so short with never enough time to accomplish all that needs doing. Your sister is taking good care of me and yet it does not take the place of the joy I felt when you were beside me.

Your Husband,
Henry Plumer

Now that I am on the mend, I am able to reflect on the terrible sickness that came upon me. It all started with a deep tiredness that soon turned to a cold. My nose was running and my head felt like it would fair explode. For the next few days Sadie nursed me with hot lemonade and brandy. Then all my muscles commenced to ache and my lungs filled with a phlegm that crackled and crackled when I coughed, and I could hardly get enough up. It's well that Sadie had not removed the cot from the library, as I've spent the last month there. I haven't a memory of much outside of the smell and the heat of the mustard plasters Sadie fairly blistered my chest during the most of the month and isn't Daniel teasing me about what I've said whilst I was most out of my head?

A melody kept floating through me, and now I've been informed of the why. Grandpa wrote a tune for Daniel which he calls "Sadie's Waltz." I find it so beautiful it brings me to tears. Daniel claims I kept saying, "I must learn to waltz. My true love is coming and I must be waltzing, waltzing when he comes to me." I'll send my Love the words of the song, and I wish I could send the notes, but, alas, I know not how.

SADIE'S WALTZ
REFRAIN:
COME WALTZ WITH ME SADIE
  COME WALTZING WITH ME
COME WALTZ WITH ME SADIE
  ACROSS THIS GREAT SEA

Sadie's Waltz

It's been so long Sadie
  since I've danced with thee
The Devil's fair taken
  your sweet memory

Her dreams were of silver
  but her heart it was gold
So she settled for children
  and my arms to hold

And it's sail away, sail away
  out to the sea
Of satins and laces
  and Sadie and me

When I dream of Sadie
  she's the lass on my arm
And I'm the young lad
  who'll keep her from harm

Lord if I must die
  let me die in this sea
Of satins and laces
  and Sadie and me

Do stop the guns Sadie
  they've not left one tree
To shelter my darling
  who once danced with me

I feel like Ichabod Crane. Sadie tells me that Jamie D. commenced another term of school on the 17th and that on that same day 13 men were arrested in Wyoming City on charges of selling hard liquor. They had a lovely Thanksgiving dinner, while I had chicken soup. After a beginning as mild as spring, November has turned into full winter. The snow started falling two days before the holiday, and the situation has continued ever since. Since the 1st, the roads have been impassable by anything but sleigh. Sadie has put the runners on her buggy.

On the 4th Gen. Sherman, with reinforcements, reached Knoxville, and on the 5th Longstreet skedaddled. It has been further reported, on Thanksgiving Day, Henry Ward Beecher, who has a farm in this county, returned from Europe. New playing cards are to be made of pictures of the faces of the men who have distinguished themselves in war. If, indeed, that's the news of the month, I haven't missed much, have I?

'Tis enough for now. I must sleep.

East Bannack
27 October 1863

Dear Wife,

We just received your letters of the 25th of September. We are disheartened to hear the news of your brother. Your sister is praying for him. I talked to Dr. Glick. On relating the symptoms as told by you, he says what he has is a type of scrofula that settles in the groin. He says, if the man is still alive when you receive this letter, you must treat him with mustard plasters. Occasionally he has saved a man in this fashion.

The weather has been nasty for days. Late afternoon, yesterday, while toasting my hide at Chrisman's, the Peabody & Caldwell express came lumbering into town a day late and the passengers in much distress, the coach having been held up about a mile this side of the Rattlesnake Ranch.

From what I could gather from the witnesses, the trip seems to have been crossed from the start. On the 26th the express driver was ill and, as a furious storm was raging, no one could be found to set out from Virginia City. Finally, someone talked Billy Rumsey into taking the coach to Bannack, as there were three passengers, Messrs. Matheson, Percival, and Wilkinson, all chomping at the bit to be on their way, as they were several hours late. Rumsey made the best time possible to Stinking Water station. When they arrived, there was no stock ready. Men were sent out to bring in the horses. After some time, the stock herder returned with only a portion of the stock. Rumsey ordered them to hitch up what they had, and he started out on a run.

At Dempsey's they went through the same scene again because of their stock not being ready. Daniel McFadden (who had been visiting the past several days at the stop) joined the other passengers on the coach. At Coplands everything was ready, the horses were quickly changed, and all possible speed made to the Rattlesnake Ranch. But, in spite of best efforts, it was almost dark before they arrived and all the stock had been turned loose.

Rumsey asked the herder to bring in the horses. He went, but came back without them. It being impossible to proceed without fresh stock, there was nothing to do but remain the night where they were. Bill Bunton treated the crowd liberally to food and whisky and all, but Rumsey spent the night gambling and drinking. At daybreak Rumsey and the herder braved the storm to look for the missing horses. However, they could not be found and he was obliged to hitch up the jaded team of the night before in order to proceed. When all was ready, he shouted, "All aboard for Bannack." Matheson, Percival, and McFadden took seats in the coach, Wilkinson announced that he was going to accompany Bob Zacchary and ride one of his horses. Bill Bunton came out with a bottle, offered everybody a nip to fortify them against the bitter chill, announced his intention of going to Bannack, and mounted the seat beside the driver.

Once inside, the passengers pulled down the curtains and lit the lamps. The horses were traveling along at a fairly good gait, Bunton doing the whipping and Rumsey the driving, but as the team was played out before they started, they soon settled down to a slow trot. Bunton complained of being cold and traded his seat beside Rumsey for one inside the coach beside McFadden. Percival and Matheson were on the front seat with their backs to the driver.

According to Rumsey they had not gone more than a mile when he saw two men wrapped in blankets with hoods over their heads and guns drawn. He shouted to the passengers to get their guns, but none did. I was not able to get a straight answer out of any of the passengers as to why. I speculate that between the sounds of the storm, the creaking of the coach, and the muting of the curtains, they never heard him, or they may have been sleeping off the effects of the long night. At any rate, the robbers were soon on the coach, demanding that everyone throw up his hands and get out. Rumsey objected, saying he was afraid that the team would get away. Pleading for his life, Bunton offered to hold the horses. Next, they ordered Rumsey to take the arms from the passengers and throw them in a pile on the ground and after that to take their valuables and add them to the pile. McFadden offered up two small purses whereupon the spokesman swore at him and demanded he make haste to unload his dust or die. McFadden lost no time handing over his belt and two more purses of dust.

As swiftly as the bandits arrived, they were gone, and Rumsey brought them here as soon as he could under the circumstances.

McFadden first said he'd lost $2,500, but on further questioning, he wasn't so sure about the amount as he'd been gambling the last few evenings. The rest of the passengers estimated their losses at a total of $500. So I suspect the loss ran somewhere between $2,000 and $3,000.

Evidently the experience so unnerved them that none recognized the horses or the voices of the men. Zachary and Wilkinson, who were riding fresh horses, should have beat the stage to town, but have not been seen. In spite of the passengers' claim that Wilkinson was a friend, until I can talk to those two, they are suspects. I've sent Ned Ray to start at the site and to try to track the men down, and I've put all the other deputies on alert to bring in Wilkinson and Zachary for questioning.

Well, Dear Wife, I am so weary I could wish for no better than dull moments.

Your devoted Husband,
Henry Plumer

18 DECEMBER

From this great distance, Husband's letters allow a peek into his life of a depth I'd probably be missing were I at his side. I do enjoy them and shall save them for a future when we are settled into a comfortable life that may not be as "exciting" as the one he is leading. I'm proud to be the wife of a lawman, but I worry he is working far too hard for his health.

Looking at the basket of presents my husband and Martha Jane have sent, I wonder if my Christmas package made it to the Territories. I hope so. God willing, we will never spend another apart.

Esther wrote—she and her beau will be coming to visit during Christmas vacation. This is Jamie's last day before their two-week vacation begins.

Since last week, the weather has been cold and cloudy, and that leaves me gloomy. I can hardly believe it—I'm missing the brilliant blue of the Idaho Territory skies?

The *Anamosa Eureka* reports on the last battle of Chattanooga. Federal troops, under the overall command of General Grant, have stormed and taken Lookout Mountain, and after a wild bayonet charge, Missionary Ridge has fallen to the Union Forces. We hope this proves a staggering blow to the Southern hopes.

According to the papers, the president, like myself, has been quite ill, but is getting better.

I've become a regular lay-about. Have been embroidering on a hanky for Esther and reading *Harper's*—beyond that, mostly, I just sleep.

SUNDAY 20 DECEMBER

HE RULES THE WORLD! THE SAVIOUR REIGNS:
LET MEN THEIR SONGS EMPLOY;
WHILE FIELDS AND FLOODS,
ROCKS, HILLS, AND PLAINS,
REPEAT THE SOUNDING JOY
REPEAT THE SOUNDING JOY.

—*Isaac Watts, 1674–1748*

As I sang this joyous song, my voice cracked from a longing that this babe was born and our little family settled in a home of our own in the States. Now wouldn't that be Christmas?

23 DECEMBER

The letters from Bannack all came in a bunch today and I've a mind to heat myself a cup of spiced milk and settle down to an evening of feasting on them.

EAST BANNACK
SUNDAY 8 NOVEMBER 1863

Dear Wife,

I'm making your sister happy by resting on the Sabbath and writing to you.

Tell Mrs. Bryan I'm not surprised by your acumen as a doctor. From the moment I first saw you, it's been one delightful surprise after another.

Yesterday Lady Mac and I met a Mr. Webster at dusk, just before getting to the Rattlesnake. He'd lost his robe and overcoat there a few days earlier and I offered to try to find them for him. He'd been to Dempsey's Ranch and expressed his concern that a hard looking set of men seemed to hang around there. A statement I cannot disagree with, but I did point out that it was always thus at Dempsey's, even before he moved from the Deer Lodge. I told him the story of how Dempsey's wife took care of the men when she'd had enough. We had a laugh at that. Would we had a town full of Websters.

I promised Mary Eliza I'd best her in a game of checkers this afternoon. The young lady looks about to call in my promise.

Your Husband,
Henry Plumer

East Bannack
6 November 1863

Dear Sister,

We rejoice in the news that Brother is on the mend.

At last our Young Swift made it into town from the Milk River. I have invited him to board with us and I hope to add a bit of flesh to his frame as he, albeit healthy, is leaner than I have ever seen him.

Since our arrival, a Methodist preacher has taken to preaching Sunday evenings in the log octagonal building, Thompson has organized a choir, Mr. Edgerton's niece, Lucia Darling, is teaching Sunday school, two men are offering classes in French and German, and a group of young men have formed an acting club.

Mary Eliza and Harvey tell me to tell you they miss you. Dear Electa, we all miss you!

With Affection,
Martha Jane

EAST BANNACK
12 NOVEMBER 1863

Dear Mrs. Plumer,

I cannot tell you how good it is to be in Bannack, and how sad I was to find you gone. Last Monday I arrived in town with the goods for our store and have been recovering and working (some contradiction) ever since. Tonight I thought I'd have a look about Skinner's saloon. Hardly had the door closed behind me before Mr. Plumer had me collared and was leading me out with the admonition, "This isn't a place for you my good man, it draws too many of a type you do not want to cultivate." Thus, it appears to be a fine moment to write to you.

I have two new friends, Ed Porter and Webster. Ed was offered $250 per month by a Mr. Durand to tend bar for him in a billiard hall, board and washing free. Webster is boarding with Mrs. Lewis. Webster has set up shop making leather gloves at nine dollars a pair and can make two pair in a day. The other day he tanned a stone martin skin. It is a lovely thing.

Tonight Web and Ed are taking French lessons. I'm not cut for foreign languages.

Mr. Thompson spends a great deal of time at the Edgerton's. He and Mr. Edgerton seem to be in each other's pocket, though I can't for the life of me imagine why. When Edgerton's at the store (which is daily) all he does is grouse about what a dismal, lawless place this is, brags about his contacts in Washington, and tries to drum up support to return to "civilization" that he might split the territory in two. I think he fancies him-

self chief of the new division. Lord knows that's all he seems good for, hot air and chiefdom. No one's yet seen him do a lick of work.

Thompson is starting up a secular singing group. A fellow named Phill Lovel, Web, Ed, and I are planning to join. I suppose all my grousing about Thompson's infatuation with Edgerton has more to do with my missing the companionship he and I shared in the past.

I hope this letter finds you well and in good spirits.

Your Friend,
Joseph Swift

East Bannack
14 November 1863

Dear Sister,

Mrs. Zoller asks that I send her love to you. I think she misses you almost as much as I do. You'd be right proud of Harvey; he can recite his ABC's and make each one on the chalk board Mr. Plumer gave to him. He thinks he's a regular little man now that he has mastered his letters.

Three days ago Mr. Plumer ran into Mr. Yeager, one of the hired hands from the Rattlesnake Ranch, who had come to town looking for Dr. Glick. He said one of his bosses, Mr. Parish, was out of his mind with a fever.

As Dr. Glick was nowhere to be found and as Sheriff Todd had already called your husband to Virginia City, he agreed to look up Doc Palmer and send him to the ranch. The weather being yet bitter, he'd already decided he'd be better off taking the stage. Next day he returned in the company of Messers. Hauser (the same who came to the territory on the Emile *with us) and Langford. Fortunately for Mr. Hauser, the sheriff made him a loan of his good red scarf as Hauser had none. On arrival Hauser made a great fuss over his need of a safe place for some $14,000 in gold he was carrying for Virginia City merchants*

Dance and Stuart. They put it in the safe at Chrisman's, of course. They are stopped the night in Bannack to await the Mormon freighter that is leaving today for Salt Lake.

I'd best be signing off as I hope to get this sent by that same freighter.

With Affection,
Your Sister,
Martha Jane.

EAST BANNACK
15 NOVEMBER

Dear Wife,

I am sitting in the office at Chrisman's after tending to the official recording of the Frontiers Ranch claim on Horse Prairie. You would find it hard to believe how difficult such a simple task can become. If the recorder isn't at the miner's meeting it becomes catch as catch can.

I worry that you have been working over hard and urge you to rest, for your sake as well our child's, if not for me.

We'll be sending our letters with the Mormon freighter. And I haven't a notion what will pop up next, so I'd best be signing off.

Your Husband,
Henry Plumer

LATE EVENING

I am thinking so many thoughts that I could only wish we were all together and having a live conversation.

First, I feel compelled to scold and warn. Swift has written that Thompson and Edgerton have formed a close camaraderie. In my bones I feel the ill it bodes for my husband, but I can just hear him saying, "Nonsense! There's nothing they can do to me." And I cannot tell him what it is that I fear; but I know enough about that man to know that he bodes ill for all who do not hold with his rigid view of the world. He is not accepting of other classes and opinions, as is my husband. Somehow I must communicate to him that Edgerton is an unrelenting man, capable of justifying any action by his righteousness. I must state this in a way that he will not dismiss this warning. I think I must tell it plain and pray he will listen.

Enough of this! Tomorrow is dear Sister's birthday. How I do so wish I were there to bake her a special meal and a cake.

26 December 1863

Didn't Christmas feel bleak without Husband. I do so regret we did not have our likenesses taken when we were in Salt Lake City. It's pleased enough, I was, to have been able to have one of myself taken in Anamosa. By now my Beloved must have it and I pray he likes his present as much as I cherish mine. The gold locket is sweet enough in its own right, but his image staring straight into me fair takes my breath away. I pray God will not see fit that we shall ever spend another long patch apart.

This evening the whole family gathered around the table to send greetings and write their Christmas thank yous.

In other important events I want to record and remember, the Christmas edition of the paper reports all quiet in the opposing military camps and that the president is now quite well.

Yesterday Esther brought her beau out for my inspection. He seems a bright enough fellow, if a bit full of himself. Of course, compared to my husband, his features are coarse and his build is more that of an ox than a cultured gentleman. I'm sure Esther is confident she has materials enough that she can make him over to her liking.

He's young (younger than she by at least two years) and follows her every word. Personally, I prefer a man who's a bit more of a challenge. While they were here, Rose and her family stopped by and there was nothing for it but Jamie D. and Grandpa playing for us. On that note, I do hope my husband will not think me too extravagant. I commissioned Grandpa to locate a good mandolin at a good price, that I might buy it for a Christmas present for Jamie D. He bought one off the widow of a friend of his, and wasn't Jamie happy? In spite of the fact that I now look fair like a triangle, the crew insisted it was time I learned to waltz. Grandpa is a gentle teacher and I did manage to follow, if without Sadie's grace. Grandpa says it will come out smooth when I am again but one. It was great fun, but wasn't I wishing my husband were here?

Tomorrow Jamie plans to take the cutter to town, so I'll send my letters off with him and go to bed dreaming of waltzing in my darling's arms.

28 December

What a glorious batch of letters I've come into this day and all of it thanks to my good nephew Jamie D. Having smoothed them out I've arranged them all in order, starting with Sister's of 15 November and ending with Mr. Plumer's of 27 November. I'm going to tease myself and read them in order instead of my Beloved's first and after all are finished rearranging them as is my usual practice.

East Bannack
Sunday 15 November 1863

Dear Sister,

Early yesterday morning, Mr. Bunton came into town looking for his partner, Mr. Pickett, to report the doctor's prognoses on their other partner, Mr. Parish, who was like to die, and to announce that if any whose horses were pastured at the ranch wanted to keep them, they'd better get over and round them up before his wife's Bannack relatives got to them. The men then came to Mr. Plumer and again asked for his assistance, this time to help round up the horses. It's cold yet today and they are not back.

But what a row we had at the table! At supper Thompson said that yesterday he overheard Edgerton telling his nephew he was sure the group was going after silver, not horses, and sent the poor man after them on a reluctant donkey. A friend of theirs ended up dragging the poor beast to the top of the hill and then beating on him to get him to move off in the general direction of the Rattlesnake Ranch. That prompted Swift to start laughing. He said he overheard Mr. Plumer tell Mr. Sanders he'd stake him to a silver claim if they found any, but wouldn't you know, the fools would not be satisfied.

Thompson defended his new companions saying, "Everyone knows the miners always ask Mr. Plumer to accompany them to a new silver strike to evaluate the ore. In exchange for his expertise, they stake him a claim near the discovery—therefore it is not so outlandish of Edgerton to speculate that staking claims is their real goal. I say, Edgerton merely dispatched Sanders as an emissary to the group."

Swift scowled at Thompson. "You heard him ask Mr. Plumer where he was going, and you heard the reply that they were on their way to get the herd of horses quartered on the Parish Ranch. You, as sure as I, listened to at least half a dozen people worrying about the possibility of losing their livestock to his wife's people over on the other side of the mountain, should Parish die. We were both there when Sanders insisted he was certain the horsemen had other intentions, namely staking quartz claims, and you heard Mr. Plumer answer that he knew nothing about them. You heard Sanders all but call him a liar. Mr. Plumer said, 'All right get your horse and come along, but I doubt there will be any claim staking done.' To which Sanders again cast aspersions on Plumer's integrity. The little toady kept it up until Plumer in exasperation said, 'Mr. Sanders, if you do not care to come along, I'll personally stake a claim on your behalf should the opportunity arise.' That should have been the end of it. You know as well as I that Plumer has never told us any untruth. With due respect, Mr. Thompson, whereas your new-found companions are certainly a cut above those blackguards you escorted into town a couple of months ago, I do question their wisdom."

At that point it looked as if Thompson and Swift were about to deliver unto each other the type of words from which no friendship can recover. Mr. Vail pushed his chair back saying, "That's enough." And would you believe they stopped?

Well Sister, one cannot say it's not an exciting place to be, although, only the Lord knows what to make of it all.

The children are well, and life in Bannack is better to us than life at the Sun River.

Know you are always in our prayers,
Martha Jane

East Bannack
16 November 1863

Dear Wife,

Night before last I hope to never repeat. Bunton, Pickett and a few men who have horses boarded at the Rattlesnake expressed their concern that the demise of Mr. Parish might precipitate some unwonted action on the part of his wife's Indian relatives as regards the herd and asked that I help round them up. In the morning the weather was crisp, but by mid-afternoon we could feel a storm brewing, so Bunton headed for the ranch in case he was needed there, and we headed north of the home place in an attempt to gather the livestock before it hit. Unfortunately, the squall found us in the hills. There was plenty of brush, so we quickly hacked out a wickiup and kept a small fire going.

Yesterday, we trailed most of the ponies back to the ranch only to find that Parish had rallied and his fever had broken. His ample wife fed us well from the larder—good passenger fare. I think the good man will make it, though having frozen his feet down to stubs last winter may delay his recovery. Of all people, he certainly deserves a chance. He saved near every penny he took from his share in his mine so that he could buy into a share in the ranch. His wife certainly pulls her weight. They've built the Rattlesnake into a good stage stop.

When we arrived at the ranch, Bunton related the strangest tale. After the brouhaha Sanders made the morning of our leaving, didn't the sorry creature take it into his head to follow us to the Rattlesnake Station? Lucky for him Mr. Yeager was still about and offered to share his grass mattress, which was already spread before a fire burning on the hearth. Sanders availed himself of the comfort, and they all promptly fell asleep.

Everyone was wakened three times in the night. All, that is, but the doctor who had not slept a wink in three days on account of a poor babe that died in his care the night before I enlisted his services in the aid of Mr. Parish. The good man staid in attendance on Parish until at last he got the fever broke, a bit past suppertime.

About midnight a great pounding on the door brought Yeager armed with a double-barreled gun to his feet and a shout of "Who's there!" A voice answered "Jack!" and in tumbled Jack Gallagher, his temper badly warped by a long search for the cabin in the snowstorm. He demanded something to eat and drink, which necessaries Yeager furnished, trying all the time to keep him quiet on account of Parish's condition. Then Sanders got up and standing at the bar grabbed Yeager's shotgun. Pointing it at Gallagher he asked if he knew where Plumer was. Gallagher said, "Be damned if I know." Then tearing open his shirt, he said, "Go ahead, ya little weasel, shoot." Then Sanders backed down and said, "I have no desire to shoot anybody, but if there is shooting to be done I intend to have the first chance." Everyone thought that a bit of a strange speech from the man who drew the gun in the first place, but things quieted down and Gallagher did the handsome thing and treated everyone to a nightcap.

Toward morning another alarm roused the sleepers. This time it proved to be caused by Sander's friend who'd came to rescue him at the behest of his distressed wife. What a carnival!

Mrs. Parish says her people foretell of a hard and early winter to come. I sincerely hope them wrong.

While we were gone Edgerton's flunky, Tilden, claimed to have been accosted by three armed men on his return from an unsuccessful cow chase that lasted till long after dark.

This morning when I interviewed him at the Edgerton's, he cowered like a rabbit, poor fellow. It seems, Edgerton had sent him westward to get some cattle left on Horse Prairie earlier in the fall and drive them back to Bannack. As a courtesy to his discomfort, I asked what the robbers took, knowing full well that the lad turns over what little he earns to Edgerton. He said, "Why nothing, I had only a comb and a picture of my girl on me." Edgerton then interjected that the would-be robbers had ordered him to hold up his hands while they searched him. Finding nothing in his pockets but a comb, and a picture of his girl, they let him go, and he went without delay, speeding toward Bannack and straight to Sander's house. I asked Tilden why he went past Edgerton's house and on to Sander's, when it was Edgerton's cows that he was to have brought home. Tilden turned quite ashen at the question. I suspect he was delaying an unpleasant confrontation. At any rate, Edgerton blustered, "The lad was so affrighted he raced home, and in the process his horse tumbled into a ditch, landing on top of him. We all heard his cries, and if you'd been in town you would have heard them as well." How like an attorney to deflect the answering of a question with irrelevant posturing.

Well, Wife, it's past time to be sleeping, so I'll sign off.

Your Husband,
Henry Plumer

EAST BANNACK
19 NOVEMBER 1863

Dear Sister,

Husband has been asked by the agent who replaces Reverend Reed to return to Sun River. I would prefer he staid here and set up a school for the winter. But he feels obligated to go and attempt to ready the place for new overseers come spring. Besides, Miss Darling is planning to open a school, and I suppose he's right in that there is not room here for two.

On the bright side, Mr. Plumer has suggested we have a party like the parties his family was used to having on for the holidays. Mrs. Zoller and I are working on the invitation list. Besides Thompson, Swift, and our neighbors on either side, the Sanders and the Zollers, I've decided on both the Burchett families, Dr. and Mrs. Burris, and Lucia Darling. Mr. Plumer says I cannot invite the Sanders and Miss Darling unless I also invite the Edgertons. I do so wish I didn't have to. The mister is a Godless man, an avowed atheist, and his wife keeps her nose in the air. According to Mrs. Zoller, she says she doesn't attend Sunday services because they are "conducted by a good but ignorant man in a house where dogs and cats stroll in and out among the congregation." I notice that doesn't stop her from sending her children. Mr. Plumer says not to worry about them, we can easily out snob the snobs and we have a moral obligation to do so. We plan to have 18 at the table. Mr. Plumer is making up the menu. Emma Zoller has already agreed to take the children for the evening.

The day before yesterday Mr. Plumer and I went about delivering invitations.

My Darling Sister, the hustle and bustle reminds me of those holidays of our youth, and I cannot tell you how I ache wishing you were here.

Affectionately,
Martha Jane

EAST BANNACK
20 NOVEMBER 1863

Dear Wife,

A fellow came in from Virginia City saying he'd heard a man had been murdered 20 miles below Virginia City. Speculation has it that robbery was the motive. Rumors abound of several robberies on the road between Virginia City and Bannack. This may or may not be so. No one has come charging they were robbed, so it might be idle talk.

Your sister has expressed an interest in holding a holiday dinner in honor of Thanksgiving. I have agreed to meet the expenses and have ordered from Salt Lake tins of oysters for a soup, a 40-pound turkey, an assortment of fine wines, and the trimmings.

Perhaps next year we shall be doing the same in a new place with new acquaintances.

Your Husband,
Henry Plumer

EAST BANNACK
26 NOVEMBER 1863

Dear Sister,

Wasn't Thanksgiving Supper a great success? Everyone showed up decked out in their finest. The men looked so handsome in their crisp white shirts and the women lovely in hoops and satins and velvets. I dressed up my old black silk with a new collar I've managed to tat when I should have been mending. And my, didn't your husband cut a charming picture? He always knows just what to say no matter the company. I chalk it up to his good education. Lucky for myself, the conversation flowed so freely, it hardly needed comment.

Everyone we invited accepted our invitations. Mrs. Edgerton said it was the finest thing to happen since they came to this "God-forsaken pit."

I must have looked aghast, for Miss Darling stepped in saying, "I shall never forget our first sight of Bannack. We all stood on the hill above town looking down at the gallows. Not a ray of sunlight enlivened the scene. The grey clouds above and around us made the bare mountains and the log cabins between them looked extremely forbidding."

Mrs. Edgerton rolled her eyes as she exclaimed, "It is a great country, all right. There are two things that it abounds in, hills or mountains and sage bushes."

Mrs. Sanders got a lively laugh out of a tale about one of the children stamping his foot impatiently and piping, "I think this Bangup's a humbug." She added, "I think there was not one of us who did not feel a keen sense of disappointment at the prospect of having to stay over in this place, however short the duration. I think, all that held our spirits up was the promise we will be leaving the place in spring."

In all fairness, Mrs. Edgerton did concede, "I think the town is very quiet and orderly for a mining town—much more so than I expected to find it."

Mrs. Sanders thought the community would be much enhanced as soon as we acquired a teacher. But Mrs. Edgerton did not agree. Her sentiments were that she would hardly like to send them to school here, if there was one, for they would learn so many bad things that would injure them more than all the good they would learn. She said that most of the boys here swear as soon as they can talk. She said that her boys had not acquired any of those habits yet, that she'd heard Wright and Sidney have the reputation of being the best boys in town.

I can't but wonder how Miss Darling felt about that speech as she plans to open a school and I'm sure is counting on the Edgerton children attending her class.

The only shadow on my pleasure came when Mrs. Edgerton enlightened us as to her opinion of our Indians, saying, "My family finds they must waste a good deal of their time trying to avoid them." She continued, "They make such beastly pests of themselves, pressing their noses to a window and peering inside or tapping on the door to beg for food. And they are so disgusting. They pick up all the dead chickens and pigs and all the old bones and bits of meat that the hogs don't get and carry them up to their wickiups. There they cook and eat them."

Poor creatures, they seem to try to make do with so little and remain peaceful. I should think we would be grateful for that. A young woman comes to the door with her little girl. I save the scraps and sometimes have a bit more to spare and give it to her. I can but thank God I am able. A few have begun to attend services, and I do believe there's hope in this.

Mrs. Zoller reports that our supper has been the talk of the town. Yesterday she heard that Mrs. Edgerton said she'd tasted butter for the first time since they came here. We wondered if it was because her husband wouldn't spend the money for it or if she was the one who was too tight fisted. She's let it be known about town that she was compelled to leave behind their fine china and damask chairs. It's also rumored those women walked across the prairie under sharkskin masks to prevent damage to their complexions. Mrs. Zoller says, "The finest complexion in the world can make up for neither coarse bone structure or poor disposition."

She says that when Mrs. Burris came into her husband's shop he overheard her telling Mrs. Biddle, "An assembly of the most prominent citizens was present to enjoy delicacies that had never before graced festal board in Bannack. And Mr. Plumer was the soul of hospitality. His easy flow of conversation . . . his well modulated voice entertained with compliment and jest . . . his elegant manners, his gracious attention to his guests made him an ideal host."

A sampling of the thank-you notes goes thus: "Mr. Sanders and I wish to thank you for the invitation to one of the most sumptuous dinners we have ever attended. Everything was delicately cooked and served with all the style that would characterize a banquet at 'Sharry's'. We shall long remember the charming evening in your company."

"Mr. Burchett and I are pleased to have been included in your fine Thanksgiving celebration. The enchanted evening at your home will not be forgotten."

Dear Sister, the only thing that could have made the affair better would have been your presence.

With Deepest Affection,
Martha Jane

East Bannack
27 November 1863

Dear Wife,

The only fine thing missing Thanksgiving evening was you.

Mr. Edgerton attempts to conceal his political aspirations under the guise of the importance of splitting the Idaho Territory in two. He thinks it should be split through the Bitter Root Mountains. The old man touts "connections" that can get the deed done, and plans to leave as soon as he can get up contributions to send him east. Both he and his nephew are certain they can drum up support for the adventure on the grounds that the Territory is vast and justice cannot be well served in it. They cite the recent spate of robberies and killings as argument in favor of separation. It is the fodder they'll use to fuel a stampede for a separate terri-

tory. When I pointed out that there had been fewer altercations here than any the states see on an average year, Edgerton moved the topic to gold mining, a subject he knows pitifully little about and could care less about excepting he aims to get in on his share.

You would have been amused to watch his nephew waltz about him, obviously nervous under the eye of his benefactor. A stiff-necked teetotaler at heart, Sanders is a great embarrassment to the old man. He's smart enough to know it and thus left the old man to carry the show. Then there was Thompson, fairly dipping and curtsying about the two of them and bobbing his noggin in agreement with their every word. Ah well, we know of his great powers of judging his fellow men!

Both men are fairly easy to read. Edgerton is a shrewd opportunist of the first order and an honest day's work has never and shall never cross his desk. He will always find toadies like his Nephew to do his dirty work. The miners recognize him for what he is, therefore I do believe I have nothing to fear from him. If he can get the territory divided in two, I have no doubt he can get himself appointed Territorial Governor. In a position of power, I doubt he will be very effective; honest, hard-working men will see through him and he cannot garner their support. Without that, no man can accomplish much. What he can do is muck the system with his petty demagoguery. Thus, any person he does not favor, such as myself (yes, my dear, I am not blind to his disdain for me—though I'm not at all convinced it isn't an extension of his disdain for all men) he will block their involvement in his government. However, we shall not be here, so we have nothing to worry about on that account.

Last night at a miner's meeting I finally got the Ottowa Lode west of the Discovery recorded by our recorder of the evening.

Your Husband,
Henry Plumer

29 December

Oh dear! Just when I am feeling secure in the knowledge that sister and family are all together safe and snug she tells me she too is about to join me in "widowhood." Having survived the misadventure we got ourselves in, I don't see that Mr. Vail's return to the Sun River can accomplish any good thing. However I do suppose they need the money this reemployment will bring. Sister does not say whether she and the babes will follow in the spring.

Equally distressing are descriptions of Thanksgiving supper sent by both Martha Jane and Husband. Now I must congratulate them on their social success. However, I see them getting deeper and deeper into relationships with Edgerton and his nephew. Husband says, "Thus, any person he does not favor, such as myself . . . , he will block. . . . However, we shall not be here so we have nothing to worry about. . . ." I must point out that Edgerton does not know Mr. Plumer's future plans, and again I must warn Husband to watch his back.

I don't remember a winter so cold as it has been these last days—not since those of my childhood. It settled in, this burning cold, on the last day of '63. If winters are this cold in Mr. Plumer's home country and if we decide to settle there, I wonder what are the chances of designing the back-house to include a stove to ward off freezing one's under parts during these spells?

Sadie and I have been taking turns spinning flax and wool. The flax takes all the moisture from the hands and leaves them dry and chapped. The wool turns around the process and leaves the hands comfortable and smooth. I am sending Husband a picture out of *Harper's* of a dress I believe I'll make up when we've finished the cloth. I do believe it will be lovely done up in either dark green with deep brown velvet trim or dark brown with black velvet trim. I wish

I could know his preference. Alas, knowing him, I might speculate with fair accuracy his answer to the question, "Please yourself and you'll please me." Sadie gave me a goodly piece of each shade of velvet for Christmas, and I've already cut out a light-weight, dark canvas lining. Sadie picked up the canvas at Fisher's sometime last fall and says it was more than she had need of—just was selling for such a good price she bought the whole bolt.

8 January 1864

Sadie was going through her old linens and pulled out a large yellowed damask tablecloth worn thin through the center. The cloth had once belonged to Mother, so for both of us there was a bit of sentiment attached to it. Since both of us have capes that are showing signs of wear at the bottom we decided to cut the stout from the thin, die it black, and stitch it in a wide four-inch band across the bottoms of our capes. Hers is a dark brown wool and doesn't the band look as fine on it as does mine against the black plush?

Last night we had a fall of snow to the depth of eight or ten inches and not much drifted. Last Monday the morning train from Springville passed Anamosa an hour and a half behind time on account of having to plow its way through the snow. We've had no eastern mail in over a week and none from the west since the end of the first week in December.

It seems the snow has been falling for as long as memory serves. It keeps falling in great white flakes, one flake at a time, spinning a cocoon around the house, insulating me and the babe, spinning our time of confinement into a shrouded dream. Sometimes Babe sets up such a fluttering I am caused to laugh aloud. And sometimes my time in the wilderness seems but a dream—some story printed in a book. It's then I take out my letters and know it was real. I read my

Husband's cramped script and know what a struggle it is for him to write, handicapped to the left hand, and I care for him so much more for his devotion to the effort.

I close my eyes and I meet the image of my beloved in that private place, and I see in his eyes the blue ice of his devotion and I see the soft curve of his lower lip and I am breathlessly drawn to it—to taking the fullness of that lip gently between my teeth and—oh My Beloved, I shiver. This winter is dragging on long—much too long.

15 January

Cold foul Weather—Several Stage Drivers have been frozen to death in Iowa, and in Minnesota the robbery of Hecht and Reed filled the thieves' pockets with $4,000 in greenbacks. I cannot imagine where these men get the energy to brave such weather for such a deed. It puts teeth in the old saw, "the weather's too cold for honest men to be about." It is so cold, Jamie D. has been boarding with the Cooks for the duration. One and a half miles in this weather is too risky to have the lad travel each day even with the trusty Morgan mare.

21 January

Marks Haberdashery of Anamosa was robbed last week. The unprecedented cold spell ended either Friday or Saturday when the mercury rose to eighteen above zero. Since then a slight thaw has been going on during the day.

The babe is turning my insides raw. I'm told this is what is to be expected and that it means all is well. Jamie will post my letters tomorrow so I must gather them to send off with him.

22 January

The earth is shrouded in white and I feel further from Bannack than ever. It is late at night, Babe keeps me awake, and I keep thinking of my husband. I have had a reoccurring dream of him these last two weeks. In my dream the night is dark as Egypt. We were holding hands and walking toward a night campfire. My foot becomes caught in some tangle of weed, and I cannot hang on to him. He calls out my name, and I cannot answer.

I woke to the sound of my Christian name ringing through the room as if my beloved were shouting it from a great distance. Oh, Husband! I feel so all alone.

Today is Mary Eliza's Birthday. I hope she received my package and enjoyed her special day.

Sunday 24 January

Savior like a shepherd lead us,
Much we need Thy tender care;
In Thy pleasant pastures feed us,
For our use Thy folds prepare:
Blessed Jesus, Blessed Jesus!
Thou Hast brought us, Thine we are,
Blessed Jesus, Blessed Jesus!
Thou Hast brought us, Thine we are. Amen.

—Dorothy A. Thrupp, 1779–1847

Sadie reassures me my estranged feelings are just those of one in my condition and not to pay it any mind. She says read, do needlework, anything to occupy my mind. Grandpa went her one better, he brought out his mandolin and didn't that liven our world?

29 January

Weather for the past week has been moderate—freezing point or a few degrees above.

Thackeray was found dead the morning of the 24th of effusion of the brain. It seems a lifetime ago when on the *Emilie* I so enjoyed reading his work.

1 February

Sadie has the laundry drying all about the house. She will not hear of me helping, says I must go easy now—go easy until my time comes. At this rate I fear I'll lose my mind to idleness in the next six to eight weeks. Received letters from the family in Ohio. They are on the receiving end of weather such as we've been having.

5 February

I see that Valentines are on sale for 2 cents at Fisher's. If the mails have gone through, all of my loved ones in Bannack will have received the ones Sadie, Jamie D., and I made just after Christmas. Wouldn't I like to see the wee ones' faces when they open theirs?

For a second time this winter we are without mail from the East for over a week. Only the good Lord knows when we'll be hearing from the Territories. I suppose the horrendous weather has held many of them hostage. I should not complain, in all fairness, my loved ones are in the same boat, I'm sure.

12 FEBRUARY

It snowed last Sunday, and it's drifted again.

We are at last in possession of the returns of the recent Territorial election in Idaho. The total vote polled was 7,912 of which Governor Wallace received 4,389 against Copperhead Judge Cannady's 3,523. We are heartened that Idaho has thus placed herself clearly and decidedly in the camp of the Union.

18 FEBRUARY 1864

Yesterday was foggy, and the wind whisked around from west to east. The night was rainy with thunder and lightning. This morning thin ice covered the water bucket in the kitchen, and icicles hung pendant from trees. At sunrise, the mercury had risen to 34 degrees already. Jamie D. braved the weather to bring us home a great bundle of letters. I am troubled by them and have need to reread them to digest them further.

EAST BANNACK
14 DECEMBER 1863

Dear Wife,

Just received a batch of letters and packages from you. I can almost smell your fine crock of mincemeat all the way to Bannack. My family always called it funeral pie as it traveled well long distances and kept long past the event.

At dinner last night, Thompson mentioned that Edgerton was planning a trip east. Naturally, first thing this morning found me at his "salon" desiring to know when he planned to leave and if he would carry a couple of packages for me. Alas, the man didn't seem to know when he'd set out, so I'm still looking for passage east, that I might send packages to you, Mother, Rebecca, and Willmot.

The weather has turned decidedly into winter, but trains are yet coming in and leaving for Salt Lake. We worry more about typhoid, as there have been a few cases in town.

Mrs. Vail no longer takes the children to town, as she has some notion that they will stay healthier if they're kept at home.

19 December 1863

Yesterday morning, under a directive of the Miner's court, I left on a mission to Centerville to sell a house in settlement of a dispute between the home's owner and his partner. Sunney, the partner, later won the case. As it turned out, the partner bought the house for $50, he being the highest bidder.

The last time I was in Virginia City a couple of packers, Messrs. Largent and Carroll, expressed their desire to travel to Fort Benton with two canteens full of gold dust and their fears of robbery along the way. I then asked them when they were planning to head out from Virginia City. They said on the 17th and I let it go at that, as I couldn't at that time know if I could be available to help.

After the auction, I headed over to Dempsey's where I gathered up Lady Mac as I'd determined that should the packers come into Bannack yet looking for protection, riding advanced guard, I'd escort them up to Fort Benton. I figured that would be better than moping about your sister's house and further, Mr. Vail might welcome my company.

Last night I bunked at Dempsey's. Largent and Carroll did come in today and tonight we are all bunked together on Thompson's floor. In the morning, before we leave, I'll get this to the express office as I want you to know I've deposited a good sum of monies with Thompson to be divided between yourself and my family should anything happen to me.

Your Husband,
Henry Plumer

Fort Benton
24 December 1863

Dear Wife,

Largent, Carroll, and their gold are safe at their destination. I plan to head out soon as I finish this coffee. I spent the night before last with Mr. Vail who is in good condition and wishing he could return to Bannack. We both question the wisdom of trying to repair the farm. He hopes to gather up his family in the spring and talks of heading east, possibly to take up farming in Dakota. He says he was quite taken with the land in the Dakota Territory near the Iowa border—claims that land is available there at a reasonable price. As for me, today, I'm ready to sell out as soon as my term is up and join you. Come July, if you are ready to travel, I should like to take you to meet my family. I shall write to Rebecca and Willmot when I return home. Next summer we shall decide where we will invest our future.

It's well I'm traveling with two horses. The cough is back. I'm weary beyond measure and cannot seem to get warm. It will be a relief to return to your sister's fire.

Your weary Husband,
Henry Plumer

East Bannack
24 December 1863

Dear Sister,

Your lovely presents certainly brightened what most assuredly would have been a bleak day with neither my husband nor yours in attendance. It is some consolation that our men at least are in each other's company this evening. I really must not complain. Young Swift has remained at our house, and thus I cannot say I am deserted. He even brought me a pair of candlesticks for my birthday and, bye-the-bye, thank you for the lovely duster and slippers. I shall think of you as I don them when I'm up at night. I probably need not tell you how I miss Husband and how eager I am for Mr. Plumer's return that I might hear news of him.

While our men are gone, I've been visiting with Mrs. Sanders who this week is also a "widow" (last week Edgerton sent him over to the Stinking Water to drum up support for his scheme to split the Territory and become appointed Governor). She just received a letter from her husband. And wasn't she excited by the news he sent? While in Nevada City, a murdered man was brought into town and so angered the populace that they formed a posse and found the murderer. Her husband offered to prosecute the man and did such a good job that, singlehanded, he got him hanged the same day the verdict of guilty came in. The people were so pleased with him they took up a collection to pay him. She said they already have several hundred dollars and are talking about getting him a gold watch. Isn't she tickled pink? Lord knows they need the money. I'm under the impression that Edgerton does not pay him much for his services and is not impressed with his efforts to garner them mining interests. He says he can't come home yet as he is under protection by his clients. I know you are not much impressed by these people—but Electa, she is always such a cheerful soul.

My Darling, I miss you.

Your Sister,
Martha Jane

East Bannack
27 December 1863

Dear Wife,

It is good to be home. Had I known how terribly cold the weather was going to turn, I should never have attempted the trip. Try as I might I cannot get warm, and yet all night I keep waking in sweats. Strange combination this.

Dear Wife, I am taken with the fine watch you sent to me and I treasure your image inside its lid. I've traded my old watch for it and put the lovely horse hair fob on it, thus I keep both of my lovely ladies at all times close.

I'm told, while I was gone, in Nevada City, Ives was tried by a jury and hanged. George Lane was sent to find me in the hopes that I might come to his aid, but he didn't know why they were after Ives. The couple of times I met Ives, he certainly seemed like a competent and honorable man. Thompson says he has little to add, but I felt he was holding back. I did not push the topic. I'll find out more on the morrow.

You will be pleased to know that this day I have sold my one half interest in the #7 Dakota Lode for the amount of $3,500. I gave Chrisman power of attorney to settle with parties owing. As he is always at the store and I tend to be in and out, we all thought this expedient.

28 December

Dragged myself about town today talking to the deputies and others. As much as I can piece together is this: while I was working guard for Largent, the following events transpired. A man was found murdered and his body brought to Nevada City; four men were arrested and brought to trial; one was hanged for the deed and the others released. In the meantime, word raced up and down the gulch that Magruder's train has not arrived in the Lewiston area. Magruder is a well-liked merchant who brought a large amount of goods from the other side to Virginia City. His friends feel certain that he had been robbed and killed somewhere along the mountain Indian trail he returned on. I'm told that Doc Howard, and Romaine (the same band of "cutthroats" Francis Thompson ushered into Bannack last) were members of his party. If this is the case, I have no doubt the man is indeed dead. When on the other side these men were notorious thieves and killers. As if this weren't enough, V.C. merchants (partners in fact) had a falling out that ended in one shooting the other to death. Adding insult to injury, a couple of men entertained a drunken brawl in which one was wounded and another killed. The citizens of Virginia City are understandably outraged. Unfortunately, I am led to understand that these events stirred the citizenry from the other side into the formation of a California-style hanging party, every one of them panting for blood. I understand they have headed to Gold Creek in search of someone to hang. With a bit of luck, a cold and fruitless trek to Gold Creek will take the steam out of them and they'll allow more sober heads to prevail.

Will write more tomorrow. Now I need to sleep.

Your Husband,
Henry Plumer

East Bannack
28 December 1863

Dear Sister,

Your husband has returned with news that Mr. Vail is in good spirits in spite of the weather and the work ahead of him. Of course he brought back the most treasured gift of the season, letters for the children and me.

I don't know as the trip did Mr. Plumer any good, though. He has returned with a cough that fair wears him out, and I've never seen him so pale. But do you think I can keep him abed? No, I cannot. The gentleman has a "job" to do, don't you know? Bannack has been quiet, but over in Alder Gulch there fair seems to be a war going on. With the weather so cold, the men congregate in great numbers in the grog shops. He says that's where the mischief begins, and he's hoping to keep our city under control till the weather warms and honest work takes up their energies.

As to the cold, it's so bitter the children have not been out of the house since the day after Christmas—so bitter I do not even allow them to leave to use the back-house.

I'm hoping the weather is better in your part of the country.

Affectionately,
Martha Jane

East Bannack
29 December 1863

Dear Wife,

The more I hear about the events over on the Stinking Water the less I understand. I'm told the same day Largent and Carroll left Virginia City for Benton the body of a fellow named Tiebalt or Tiebolt, a Dutch immigrant, was found and brought into Nevada City. He had disappeared after being sent to pick up a mule team from Ives. When the corpse was brought into Nevada City, those who examined it found the head and shoulders badly pecked by magpies, further there were rope marks on his neck and pieces of sagebrush in one of his hands, indicating he may have been dragged into the brush while still alive. Others state that he was shot in the back of the head, and some say he was shot twice, once in the back and once in the back of the head. No one thought to have a doctor examine the body.

As best I can follow, Mr. Tiebalt owned a fine pair of mules, which he boarded at Ive's Wisconsin Creek Ranch. He sold them to the men for whom he worked and they, needing to use them, sent Tiebalt to bring the mules to Virginia City. Several days elapsed, and the employers heard nothing of Tiebalt or the mules. Then one day Alex Carter, one of Ive's wranglers, showed up with them and they concluded their hired hand, Tiebalt, had gone to the States.

Some time passed and Tiebalt's body was found by Mr. Palmer, a Stinking Water businessman. Traveling toward his home in Nevada City, he shot a grouse above the Dempsey Ranch. While searching for the bird he found the frozen corpse in a ravine near the road. At a wickiup on the ranch, he roused its residents, Long John Frank and George Hilderman, and asked them to help him get the body into his wagon so he could take it to Nevada City. They refused. Palmer went back and loaded the body into his wagon on his own.

Having decided Hilderman and Frank, by reason of their refusal to help, were guilty, an angry group of well-armed men formed a posse and headed for Dempsey's Ranch. Leaving Nevada City at ten o'clock that night, they reached the ranch at daybreak and arrested the men. John Frank denied having murdered the man, but after toying with him at the end of a well-placed noose, he told them that George Ives had done the deed. That I find hard to believe, as I've never heard Ives touted as anything but a conscientious businessman who returned the stock in his care to their owners in better condition than when he took them in. His good reputation did not slow down the posse's trek to Wisconsin Creek, where they arrested him and were back in Nevada before sundown.

Mr. Sanders, being in Nevada City on other business, insinuated himself into the position of prosecuting attorney. The men say that Sanders was so longwinded, he nearly drove them mad combining legal jargon with highfalutin' language. He further enraged some of the crowd and many a good man by calling them names. He called Caven a coward (perhaps the man confuses quiet good manners with cowardice), and belittled the list of jurors Caven presented because one of the jurors happened to be a professional gambler. With his nose high in the air, Sanders said of the jurors, "I have no desire to make their acquaintance." Yet he partnered up with Charles Bagg, lawyer and common scoundrel, who was mining in the area. Nelson Story, a miner who arrived late last Spring with the Pikes Peak Train, happened into town. He credits Long John's appearance on the stand to testify to Sanders. Evidently, the ragged little lawyer who lives next to our door promised Long John if he fingered Ives he would go free.

According to Long John, Ives stood watching Tiebalt leave, suggested they kill him for his money, and rode after him when the lot of a tossed coin fell to him. Long John claimed not to have been with him, but he said he shot Tiebalt in the forehead, took his gold, and brought the mules back to camp.

At the end of three days, Judge Byham sent the jury off to a store to deliberate. Within half an hour, a hung jury returned with a written report, the prosecution had convinced all but one of the jurors. Sanders jumped to the witness wagon and successfully enjoined the assembled crowd to ignore the lone dissenting vote and accept the decision of the majority of the jury and to hang Ives immediately. Judge Byham asked for final words. Ives said, "I am innocent of this crime; Alex Carter killed the Dutchman." Faster than a rattlesnake strike, Nelson Story and Benjamin Ezekiel stood Ives on a box and dropped a noose about his neck. When Ives asked Sanders if he would not put off the execution until morning that he might put his affairs in order, Beidler called down from his perch on the dirt roof of a cabin, "Sanders, ask him how long he gave the Dutchman!"

Story brags that he and Ezekiel kicked the box from under him before the anti-hanging elements of the crowd could prevail with a call to stay the execution.

Sanders's third motion also carried, that the court take possession of Ives's property to pay the expenses of board for the three prisoners and the nearly 100 guards employed throughout the trial. When the defense lawyer protested it was bad enough to kill an innocent man without using his property to pay the expenses of his killers, Sanders responded, "It is not unusual for the defendant to pay costs after a death sentence. If a lawyer was not aware of that fact, he should go to a law school instead of a law office."

The next day, Long John was set free in reward for his testimony, and the third prisoner, George Hilderman, was sentenced to banishment on the grounds of being a conspirator to the murder. According to Story, the blood-thirsty posse set out to arrest Carter before Ives's body was in a grave. I'm glad the mess is not in my jurisdiction.

Your Husband,
Henry Plumer

EVENING . . . 18 FEBRUARY

I do think Sister has gone to the enemy and doesn't even know it. And Husband's letters fill me with dread. I fear that all this mystery, murder, and gore will somehow contaminate his life. I know it's irrational, the events in the Idaho Territory rage no dirtier than the war in the South and even here in Iowa we are not immune to injustice and violence, but I have nightmares. I pray this will soon be over and we will be again together—together where the world's a cleaner place.

I am so lost being so far from him. We write, but we are always writing to something so long past its history. I want to urge him to slow down and take care of his health. What good will a fortune due me if he kills himself in the service of the law? I want him with me, and I pray my admonitions will reach him and he will take heed.

22 February

ILL THAT HE BLESSES IS OUR GOOD,
AND UNBLEST GOOD IS ILL;
AND ALL IS RIGHT THAT SEEMS MOST WRONG,
IF IT BE HIS SWEET WILL. AMEN.

—*Frederick W. Faber, 1814–1863*

Daniel says the sermon today was based on the theme "What Dying Worms Are We." Didn't that one tickle our funny-bones?

Am tired, oh so tired. I'll work on my letters on the morrow.

26 February 1864

23 FEBRUARY

Isn't this a delightful kettle of fish? I've hardly digested the last batch of letters when, wouldn't you know, to my great joy, Jamie brings me another. I feel a little guilty leaving all the laundry to Sadie, but she cheerfully says, "Read your letters and write, that's the proper course for you to take," and so I shall.

EAST BANNACK
6 JANUARY 1864

Dear Wife,

Word has come, day before yesterday, a party of stranglers looking for Alex Carter found Red Yeager and George Brown asleep in their wicki-ups at the Rattlesnake. They took them to Dempsey's where they held their version of judge, jury, and trial, then strung them up at Laurin's

Ranch. It is said that prior to the hangings one of the party wanted out. The rest turned their guns on him. He decided to stay.

While the stranglers were plying their trade, a group of miners asked me to ride over to White's District with them, that I might apprize them of the potential of a piece of ground below White's discovery. I'd already put up the handbills advertising the auction of a one-half interest in claim 126 below Stapleton's Discovery on Stapleton's Bar, thus I told them I'd be pleased to accommodate if they could wait till after the auction. To this they agreed, and as soon as a fellow made the final high bid in the sum of $105, we headed out.

Indeed, judging the land from its relationship to the syenite heart area, we should find clusters of rich veins. Thus we each filed claim to our allotted 100 feet.

Tomorrow evening I shall see to a proper recording of this morning's transaction.

9 January

Neil Howie has just this day informed me he has brought to town a prisoner, Dutch John. When I asked what the charge was against him, Howie responded, "I am certain he attempted to rob the Moody wagon train." So I said, "I suppose you are willing he should be tried by the civil authorities."

Howie replied, "That may come to pass, but for now I'll see to his safe keeping."

I retorted, "This new way our people have of hanging men without law or evidence isn't right. It's time a stop was put to it." My little speech fell on deaf ears, and he refused to release his prisoner. I have no notion where Dutch John has been hidden. Could be any cabin. I'm hoping Howie will be talking to someone with a level head and some respect for the law.

By afternoon the word about town is the Moody train was carrying 80,000 in dust for transmission from Salt Lake to their eastern creditors. If I understand correctly, the robbery took place on the Salt Lake road some two weeks ago. I understand that although the train was accosted and a robbery attempted, the would-be robbers were a couple of bunglers, and all the monies were retrieved.

Somewhere lost in this whole mess seems to be the Virginia City murder of one merchant by his partner. No one cares about it anymore than if they'd gone on a Sunday toot.

After reading your reports from the East, I can only suppose this universal disregard for each other and due process stems from the general violence of the war. Villainy seems to run rampant all over this country.

While in Benton, I visited with a couple of fellows from the mines in Canada. They say the situation is not the same there, perhaps because government-supported justice courts were in place before the miners arrived. Although there is attendant violence in their gold camps, they do use the courts, and the citizenry does not depend on the vigilance of these ill-conceived bodies of stranglers.

I worry that the innocent will be hurt. My dream is that all people will have the dignity of a full hearing by trial, imperfect as that may be, it at least attempts the right thing—it attempts to be just. Barring the realization of that, my dream would be to get warm. Seems like a chill has taken me and I cannot shake it off.

Good Night Wife.

Your Husband,
Henry Plumer

16 January 1864

Dear Mrs. Plumer

Today it is bitter cold. The wind blows snow like grains of sand against the windows and on the floor in front of our door it marks a white line. A line Mrs. Vail, the children, and I are want to cross. Oh, Mrs. Plumer, my heart breaks to tell you we have lost our dearest companion and friend. Forgive me, harbinger of bleak days ahead, they have murdered Mr. Plumer. It is bitter cold in our hearts.

Sunday last, Mr. Plumer dragged himself out of sick bed to make his rounds. It was a reasonably quiet Sunday—the weather brittle cold. I helped him into his great cape, and your sister fussed at him and bid him wrap his neck with your scarf. We had a laugh at the sight of our elegant Sheriff now muffled hat to boot. Even so, by the time he returned home he was feverishly ill. Whilst Mrs. Vail prepared a fine meal of stewed oysters and biscuits, he lay himself on the couch. At length he began to cough and did so till the sputum in his handkerchief was tinged with pink. Mrs. Vail bid me get the brandy from the medicine chest and pour a cup, which I did and then he slept.

At supper Plumer barely touched his meal, as opposed to Thompson who took his meal leisurely, complimenting the cook and eating with great relish. After supper, your sister began to make ready to go to choir practice when Thompson said, "Oh, my dear, I forgot to tell you whilst visiting with the Sanders earlier, Miss Darling came by and suggested that since I was the choir director it was my duty to put out the word that practice was canceled tonight." Mrs. Vail was troubled by the statement. We all wondered why it would be canceled and why this was her decision as Thompson has always lead the affair.

Not long after, there came a big commotion at the door where a group of men were gathered. One carrying a torch asked the Sheriff to step outside. Mr. Plumer rose and proceeded to dress for the cold. Mrs. Vail, citing his cough, his fever, his extreme weakness, pleaded he stay put. But he silenced her saying, "It is about Dutch John. It is my duty to do what I can for him." The door closed behind him. Mrs. Vail was distraught and the children began to fuss. She took them to the bedroom to prepare them for sleep and I wrapped up and promptly quit the house.

The night was pitch dark. Near the Sanders' house I could see two more torches looking for the world like lit candles. I heard Mr. Plumer call out to Mr. Sanders who opened the door. Mr. Plumer said, "Mr. Sanders tell these men who I am. You know me. We are men of the law." Sanders said nothing and the silence rang crisp in the air. The men who detained our friend started to back away from their task when the little man croaked, "Men do your duty!" That snapped them to attention. And they marched off with our sheriff bound between them.

I ran back to the house to enlist Thompson's help. He met me at the door and hissing at me said, "Swift, this is none of your concern. It is my duty now to take care of Mrs. Vail." I turned and ran to catch up with Mr. Plumer and by the time I did, two more torch bearing columns and a great mob of drunks and curiosity seekers had emptied the saloons to join the parade.

They took the three men, Sheriff Plumer, Deputy Stinson, and Deputy Ray to the gallows. They charged them with the crime of being members of a gang, the Sheriff of being the ring leader. They did not allow them to answer the charges nor to settle their affairs. I tried to get through the crowd that I might speak out for my mentor, yet no one would make way for me. I screamed and screamed, but no one listened to me. In the end, Mr. Plumer took off his scarf and asked it be passed to me saying, "Give this to my good friend Joe Swift." But someone took the scarf for himself. In the end, I lay myself down in the snow, in the cold white snow, and I cried and I cried—willing the white pain of the cold to staunch the pain in my heart.

It is common knowledge that the most of the stranglers came from the towns lining Alder Gulch. Besides the crowd of drunks, there were not but a handful of men from our good town in attendance to this shameful affair. The murders have continued into the week, and it is whispered that the freight wagons rolled for Salt Lake City loaded with kegs of gold dust. Please know hardly anyone in Bannack believes Mr. Plumer was guilty of anything but being a very well-liked person—the only Bannack sympathizers with the stranglers being Edgerton, his nephew, a couple of merchants, and Thompson. The latter has alluded to my need to stay near him lest I meet with the same fate as my beloved mentor. Until opportunity arises I deem it prudent to do so.

These midnight stranglers are like a pack of mad dogs with the taste of blood in their mouths. Nothing this side of death shall stop them. Attempting to sate their appetite for murder, they turn all this side of heaven into hell.

Mrs. Plumer, I am so sorry. I am so sorry, sorry for our loss and more sorry for the empty spaces where the souls of the men who have instigated this black time should have existed.

Your Devoted Servant,
Joseph Swift

My God, my God, how shall I endure this? When first I read Swift's letter, I screamed, then fainted away. Sadie cleaned up the mess made by this babe, who decided to come before its time. Sadie is beside herself, wringing her hands and fussing. Over and over she repeats herself, "Electa, you must rest. Electa, please rest." I cannot rest. I must write. If I don't write my thoughts, how can I find a path through this? If I don't write, how can I weigh the situation? Lest I write, how shall I find what's in my mind? Daniel has gone for the doctor, leaving so fast but for Sadie he would have been off with neither hat nor glove. Sadie has me propped upon the pillows. Grandpa's the only sensible person around. He brought me my writing table and fixed it so that I can scribble while reclining and it can be quickly removed when the pains return—and return, Sadie promised, they shall. She tells me once the water has broken, there's no staying the event. One thing I know, the bastards have framed my husband. God is my witness, I warned him against them. Would he take heed? No! He was a man of principle, a man of honor! How often did I hear him say, "A man who lives by honor will engender honor in others of breeding"? How often did I hear him say, "Ultimately honor is vindicated"? They have caused his death as certainly as if they had wrested his life from him with their own hands.

God be my witness, one day the world shall know the truth. What is this pain I am feeling? Is it mind or body? I know not whether to pray for this babe's life or its death—my life, my death. If the babe lives, it will be forever marked by ignominy. It hardy matters my beloved is innocent, the way of this world is to revel in the artful inventions of the liar and to hate the harsh truth.

Child of my womb, I want you to know, our romance on the Sun River was idyllic—unlike the life we had to lead in Bannack. There the people claimed his time and his tongue. When we were together on the Sun River, my Betrothed was quite open and we shared so fine a love. Oh, if you could but know, in Bannack I was terribly alone. I just knew things would aright themselves if we could be shed of that place. I want you to know, he would have followed me back. I never would have ridden out of Bannack if I'd doubted his following. He did have responsibilities that needed to be finished. But, oh, I knew if I staid we'd end up raising our babies in that godforsaken place. Those people would never let him go. Like me, they needed him. Unlike me, they weren't about to birth his child. He agreed to follow. My darling, he would have. East is the direction he was heading when he met me.

Perhaps I should spare this child the shame and give it to be raised by another. But could I give away a part of myself and my Love—this life that is the issue of our love? I do not doubt he loved me as deeply as I loved him. I would be unselfish if I could do it, but I would rather die. Ah, if only Sadie could claim it. Alas, there is no hiding the fact that she's long been barren. No, the gossips would insure the child be not spared. I should be praying for our death, yet every fiber of me wants life—life for both of us, and I can only pray God's will be done. Oh, Sadie help me! God help me. . . .

When seeming respectable men arrogate unto themselves the power to direct the fate of their fellow man, so excellent a counterfeit of right it seems, few men have moral force enough, nor strength of fortitude enough to challenge their will. To bear the slander marks no shame. We lived lives given, in God's name.

Afterword

AUTHOR'S NOTE

Very few facts are known about the "real" Electa Bryan: She was born on May 8, 1842, in Findlay, Ohio. On June 20, 1863, Electa's marrige to William Henry Handy Plumer at the Sun River Government Farm was witnessed by her sister Martha Jane Bryan Vail, her brother-in-law James A. Vail, their two children, Francis Thompson, Joseph Swift, three Indians, and a crowd of pilgrims. Details of her life are then lost to history until 1865, when we know she was teaching in Emory, South Dakota. On January 19, 1874, Electa married wealthy, widowed farmer James Maxwell. They had three sons together (one died in infancy), and she raised his children from his first wife. Electa died on May 5, 1912, and is buried in the cemetery at Wakonda, South Dakota.

To write *Strength of Stone*, I began with these few known facts about Electa. From there I searched in all directions. The details of weather come from diaries, journals, and newspaper clippings of that time and place in history. I then filled in the events of the Civil War. I cataloged each mention of the Sun River Government Farm gleaned from the diaries of the emigrant parties traveling the Mullen Road. The events of Plumer's life are recorded as I found them in newspapers, legal documents, mining records, and the writings of the Vigilantes.

The plot, ninety percent or better, has been developed from the facts reported by the Vigilantes, their relatives (Mrs. Edgerton and her daughter Mattie Edgerton and Mrs. Sanders), newspaper accounts, and court records. I filled in further details using histories of Missouri River steamers, overland mail delivery, stagecoach routes, and stage companies. I consulted magazines of the times and Methodist and Catholic literature. I reviewed more diaries, journals, and letters (both published and unpublished) of western pioneers. I was even able to locate writings and correspondence from individuals who were a direct part of Electa and Henry's lives (including Francis Thompson, who published a late version of selected portions of his journal writings). The descriptions of landscapes are authentic and come from my personal observations during travels through the regions described. Electa's voice and mind are my creation.

The writings of the Vigilantes nicely filled in the details of Bannack days and ways, including what became Swift's descriptions of the day Plumer was hanged. Much has been written about the Vigilantes's actions. The Vigilantes themselves hired Thomas. J. Dimsdale to tell their story and defend their actions (they were under Congressional Review at the time). The Vigilantes claim that Henry Plumer was the leader of a band of road agents and thereby guilty of robbery and murder. Until the publication of R. E. Mather and F. E. Boswell's *Hanging the Sheriff,* most historians accepted the Vigilante's version of the dealings. Mather and Boswell successfully cast doubt on issues such as whether there ever was a gang of road agents operating in Bannack. If there was no gang, then Plumer could not be guilty as its leader and, therefore, was hanged an innocent man.

By the time he became sheriff of Bannack, Plumer had gained a reputation as a successful businessman (he had gold) with a dubious past. Plumer was an easy target for the likes of Edgerton, who stood to gain a great deal—politically and financially—from rumors of a lawless territory and a rogue sheriff.

We can't know what Electa really thought or knew about Mr. Plumer's past and his activities in Bannack. This novel presents one possibility—another side of a fascinating story.

Plumer's grave and Hangman's Gulch in Bannack.

E. C. Schoettner photographer.
Courtesy Montana Historical Society, Helena.

Goodrich Hotel and Skinner's Saloon in Bannack. Plumer frequented these very establishments as a bachelor in Bannack.

Courtesy Montana Historical Society, Helena.

BANNACK JAIL BUILT IN 1862.

Courtesy Montana Historical Society, Helena.

1860S BANNACK STREET SCENE. THIS IS PERHAPS WHAT GREETED ELECTA AS SHE AND PLUMER RODE INTO TOWN AT THE END OF THEIR HONEYMOON.

Courtesy Montana Historical Society, Helena.

This 1863 residence was that of Montana's first governor when Bannack became the state capital in March 1908. The log home is similar to that which Plumer would have had built for himself and his bride.

Courtesy Montana Historical Society, Helena.

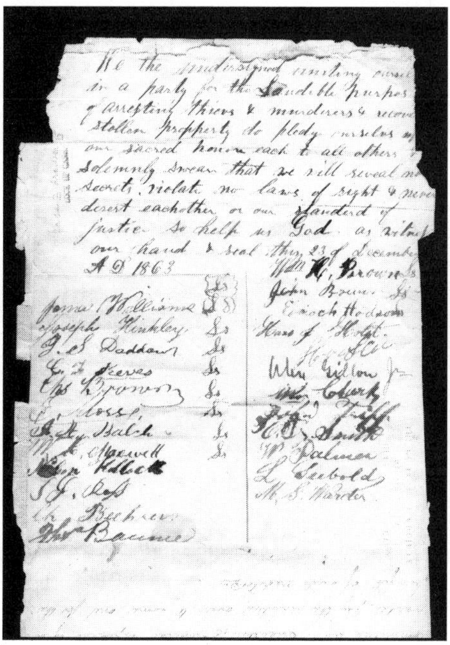

We the undersigned uniting ourselves in a party for the laudible purpos of arresting thievs & murderers & recovering stollen propperty do pledge ourselves upon our sacred honor each to all others & solemnly swear that we will reveal no secrets, violate no laws of right & never desert eachother or our standard of justice so help us God as witness our hand & seal this 23 of December A D 1863

Wm H. Brown
John Brown
Enoch Hodson
Joseph Hinkley
Wm Gillow
Wm Clark
M. S. Warder

Vigilante oath.

Courtesy Montana Historical Society, Helena.

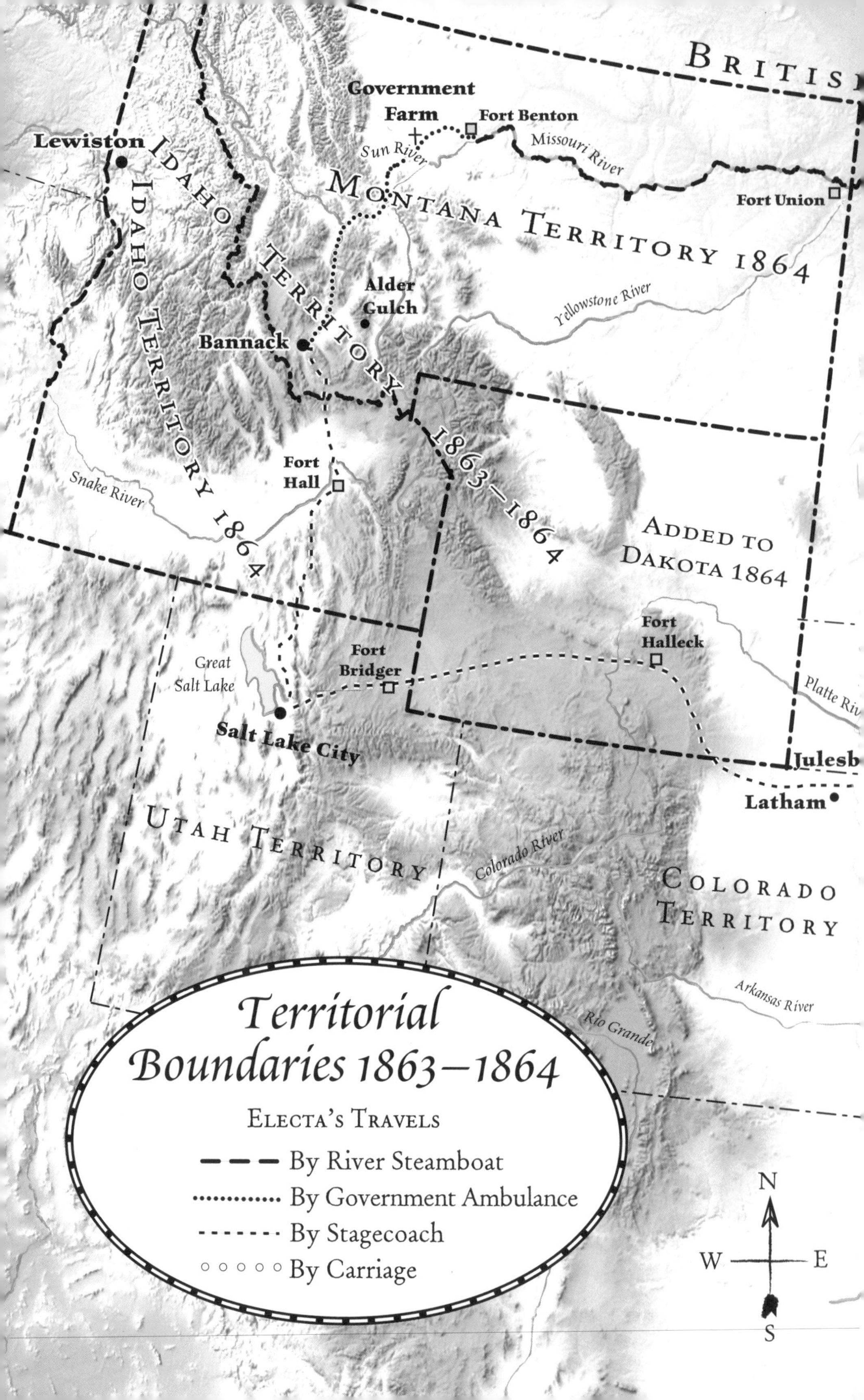

British
Government Farm
Fort Benton
Missouri River
Sun River
Lewiston
Idaho Territory 1863–1864
Idaho Territory 1864
Montana Territory 1864
Fort Union
Alder Gulch
Bannack
Yellowstone River
Fort Hall
Snake River
Added to Dakota 1864
Fort Halleck
Platte River
Fort Bridger
Great Salt Lake
Salt Lake City
Julesburg
Latham
Utah Territory
Colorado River
Colorado Territory
Arkansas River
Rio Grande
Territorial Boundaries 1863–1864
Electa's Travels
By River Steamboat
By Government Ambulance
By Stagecoach
By Carriage
N
W
E
S